D1280085

Rights of Union Members and the Government

RECENT TITLES IN

CONTRIBUTIONS IN AMERICAN HISTORY

Series Editor: Jon L. Wakelyn

Rights of Union Members and the Government

Philip Taft

Contributions in American History, Number 39

Greenwood Press

Westport, Connecticut • London, England

Library of Congress Cataloging in Publication Data

Taft, Philip, 1902-
  Rights of union members and the Government.

  (Contributions in American history, no. 39)
  Includes bibliographical references.
    1. Trade-unions—United States. 1. Title.
KF3389.T3   344'.73'0188   74-5994
ISBN 0-8371-7527-5

Library of Congress Catalog Card Number: 74-5994
ISBN: 0-8371-7527-5

First published in 1975

Greenwood Press, a division of Williamhouse-Regency Inc.
51 Riverside Avenue, Westport, Connecticut 06880

Manufactured in the United States of America

To The Memory Of My Grandson
John Philip Blake
1955-1974
This Book Is Lovingly Dedicated

Contents

Tables

Acknowledgments

An evaluation of the effect of the Labor-Management Report-ing and Disclosure Act (LMRDA) is the major purpose of this study. Enacted in 1959, largely as a result of the disclosures of the Select Committee on Activities in the Labor or Management Field (McClellan Committee), the law was the most detailed regulation of internal union affairs yet made by any unit of government in the United States.

Even before the emergence of the McClellan Committee, rep-resentatives of state legislatures and law officers of a number of communities exposed undesirable practices in the labor area. Nevertheless, it was the assembling of a vast amount of evidence which induced Congress to act. In addition to dealing with cor-ruption and violation of trust, the LMRDA concerns itself with the problem of the denial of rights to members of unions, rights such as free speech and free assemblage and the fairness of the disciplinary procedure. Information on these questions is reasonably abundant, but it is far less voluminous and persuasive than the mass dealing with corruption. The material on rights of members consists largely of occasional and partial reports of factional disputes within a number of unions, the pamphlets of the American Civil Liberties Union on the subject, articles in legal and popular journals, and the records of court cases in which members sought relief against penalties imposed upon them by unions. While there existed general agreement that action was needed to contain improper activities in financial matters, there was a difference of opinion on whether federal regulation was desirable in the protection of members' rights. The skepticism was based on the belief that adequate remedies could be obtained on the state level.

I have had the benefit of assistance from many persons connected with government, labor organizations, employer associations, labor unions and universities.

May I express my thanks to Morris Iushevitz, secretary of the New York City Labor Council, AFL-CIO; Thomas Harris, associate counsel, AFL-CIO; Andrew J. Biemiller, director, department of legislation, AFL-CIO; Stephen Schlossberg, general counsel; John Fillion, associate counsel; William J. Beckham, administrative assistant to the President, United Automobile Workers; Louis Sherman, general counsel and Thomas Dunn, associate counsel to the International Brotherhood of Electrical Workers (IBEW); and Robert J. Connerton, general counsel of the Laborers' International Union of North America. Mr. Connerton turned over papers on more than 100 appeals for my examination, including cases which ended in the courts; I also had the benefit of his penciled and typed observations.

The International Association of Machinists opened its files on election appeals. These records contained all the information on dozens of cases, and letters and briefs from attorneys or individual members acting for themselves or other members. I should like to thank Roy Siemiller, president; Alex Bauer, grand lodge representative at the national headquarters; Gordon H. Cole, editor of *The Machinist*; Plato E. Papps, chief counsel; and Albert Epstein.

Justin McCarthy, editor of the *United Mine Workers Journal*, was also helpful, as were Martin Rarback, former secretary, District Council No. 9, New York; William T. Dodd, former executive vice-president of the Plumbers' Union; Paul Hall, president of the Seafarers' International Union; Herbert Brand, director of Organization and Publications; President I. W. Abel, John Rooney, assistant to the president; and Lawrence Spitz, Harry Guenther, and Irving Dichter, staff representatives at the

Pittsburgh headquarters of the United Steelworkers of America. Several staff members of the Teamsters' Union have been of assistance: Florian Bartosic, house counsel; David Previant, general counsel; Jules Bernstein, at the time a staff lawyer; and Abraham Weiss, economist. The late president of the International Typographical Union, Elmer Brown, James S. Schell, director of the Bureau of Statistics, and Scoop White explained the meaning of expulsion in the union.

A number of officers of employer associations were kind enough to give me the benefit of their knowledge: Harold H. Brodeau, American Trucking Association; Paul Richards and David W. Ferguson, respectively director and assistant director, General Building Contractors of New York State, Inc.; William E. Dunn, executive director, Associated Building Contractors of America; Joel B. Leighton, General Contractors Association of America; John E. Gibbons, Associated Building Contractors of the Triple Cities, Inc.; Lewis Whiteman, Investing Builders and Owners Association; and Daniel F. McKnight, vice-president, United Parcel Service.

My thanks to Professor John H. G. Crispo, director, Center for Industrial Relations, University of Toronto; Professor Robert Ozanne of the economics department, University of Wisconsin, and director of the School for Workers at that institution; Dr. H. W. Woods, McGill University; William Caples, president of Kenyon College; Professor Marten Estey of the Wharton School; Professor Bernard Meltzer of the University of Chicago Law School; and Professor Emanuel Stein. I also wish to express my sincere gratitude to the officers and staff of the Graduate School of Business of the University of Chicago who provided typing and copying services and for their continuing assistance while I was at that institution. The librarians of the law school were helpful, and I thank them for their kindness to a stranger. The School of Labor and Industrial Relations at Michigan State University and one of its staff, Mary Anne Merrill, made it easier to make the final corrections and changes.

May I also thank Alfred J. Scotti, chief assistant district attorney and head of the rackets bureau, New York County, New York; James Featherstone, formerly chief of the labor section, U.S. Department of Justice; William Simkin, former head of U.S. Federal Mediation and Conciliation Service; Charles L. Tilton, national representative; M. P. Catherwood, Industrial Commissioner of New York; William J. Hurley, director, division of labor-management practices in New York State; and Jay Kramer, chief of the New York State Labor Relations Board. Both Mr. Kramer and Mr. Hurley discussed the problem of containing racketeering in the labor-intensive industries in the New York-New Jersey region.

A number of members of the Office of Labor-Management and Welfare-Pension Reports discussed problems covered by the study: the late John Holcombe, who headed the Office when it was first established under a different title; Frank M. Kleiler, deputy assistant Secretary of Labor; Leonard Lurie, the head of the Office; Benjamin Naumoff, A. S. Friedman, regional directors; Edward Gordon, statistician; Herbert Lahne, economist; Herbert Raskin, attorney; James R. Beaird, formerly associate solicitor; Mrs. Elsie Goodman, Chester Skibinsky, of the Boston office; and many others.

Lawyers in private practice supplied insights and information which could not be normally obtained from the records. I thank Stephen Vladeck, the late Aaron Benenson, Harold Berg, Bernard M. Mamet, Lawrence Gold, Herbert Thatcher, Henry Kaiser, George Kaufman, Samuel Kates, and Ronald Rosenberg.

Hy Fish, an old Chicago friend, read the manuscript and suggested some additions.

Closer to home, the State of Rhode Island Law Library in Providence has been opened to me, and I want to thank the staff for its continual aid. My colleague, Professor Jerome Stein, has offered his usual good advice. A grant of the Ford Foundation helped to finance the research.

Theresa Taft has been helpful in every phase of this study; without her assistance I could not have completed it.

When I began the final draft, I had no intimation of the tragedy which was to befall my family. My older grandson, John Philip Blake, was killed in an automobile accident on March 29, 1974. The book is dedicated to his memory.

Brown University
Providence, Rhode Island

Rights of Union Members and the Government

1

Introduction

The enactment of the Labor-Management Reporting and Disclosure Act was the result of the evidence of corruption and denial of democratic rights to members of labor unions presented before the Select (McClellan) Committee on Improper Activities in the Labor or Management Field.

It was somewhat accidental that the McClellan Committee undertook its extensive investigation of union wrongdoing. Informed of serious misuse of funds by a number of union officials, a sub-committee of the Senate Government Operations Committee undertook an investigation in December 1956. Four witnesses—Einar Mohn, a Vice-President of the International Brotherhood of Teamsters; Frank Brewster, Chairman of the Western Conference of Teamsters, one of the powerful units of the above international union; Nugent LaPoma, Secretary-Treasurer of Teamsters Local Union 174; and Harry Reiss, Administrator of the welfare fund of Allied Industrial Workers —refused to answer the committee's subpoena on the ground that it lacked jurisdiction to investigate in the labor area. Tried and convicted for contempt of Congress, they appealed and won when the Court of Appeals, Ninth Circuit, reversed the lower court's decision.

Mr. Justice Stanley Reed, serving as an appellate judge, claimed

that the committee was "within the scope of its authority" when it\
sought the books, records and testimony of the union officers. \
However, the majority disagreed because the acceptance of the
committee's jurisdictional claims would allow the committee to
investigatte every issue affecting persons and corporations and
thereby undermine the rights of other committees to investigate
issues falling within their assigned areas.[1]

The Senate did not allow the witnesses to escape on a technical-
ity, but a dispute arose over which committee of the Senate was to
make the investigation. Irving Ives, a Republican senator from
New York, wanted the Committee on Labor and Public Welfare
to perform this task. On the other hand, Senator John L. McClellan, Chairman of the Committee on Government Operations, was
not inclined to allow others to exploit the bonanza his committee
had uncovered. The Senate, which might have insisted on the
regular order, was, according to Senator John McClellan, influenced by the directives from the Teamsters' Union for the officers to refuse to testify. It therefore established, in January 1957,
the Select Committee on Improper Activities in the Labor and
Management Fields, which functioned through January 1960.
Made up of eight senators, equally divided between the two
parties, the committee heard 1,526 witnesses in 270 days of public
hearings which filled 20,432 pages of record, a large number of
them devoted to the Teamsters' Union.[2]

Although the McClellan Committee went over some of thhhe
ground covered by earlier investigations by Congress, committees of state legislatures and law-enforcement officers, its attention was mainly directed at the mishandling of the finances of
some labor organizations and the denial of democratic rights to
the members of a number of unions. It showed that some union
officers were guilty of a conflict of interest in that they operated
or held an interest in businesses that sold goods and equipment to
employers with whom they bargained on behalf of their members. The revelations were not entirely new as one of the more
venal union officials of the 1920s, Sam Kaplan, a business agent
for a New York City local of motion picture operators, sold film
and other goods to theatres employing the members of his or-

ganization. Patrick Comerford and Joseph Fay, both operating in the New Jersey building trades, were also known for using their position for private gain, and there were others equally unscrupulous.

More serious than the conflict of interest was the disclosure that union officers borrowed thousands of dollars in interest free loans from the organizations they served, that the funds were used in risky investments and the gains pocketed by the union official. Two high officers of the Teamsters' Union, President David Beck and Frank Brewster, Chairman of the Western Conference of Teamsters, were among several shown to have abused their trust. The committee went much further. It showed, in the case of the United Textile Workers of America, and the Bakery and Confectionary Workers Union that hundreds of thousands of dollars could be systematically diverted by crooked officers without the membership's knowledge, and, even when exposed, there was no method by which such thievery could be prevented. Other Congressional committees had discovered abuses of welfare and pension plans, but the McClellan Committee was the first to show by many examples that union resources were in fact unprotected from mishandling.[3]

The committee also investigated a number of organizations in which the officers had engaged in ballot stuffing, had penalized those who opposed the incumbent officers, and denied members a voice in determining policy or control over finances or officials. It also showed that in some organizations elections were only a formality and that the members had virtually no opportunity of challenging those in office.[4]

The committee found that the imposition and the administration of trusteeships were seriously abused in a number of orgaanizations. This procedure allows a parent union to take over a subordinate unit for a variety of reasons such as factional disputes, failure to manage affairs or finances of the union or administer the contracts with employers satisfactorily. In some instances, the trusteeships appeared to have been imposed for no reason except that the top officers were tempted to seize the local union and its assets. Although very few unions were guilty of those practices, several were shown to have imposed trusteeships arbitrarily and for periods far beyond the time necessary for eliminating the shortcomings that presumably affected the subordinate unit.

Attention was also given to the dictatorial methods followed in some unions and the denial of democratic rights to members. Yet, prior to the enactment of the LMRDA, there were no legal requirements that unions be democratic; recognizing the desirability of democracy introduces, and not ends, a series of problems. Conflicts between units of the organization are sometimes inevitable. Jurisdictional disputes between locals, between locals and intermediate bodies, and between the latter have taken place, and it is not always easy to determine where justice lies. Sometimes disputes are the result of political or ideological differences, but frequently they may result from an effort by the parent body to impose a common policy upon its subordinate units.

Nevertheless, the democratic principles which govern American society and the quality of union organization were sufficiently influential to impose democratic standards in virtually all unions. No one ever seriously questioned the desirability of allowing the members to control their organizations through democratic means.

Some of the most bitter controversies have been occasioned by the attempt to shift power from the local or regional units to the national organization.[5] Changes in competition in the labor or product markets in which members operate, control of the strike fund, rules of admission to the union or training of apprenticeship, as well as others, may cause friction and warfare. The national organization may have been directed by the union's convention or by some other means to insist upon specified terms being incorporated in the contract with employers, or others eliminated. Some locals may believe that the national rule prejudices their interest or position and may seek to resist. Cases in which the International union intervened to eliminate corruption or oppression of members are not unknown.

It is obvious that local dominance may not be more uniformly acceptable in union government than states' rights are in all questions that affect the citizen. One may ask if the power exercised has been granted to the officers and whether it has been carried out so as to allow for protest through a hearing of opponents. Once the organization has met those standards, and the contemplated act is not against the public interest, the parent body's actions meet the test of being democratic. A national policy sometimes requires that some units in the organization surrender advantages, but the repression of local advantages does not demonstrate that the action of the central body is oppressive or unwarranted.

It is unnecessary to observe that disputes between factions within unions are not always conducted on the highest plane, or that the disciplinary proceedings are not always models of judicial impartiality. However, until the great upsurge in union membership, there appeared to be no great concern with the internal government of unions. Aside from an occasional stricture from the bench, few criticisms of the operation of union judicial tribunals were made. The increased membership and rising complaints induced the American Civil Liberties Union (ACLU), in 1943, to issue a statement urging unions to allow admission of all workers qualified for membership, end racial discrimination in admittance or job assignment, and observe due process in proceedings in which members are charged with violation of union rules.[6] However, the statement stressed self-correction rather than government intervention.

Nearly all of the amendments submitted, when changes in the National Labor Relations Act were considered, aimed to reduce or, as it was more euphemistically expressed, to equalize bargaining power between labor and management. Concern with union abuses brought the ACLU to Congress with a sheaf of suggestions to outlaw segregation of members on the basis of race, creed, nationality or citizenship, and requiring a fair hearing and "reasonable cause" before a member could be disciplined. Unions would have also been compelled to hold periodic elections, release financial reports to members, and would have been prohibited from charging excessive initiation fees or imposing unequal or discriminatory rules. The American Civil Liberties Union described these proposals as a "basic 'bill of rights' for actual or prospective union members."[7]

In its proposals for amending the Wagner Act, in 1947, the House Committee on Education and Labor included section 8 (c) which contained a "bill of rights for union members" incorporating suggestions of the ACLU which were eliminated in conference. Congress did require that union dues and initiation fees be reasonable, and unions deposit their constitutions and bylaws, and file annual financial statements with the Department of Labor.[8]

Other efforts to reform union practices were made subsequently by Congressman Andrew Jacobs, of Indiana, who headed a subcommittee investigating practices of labor organizations.

The Jacobs bill did not get out of committee. Nor did a proposal by Joseph Kovner, a former assistant counsel of the Congress of Industrial Organizations, gain any legislative support. His was a simple statute which contained protection of union members against improper discipline.[9]

The ACLU also continued its campaign for union reform. In 1950, a summary of the 1943 pamphlet was issued, and in the same year the ACLU issued a statement: "Disturbed by reports of 'illegal and undemocratic procedures in disciplinary proceedings of trade union members by several CIO and AFL organizations, the Board of Directors announced . . . a preliminary study' of these proceedings . . . to discover if, and to what extent, the civil liberties of union members have been violated."

The ACLU continued to be concerned with the problem of civil liberties in labor organizations. A preliminary inquiry was started, but the response to its plea for documentation of its concern was not forthcoming.[10] A preliminary report was nevertheless issued, as was a summary of the 1943 statement. It reiterated the need for "direct protection" of the fundamental rights of a worker within his union "including the right to vote, honest elections and the right to fair and equal treatment in collective bargaining; and the right to a fair trial on all charges."[11]

While nominally supporting union self-control, the report suggested that if the legislation were enacted, "enforcement should be placed in the hands of an administrative agency which is readily available to union members, which can act quickly and can exercise continuing supervision where it is necessary."

The McClellan Committee Hearings offered another opportunity to the ACLU to present its proposals for reform of union government. In 1958 it submitted to Congress a "Labor Union Bill of Rights." The statement proposed that union members have access to official union publications to express their views, be allowed to circulate petitions among the members, publish and distribute leaflets, newspapers and other written material and assemble freely with other members for discussing union policy. In addition, the statement called for free union elections by secret ballot, hearings before the imposition of trusteeships, full and complete accounting of funds, equal treatment of members and the prohibition of discrimination on the basis of sex, race, national origin or citizenship. Finally, the statement outlined procedures that would assure fair trials for those charged with violations of union rules and regulations.[12]

Background of Legislation Dealing with Corruption

The protection of membership rights was only one of the purposes of the Labor-Management Reporting and Disclosure Act. Labor racketeering had been exposed, the first revelations coming at the turn of the century. In some instances, these practices involved arrangements with employers for the sharing of gains. In others the officers used the unions' power to extort monies from the employer. The diversion of union funds had also been practiced, and compelling members to pay tribute for favorable assignments through a hiring hall had also been known.

Corruption appears to be of several kinds. It can be occasional, under circumstances such as the payment of a bribe for a steward or a business agent for a concession in work rules or for allowing a practice that is not permissible under the agreement. Systematic corruption is also found. It is a situation whereby the employer may make periodic contributions to a union officer, or an arrangement may be devised whereby gains are shared, as in the

New York and the Chicago building construction industry. Jobs were allocated, costs were centrally determined and bidding eliminated, and the monopoly profits divided among business agents, contractors and material dealers.

The systematic types of industrial corruption are much more serious than the occasional ones because of their superior organization and greater power. Many of those who have used the union for personal gain have been members risen from the ranks. The outsider who has taken the union over by guile or force is a later phenomenon than the union officer grown corrupt. The latter presents a more serious threat to the union because he is likely to be a member of the underworld with criminal connections.

Exposure of the misdeeds of union officers has inevitably led to demands for government intervention. However, legislators have generally been convinced that such problems should be dealt with by the normal government processes, and that unions should themselves seek to bar the corrupt and venal from places of power within the organization. Another reason was that exposure was likely to involve only relatively few local or regional union officers. The phenomenon was generally observable in a number of labor-intensive industries in which union officials were able to exact a toll upon some of the firms in which their members were employed or engage in a profitable collusive arrangement with the employer or/and others. While the building construction industry appears to have been especially susceptible to such arrangements, shakedowns and extortion were also observed in the clothing manufacturing industries, retail distribution, building service, trucking, the entertainment industries, and the port of New York.

Larger cities seem to have been the principal centers for such activities, but the massive shakedown attempted in the construction of the atomic energy project in southern Illinois and Kentucky shows that size is not a necessary condition for such operations.

The growth of health and welfare programs, financed by employers or jointly by employers and employees, can be said to have introduced another dimension into the problem of labor racketeering. Their spread was an unforeseeable development of the system of wage controls established by the government during World War II. The Little Steel formula, elaborated in the summer of 1942, by the National War Labor Board, limited increases in hourly wage rates to 15 percent above the amount prevailing on January 1, 1941. Allowance for higher increases were made, but the formula governed, with few exceptions, the entire economy.

As the war continued, the ability of unions to gain approvable wage concessions was virtually exhausted. They then turned their attention to improvements in fringe benefits, such as vacations, paid holidays, health, welfare and pension programs. Facing severe labor shortages and high excess profit taxes, employers were not generally opposed to those measures. Once inaugurated, the push for these benefits spread, and the impetus continued after the ending of the war and wage control. A ruling that employers were obligated, under the National Labor Relations Act, to bargain over pensions gave added impetus to demands for the establishment of these programs.[13]

Health and welfare programs, and pensions can be financed in a variety of ways. The programs can be jointly administered by representatives from labor and management, or the benefits might be purchased from a bank or an insurance company. Brokers and underwriters are interested in selling coverage. A number of unions have operated beneficiary programs for their members, but these were simple and modest ventures administered out of the secretary-treasurer's office. These were financed by the members through their dues payments or as an addition to dues. The union-operated programs did not usually involve purchase of policies from banks or insurance companies, nor did they raise problems of contributions, commissions or retention fees.

The new programs enlarged the problem of corruption. While the overwhelming number of these plans are efficiently and honestly managed, there was exposure of grave disregard of the interest of those who are covered. Moreover, the absence of competitive bidding and standards for compensating trustees and managers of the program makes corruption and violation of fiduciary duty relatively easy. As a result, some of the programs, usually covering low paid workers, were looted or their funds wasted.

The Subcommittee on Welfare and Pension Funds of the United States Senate Committee on Labor and Public Welfare noted that the "unsupervised development" of these funds brought with them "many problems that merit public attention. Nor is it surprising that, with so much money involved and the absence of supervision, our investigation has indicated that an unscrupulous minority has preyed upon such funds; nor that there has been shocking abuses, such as embezzlement, collusion, kickbacks, exorbitant insurance charges, and various other forms of malfeasance."[14]

Outright embezzlement of funds by union officials or by agents appointed by them was also found. The outstanding example was the looting of the Laundry Workers International Union by its "insurance agent," Louis B. Saperstein, in collusion with one of the union's officers, E. C. James. More than $900,000 belonging to more than 50,000 beneficiaries was stolen from the fund.[15]

The initial involvement of the federal government in labor racketeering was the indirect result of an effort to contain inter-state criminal activity by roving gangsters. It followed the investigation of a Senate sub-committee headed by Senator Royal S. Copeland. The Coleman Act, as it was called, provided: "Any person, who, in connection with or in relation to any act in any way or in any degree affecting trade or commerce (a) obtains or attempts to obtain, by the use or attempt to use or threat to use force, violence, coercion, the payment of money or other valuable considerations, or the purchase or rental of property or protective services, not including, however, the payment of wages by bona fide employer to a bona fide employee," shall be a felony.[16]

The prohibitions against illicit payment were applied to Teamsters Local 807 in New York. Large volumes of merchandise entered New York City on over-the-road trucks driven by chauffeurs from points at which cargo originated. Local 807 claimed that work within its jurisdiction had to be performed by its own members. As the out-of-town drivers refused to turn over their vehicles to members of 807, the custom was established that entering trucks paid to the union $9.42 for the larger truck and $8.41 for the smaller one.

Following complaints from shippers and trucking companies twenty-six members of New York Local 807, including several officers, were indicted for violating the anti-racketeering statute. The charges were dismissed by the United States Court of Appeals Second Circuit, and the case was subsequently reviewed in *Local 807* v. *United States*. The crucial question was whether the money had to be paid to a permanent employee in order to come under the ban. Mr. Justice James F. Byrnes, writing for the majority, held the statute was not restricted to an employee who had attained status prior to the time at which he obtained or attempted to obtain payment of wages from a bona fide employer, and consequently the union's demand for taking over the driving of the trucks into the city was not illegal. Moreover, the majority opinion said the statute was designed "to close gaps in existing Federal laws to render more difficult the activities of predatory criminal gangs of the Kelly and Dillinger types."[17]

In 1946, the Hobbs Act was passed by the Seventy-Ninth Congress to close the gap opened by Mr. Justice Byrnes' decision. The earlier prohibitions on obstructing or delaying commerce were repeated, and extortion was defined as: "The obtaining of property from another, without his consent, induced by wrongful use of actual or threatened force, violence, or fear, or under the color of official right." In *United States* v. *Green*,[18] the Supreme Court upheld a conviction under conditions similar to those reported in the New York labor market in the Local 807 case. In upholding the conviction, Mr. Justice Reed, writing for the court, said the prohibitions covered offers of "superfluous services." The Hobbs Act and Section 302 of the Taft-Hartley Act were the major anti-racketeering statutes affecting labor union officials and the organizations of labor prior to the enactment of the Landrum-Griffin Act. Between 1946, the date of the enactment of the Hobbs Act, and March 1959, 134 convictions took place under the above laws.[19] These statutes, however, prohibited acts which affect employers and did not provide a remedy for many of the abuses publicized by the McClellan Committee.

The American Federation of Labor, almost from the beginning of its history, was confronted with reports of wrongdoing by labor officials. In 1898, it appointed a committee to investigate, but its lack of power over its affiliates precluded any action beyond a call for virtue,[20] although efforts for higher standards of behavior were often made by the leaders on an unofficial basis. Finally, in 1940, the AFL authorized the executive council to seek correction of irresponsible conduct by trade union officials through appeals to the heads of the international union with which the offending member or members were affiliated.

While this directive was scarcely a severe restraint upon undesirable conduct, it served as a basis for the AFL's intervention in the Port of New York, in the early 1950s, after the New York Crime Commission had exposed violations of trust, tolerance of loan sharking, and kickbacks to foremen for an opportunity to be picked from the "shape up" for a job. When the International Longshoremen's Association (ILA) refused to introduce reforms, it was expelled from the federation and another union chartered in its jurisdiction. The effort to replace the ILA by the union failed as a result of an unofficial alliance of the stevedores, the ILA, and the National Maritime Union (NMU). After a sojourn of several years outside the ranks, the ILA reaffiliated with the AFL-CIO.

The merged federation, American Federation of Labor (AFL)-Congress of Industrial Organizations (CIO) was authorized, under the constitution, to "protect the labor movement from any and all corrupt influences," and a standing Committee on Ethical Practices was established to investigate if an affiliate was "substantially influenced in the conduct of its affairs by corrupt influence." In addition, the executive council was given power to suspend such affiliates by a two-thirds vote, with the right of the latter to appeal to the convention.

The Committee on Ethical Practices subsequently recommended six codes embodying desirable rules for issuance of charters by national and international unions, the management of health and welfare funds, the exclusion of racketeers, crooks, communists and fascists from union office, investments and business interests of union officials, financial and proprietary activities of unions, and a supplementary code for proper accounting and financial controls. Unions were also advised that democratic processes were necessary for the proper functioning of the organization. The AFL-CIO also announced that it was its "firm policy" to cooperate with proper legislative committees and law enforcement agencies seeking "fairly and objectively" to expose corrupt influences within the labor movement.[21]

The Ethical Practices Committee did not wait for the government exposure before taking action. Its first hearings in 1955 were held before the McClellan Committee was on the horizon. It reviewed the activities of Angelo Inciso, President of Local 286, Allied Industrial Workers, a catch-all amalgamated local in Chicago. Inciso was charged with making verbal agreements with employers on payments to the health and welfare fund, comingling insurance premiums with union dues, not keeping adequate records, and making questionable expenditures.[22] The same union allowed John DioGuardia (Dio) to organize locals in New York City. The Allied Industrial Workers was directed to clean house in ninety days or be suspended from the AFL-CIO. It was placed on probation, which was lifted on October 24, 1957. The Ethical Practices Committee pointed to the "splendid record of the Allied Industrial Workers . . . in complying with the provisions of the Ethical Practices Committee."[23]

The Distillery, Rectifying and Wine Workers' International Union, and the United Textile Workers of America were also placed on probation, and both were subsequently granted complete autonomy: In both unions, officers embezzled hundreds of thousands of dollars. Sol Cliento, Secretary of the Distillery Workers, was indicted for diverting monies from health and welfare funds financed by contributions from about 600 employers and covering 23,000 workers. He was found to have received about $300,000 from Louis Saperstein, a broker whose name appeared in several Congressional investigations. After the death of Saperstein, under mysterious circumstances, it was revealed in the trial of a leading New Jersey gangster, that Saperstein had been mercilessly beaten for refusal to share some of the proceeds from union contracts on health and welfare programs.

The United Textile Workers of America was another union whose tolerance of defalcations by its top officers became publicly known. The conduct, especially of Secretary-Treasurer Leonard Klenert, was one of the most sordid pieces of thievery to come to public attention.

In addition, three unions refused to make' the changes requested by the AFL-CIO and were expelled. The largest affiliate was the International Brotherhood of Teamsters, Chauffeurs, Warehousemen and Helpers of America; the two others, the Bakery and Confectionary Workers, and the Laundry Workers Unions. In his demand for the ousting of the Teamsters' Union, Alex Rose, Chairman of the AFL-CIO's convention Committee on Appeals, expressed his frustration with the behavior of the convention of the Teamsters' Union. Rose believed "that the behavior, the arrogance, the defiance of the Teamsters Convention has created a climate for all the anti-trust legislation that we fear, and I think the decisions of this Convention will straighten out and put labor in its proper role and in its proper light before public opinion.[24]

Rose's belief that disciplinary action against unions charged with corruption might dampen sentiment for labor reform was soon to be shown to have been false optimism. A few weeks after the adjournment of the federation convention President Dwight D. Eisenhower asked for the enactment of a labor reform measure. Congress responded by enacting the Labor-Management Reporting and Disclosure Act. It provided for the most extensive regulation of the internal affairs of labor organizations that had ever been enacted by a legislative body in the United States. The law contained a "bill of rights for union members" which guaranteed to union members the right to free speech, press and assemblage in the discussion of union business, and also provided for equal rights for members to vote and to hold office in the union. Unions were required to submit annual reports of assets, income and expenditures. Trusteeships were limited as to time, and members were allowed to challenge their imposition in the courts. Rules for holding union elections were instituted, and on the basis of a member's valid complaint elections could be challenged by the Secretary of Labor who was authorized to call on the United States district courts for the enforcement of meritorious complaints. Finally, the law defined the fiduciary obligations of union officers, and allowed members, under defined conditions, to sue for an accounting or for the return of improper expenditures.

2

The Bill of Rights
for Union Members

Title I, the bill of rights, guarantees to members of labor organizations (1) equal rights to nominate candidates for union office, vote in elections, attend meetings of the organization and participate in its deliberations. (2) It guarantees to every member the right to assemble and express his views at meetings of the union, upon any business of the organization including candidates for union office. (3) It requires that members be given adequate notice of voting on proposals for changing the member's contribution and that it must be made by secret ballot. (4) It forbids penalizing a member of a union for protesting an action of his organization to a government agency or a court of law. (5) It decrees that no union member can be penalized by his union without being presented with written charges and given a "full and fair hearing."

Full evidence was presented to the McClellan Committee of the denial of rights to members, and of the arbitrary imposition of assessments and of raising of dues. However, it was not conclusive, and there was opposition to the enactment of Title I on the ground that it was a needless intrusion into the affairs of labor organization. It may, therefore, be helpful to review briefly the functioning of union government and opportunity provided members to obtain relief from unfair decisions of their unions and their officers.

Unions are governed by constitutions, by-laws and the rules enacted by authorized legislative bodies of the organization. American unions, an early student tells us, in "piecing together their machinery of government, have borrowed from various sources."[1] The constitution of the first permanent national union, the International Typographical Union (ITU), was borrowed, in 1851, from the Order of Odd Fellows of the United States of America. The Molders' Union and others then borrowed all or much of their constitutions from the ITU. The fraternal societies, and unions in England furnished a number of organizations in the United States with all or part of their basic documents.

The main source has been, however, the borrowing from one another, and through these borrowings the influence of the primary source was diffused among the organizations of labor. A successful organization's system of laws tended to be imitated. As a result there developed a similarity in the constitutions of the early unions, especially if they were engaged in kindred trades.[2] In time, however, the constitution, by-laws and rules tended to be adapted to the needs of the organization, and the unions' governments were shaped by the kind of markets in which their members were employed, leadership, and the kind of problems the organization faced.

Constitutions and by-laws of the national and international unions contain the rules and powers of the various officials, the manner of their selection, the term of office, their duties, salaries and the manner by which locals and intermediate bodies can be chartered and their rights and duties. In addition, the constitution will include sections on qualification and acquisition of membership and the obligations of those who have become members. National or international unions require or allow subordinate bodies to write local constitutions in harmony with the rules of the national organization. Others prescribe a uniform local constitution for their members. A certain amount of variation is permitted by the former, but none in the latter.

Union rules are of two types, those which regulate behavior on the job and/or in the union. Work rules are more important in unions of skilled workers than in unions of production or semi-skilled, and unskilled workers. Unions of skilled workers regulate the work shift, overtime and the use of tools, and a variety of job-connected conditions which are determined in bargaining with employers by industrial unions and embodied in labor management agreements. All unions require that members obey the laws of the organization and have established procedures for punishing violators.

Union constitutions typically specify that certain acts will subject members to union discipline.[3] As an example of proscribed acts, Section 218 of the constitution of the United Association of Journeymen and Apprentices of the Plumbing and Pipe Fitting Industry of the United States and Canada says: "No member of the United Association shall be permitted to furnish tools." This rule applies to the job. What might be called a "political offense" is spoken of in Section 221, which prescribes that a member "guilty of sending out letters of falsehood and misrepresentation shall be expelled."[4]

The United Steelworkers of America does not list violation of work rules as offenses against the union. Under Article XII, "Discipline," a violation "of any" collective agreement is an offense against the union constitution. However, the specific prohibitions of given work practices are absent because the members of the union unlike a craft organization do not perform similar work. The article on discipline deals with such acts as "obtaining membership through fraudulent means or by misrepresentation," instituting action against the union or its locals without first exhausting all appellate procedures within the organization, promoting a competing or dual union, slandering a member, furnishing lists of members to outsiders, and interfering with an officer in the course of his union duties.[5] Similar clauses are also found in the constitution of the Plumbers' Union.

As the steelworkers' and plumbers' unions are typical of their group, their handling of discipline will provide a fairly accurate picture on how these proceedings are carried out. The Steelworkers' Union requires that the charges must be submitted in writing to the local union of which the individual charged is a member. The Plumbers' Union requires that the charges be made by a member in good standing who has "personal knowledge" of the offense committed. The charges must be in writing and state "with reasonable certainty the nature of the offense charged, the time and place of the occurrence . . ." Each union requires that copies of the charges be sent to the accused. In the Steelworkers, the charges are immediately considered, but in the Plumbers' Union the local must accept the charges before they can be entertained. Each constitution provides that the defendant must be given time to prepare a defense, but the Steelworkers limit the time to between two and four weeks.[6]

The trial procedure is specified in each document. In the Steelworkers' Union, a trial committee is designated in accordance with the local union by-laws, while the local executive board acts as the tribunal in the Plumbers' Union, unless disqualified from serving. In the latter, the local executive board reports its findings to the members, but the local does not assess penalties if the verdict is guilty. The trial board performs that function. In the Steelworkers' Union, the trial board reports to the membership which can act on the report and impose penalties as "in its judgement it may deem fitting and proper."[7] Suspension, expulsion from the union, or fines of more than $150 must be approved, in the Plumbers' Union, by the general executive board.[8]

Unions generally allow one or more appeals from a verdict of a local union or an intermediate body. In the Steelworkers, "the accused and the accuser" may appeal to the International and thereafter to the next international convention, provided that notice of appeal is filed with the Secretary-Treasurer within thirty days of the verdict. The executive board may reverse the decision. It has the authority to order the local union to compensate a member for the expenses incurred if the decision is overturned.

In the Plumbers' Union, the decisions which are not automatically reviewed by the executive board—expulsion, suspension or a fine above $150—can be appealed within twenty days after the local acted. The general executive board has the power to affirm, reverse, or modify the verdict of the lower tribunal. Appeals to the convention, in both unions, can be made after due notice, but the verdict of the executive board remains in effect while the appeal is pending.

Union disciplinary procedure has been attacked on a number of grounds, the most common one being that offenses are too general and that the trial bodies are prejudiced. It is also claimed that it is improper to permit the retrial of a member who has been acquitted of the charges by a local union tribunal. This procedure has been allowed because the membership may not convict a popular officer or member, regardless of the evidence submitted.[9]

Charges and trials and penalties and acquittals are events which generally take place at the local level. Under some circumstances, the international union may intervene and appoint a hearing officer, but such action is only likely to take place when a local union or an intermediate body is faction ridden, and a fair trial is not possible. Such an act might be compared with a change of venue in the courts and has no importance as far as the integrity of the procedures is concerned. Because trials are on a local basis, the international union is usually not aware of the situation, unless an appeal against a verdict is made by the accuser or the accused.

Most unions have created appellate tribunals to which members convicted by the courts of the organization can appeal. Because the judges are usually members of the union and can on occasion be friends or enemies of the defendant, each side is allowed to appeal to the higher tribunals of the organization. In a number of instances, the defendant-member may be convinced that charges were fabricated, that the jury was packed or that the verdict was unsupported by evidence. Union members could then turn to the common law courts for relief from the unfair penalties of their organizations.[10]

Professor Clyde W. Summers, "Legal Limitations on Union

Discipline," *Harvard Law Review*, May 1951, p. 1051, tells us: "On the one hand, the courts have a deep rooted reluctance to intervene in the internal affairs of voluntary associations. This reluctance is a product of long judicial experience in attempting to settle family fights in religious and fraternal associations . . . This policy of nonintervention which the courts developed in cases involving churches and lodges was early applied with equal strictness to labor unions."

The situation is not quite so simple. Thus, Frederick H. Bacon, writing in 1894, claimed:

> benefit societies have a dual existence: they are social and fraternal in their nature, yet provide for beneficiaries certain pecuniary benefits. Consequently, while expulsion in the case of a member of a church or club, or fraternity purely social, might well be enough, if the proceedings were regular, the same offence in the case of a benefit society could not be punished by expulsion.[11]

If the reported cases are any guide, it would appear that the state courts, despite any reluctance they might have had, did accept complaints of union members against the decisions of their organizations for adjudication. Summarizing the view of the courts in 1906, a New York tribunal noted:

> The well established rule governing interference by courts with the internal affairs of voluntary associations and membership corporations in regard to disciplinary proceedings is, the courts will look into the record to see whether the practice and proceedings have been in accordance with the constitution and bylaws of the organization, whether the charges are substantial, and whether the member had fair notice and opportunity to be heard. In short has the member received fair play.[12]

Between the middle 1880s and 1959, the year in which the LMRDA was enacted, I have found 358 reported cases brought to court by members of sixty-eight unions which were part of the general labor movement and fourteen independent non-affiliated organizations. The union was not identified in fifteen cases. A review of the individual cases is not necessary. Many of the protesters were charged with violating union job rules. Some arose in factional disputes or were attempts by union officers to suppress free comment. A third group was the result of opposition of a local union to being merged with another or protesting the chartering of another local in its territory. The statistical breakdown of their cases is shown in Table 1.

The above cases do not show that aggrieved union members were generally denied relief in the state courts. Critics, however, believed that this remedy against arbitrary acts of the union or its officers were "too chancy" and uncertain as well as expensive. Moreover, the critics argued that the approach of the courts in the different jurisdictions was not uniform in the matter of protecting the rights of members. As the federal government has, since the 1930s, exercised a predominant influence over policies which affect unions as collective bargaining agencies, the critics claimed that it was therefore essential that it provide standards for the protection of membership rights. In addition, since abuses such as excluding certain members from the right to hold union office or to exercise an equal voice and vote in determining union policy was legal, these discriminatory policies could not be successfully challenged in the state courts.

The court cases cited are part of a larger number which include those that have been acquitted by the union tribunal and those which the member may accept because he believes the verdict is justified or because he is unwilling to take his grievance to the courts. Because union business meetings are not open to the public, it is not possible to estimate the number of members that are brought to trial or the character of the verdicts handed down by the union trial boards.

Congress went beyond assuring a union member a fair trial. It wrote into Title I provisions guaranteeing members equal rights to vote and be candidates for union office, and to free speech,

Table 1.
Number of Cases in the State Courts Involving Discipline and Election Disputes Up to 1959, by Union

Union	Number
Automobile Workers, United	2
Bakery and Confectionery	2
Boilermakers	5
Brewery	5
Bricklayers	4
Building Service	5
Building Trades Council (Sacramento, Calif.)	1
Carmen, Railway	1
Carpenters	23
Clerks, Retail	2
Communication	1
Conductors, Railway	1
Electrical Workers, Intnl. Brotherhood	2
Electrical Workers, United	1
Engineers, Operating	14
Federal Labor Unions (AFL)	4
Fur Workers	1
Furniture Workers	3
Garment Workers, United	2
Garment Workers, Intnl. Ladies	3
Glass, Flint	1
Glass Bottle Blowers	1
Hatters	1
Hotel and Restaurant	16
Independents and Unaffiliated	14
Iron Workers	7
Jewelry	1
Laborers	9

Table 1—Cont.

Union	Number
Leather	1
Locomotive Engineers	14[1]
Longshoremen, Intnl. Association	6
Machinists	8
Marine Cooks and Stewards	4
Marine Engineers Beneficial Assn.	1
Marine and Shipbuilding	4
Maritime Union, National	5
Masters, Mates and Pilots	6
Meat Cutters	1
Mine Workers of America, United	4
Musicians	19[2]
Newspaper Guild	1
Painters	18[3]
Paper Makers	1
Photo Engravers	1
Plasterers	1
Plumbers	10
Potters	3
Pressmen, Printing	2
Pulp and Sulphite Workers	2
Radio Artists	1
Roofers	1
Sailors Union of the Pacific	1
Sheet Metal Workers	3
Shoe Workers (Knights of Labor Assembly)	1
Boot and Shoe Workers	2
Stage Employees	25
Steel Workers	1
Stereotypes	1
Stone Cutters, Journeymen	1
Street and Electric Ry. Employees	7

Table 1—Cont.

Union	Number
Teamsters	30
Tobacco	1
Trainmen	7
Transport Workers	3
Typographical Union, Intnl.	3
Upholsterers	2
Utility Workers	1
Union not identified	15
Total	358

[1]One of the suits involved ten members; each suit was separate.

[2]Nine of the cases were decided before 1907. Several of the locals were not members of the American Federation of Musicians at the time the suits were decided.

[3]Eight of the cases that involved the Painters' Union originated in New York District 9; the first one was decided by the Court of Appeals in 1916. *Solomon* v. *Brotherhood of Painters*, 112 N.E. 752 (Court of Appeals, 1916).

press, and assembly, the provisions of which will be examined in the next six chapters.

"Title I—Bill of Rights of Members of Labor Organizations"—was not included in either the Kennedy-Ives or Kennedy-Ervin bills. During the debate on the latter, Senator John L. McClellan introduced an amendment containing six provisions which were subsequently written into the final legislation. However, Section 103, authorizing the Secretary of Labor "to bring an action in a district court of the United States for such relief as may be appropriate including, but without such limitation, injunctions to restrain any such violations and to compel compliance with this title," was rejected after it had been initially passed by the Senate.[13]

John F. Kennedy opposed the amendment on the floor. In his view "such rights are dealt . . . more effectively under state law, under the Taft-Hartley Act than under the pending bill." The McClellan amendment passed the Senate by a vote of 47 to 46. Its enactment was the result of a temporary coalition of Southern Democrats and Republicans. Thomas Dodd of Connecticut, Frank Lausche of Ohio, and Dennis Chavez of New Mexico were the three non-Southern Democrats to support the amendment. A number of senators had second thoughts on the McClellan proposals after Senator Olin Johnston of South Carolina told them that the injunctive procedures included in the McClellan amendment "opens the door for such procedures in the field of civil rights," and "grants the Secretary of Labor power to obtain through the Federal courts injunctions to restrain anyone violating or threatening to violate the provisions of the bill."[14] Senator Johnston warned that the "McClellan amendment contains powers far beyond any civil rights legislation yet proposed and it similarly does not contain a jury trial requirement in cases brought. . . . This amendment effectively enforces integration in social activities of unions, and in my opinion, is the first step to a broad Federal FEPC program which will become a menace to management and industry as well as labor."[15]

In response to the warnings of Senator Johnston, an amendment sponsored by Senator Thomas Kuchel and eight of his colleagues was adopted. It eliminated the power of the Secretary of Labor to sue on behalf of an aggrieved member who, instead, was himself allowed to appeal to the courts. The newly amended bill passed the Senate by a vote of 77 to 14.[16] A different version was enacted in the House, and the two statements were compromised in conference.

3

Protection of the Union Member's Right to Vote

Equal Rights

The "Bill of Rights of Members of Labor Organizations" is made up of five sections, the first, Section 101 (a) (1), prescribing the equal rights of union members. It declares:

> Every member of a labor organization shall have equal rights and privileges within such organization to nominate candidates, to vote in elections or referendums of the labor organization, to attend membership meetings and to participate in the deliberations and voting upon the business of such meetings, subject to reasonable rules and regulations in such organization's constitution and bylaws.

The major objective of the provision was to eliminate differences in the rights accorded by some unions to certain members, with respect to voting in elections or referenda, in holding office, or voting for officers or policies of the organization. It had not been unusual for labor organizations to deny the right of full participation in the affairs of the organization to apprentices occupying a temporary status. However, as soon as they became journeymen, they were allowed to share in the full rights and privileges of other members. Differences in treatment were accorded by some unions of skilled workers to members who were recruited after the organization extended its jurisdiction to jobs requiring employees with lesser skills. The Carpenters', Electrical (IBEW), and Bookbinders' unions were among those which followed such a policy.

These practices had been in effect over a long period of time, and they were generally introduced when unions of skilled workers decided to recruit those employed at semi-skilled and unskilled tasks in their craft or industry. These discriminatory practices could not be successfully attacked because membership had been obtained when the restrictive clauses were part of the constitution and by-laws of the organization. A member of a branch or division of a union whose members were denied full voting rights or the right to hold some or all offices could not claim that such discrimination violated the constitution and by-laws of the organization. Instead, the appeal against such provisions had to be made upon their discriminatory and inequitable character, and because members of the discriminated group were denied full rights to choose the officers and policies of the union.

By enacting the "equal rights" provision, Congress declared that if a union is willing to recruit a worker performing certain tasks for an employer, it cannot on any ground grant him lesser rights within the organization than it has to other members. While discriminatory treatment of any kind by a labor organization might be challenged in the courts, the majority of complaints under Section 101 (a)(1) have been related to voting and elections. As union elections are also covered in Title IV, which deals with them in much greater detail, it became necessary as soon as the law became effective to decide when and under what circumstances an aggrieved member could appeal to the courts and when he was obliged to utilize the remedies granted in Title IV.[1]

Although in retrospect the differences in the remedies provided under Section 101 (a) (1) and 402 may be clear, the disqualifications of candidates for election by several unions were protested under Section 101 (a). In *Mamula* v. *United Steelworkers of America*,[2] the Third Circuit Court of Appeals ruled that a member disqualified from running for office could not bring suit under Section 101 (a) (1) because an election had been held. Now the remedy was a complaint to the Secretary of Labor in accordance with Section 402 of the Act. Even though a case was pending in the federal court under Title I and the court had jurisdiction, both parties deferred action on the complaint to await details on the manner in which nominations were conducted. Nicholas Mamula had been tried for misconduct by his local union and was disqualified from running for office for five years, with a proviso that the waiting period would be shortened if he restored certain monies to the union treasury. "There is nothing in the record showing any of the plaintiff's rights as a union member set forth in Title I were violated by defendants. The facts point the other way, for he participated in the meeting, was its presiding officer, and had ample opportunity to nominate candidates. There is nothing in the provisions of Title I or its legislative history that would give plaintiff standing as a candidate to bring this action."

In two cases, the District Court, Southern California, refused to enjoin union elections. In *Byrd* v. *Archer*[3] the court found that Section 101 (a) (1) "does not specifically create a right to be a candidate in a union election upon which a member may sue under Section 102, but Title IV . . . does provide elaborate procedures by which members may challenge union elections, and those procedures appear to be exclusive for any such challenge." The petition of the member of Local 440, Lathers' Union, was rejected on the above ground. The view was further elaborated in *Johnson* v. *San Diego Waiters and Bartenders Local No. 500*,[4] by the same court. Rejecting the plea for an injunction to prohibit the holding of a local election, the court said:

A close comparison of Title I and IV indicates . . . that there is no apparent overlap in protection *of the right of an individual to stand for an office in a union election.* Only Title IV . . . protects the right of an individual to be a candidate in an election. Title I . . . it is true, protects the right to nominate and vote for candidates. But the emphasis there is placed on the right of the nominator, not the rights of the nominee. The essence of the alleged wrong in this case is not the unequal treatment of nominators, but the alleged right to be nominated.

A completed election could not be challenged under Section 101 (a) (1), even though members had been denied an opportunity to nominate candidates of their choice and to cast their ballots.[5] A group of members of Local 1191, Hod Carriers, charged that they had not been allowed to nominate candidates, and that a large number of members had been unable to cast ballots because only one polling place had been established, in Detroit, while members were scattered throughout Michigan. The District Court, Western Michigan, found that there had been "a denial of equal opportunity to vote to those members who were scattered throughout the State of Michigan." Nevertheless, it was ruled that a completed election could only be challenged by a complaint to the Secretary of Labor.

The pleas that an election in a local union should be enjoined as the member's right to cast a ballot would be denied was rejected by the Court of Appeals, Second Circuit.[6] In rejecting the petition, the court noted that the plaintiff

had not been denied a right to vote and makes no claim based on any such denials. But he would have us construe the language of the statute as granting authority to the federal courts to control and direct the entire conduct of union elections on the theory that the right to vote is a right to cast an "effective" vote, and that a vote cannot be effective unless the election is properly conducted in all its aspects.

Local unions frequently impose qualifications for candidacies which members may regard as unfair or onerous. Differences may also arise as to whether certain offices should be filled by election or appointment. Because business agents had been appointed instead of being elected, a group of members complained to the district court that their equal rights to elect officers had been infringed. The complaint was dismissed on the ground that the "essence of the alleged wrong . . . does not concern itself with equal rights among members to vote for 'officers,' but whether business agents and stewards are, in fact, 'officers' who must be elected. Accordingly, plaintiffs have failed to establish a claim arising under 101 (a) (1) upon which relief may be granted."[7]

Disqualification of members as candidates for union office was unsuccessfully challenged in a number of cases. In rejecting a petition of a disqualified member that the union be ordered to place his name on the ballot, the Delaware District Court said that "nowhere among the rights enumerated therein (Title I) is the right to be a candidate found." Moreover, another district court found that the right to hold office is not protected under Section 101 (a) (1).[8] A protest by a candidate barred from having his name placed on the ballot because he had not attended one business meeting of the local union in each quarter was rejected on the ground that the requirement was not unreasonable. However, the Western Pennsylvania District Court also observed that Section 401 appeared to be the remedy for denial of right to run for office.[9]

Not all courts believed they were lacking in power to prevent election abuses or improper disqualification of candidates. The Seventh Circuit Court of Appeals ruled that the tampering with the ballots and substitution of a different ballot box from the official one constituted a denial of the right to vote warranting injunctive action under Section 101 (a) (1).

Officers of Local No. 46, Iron Workers, printed three times as many ballots as there were voters, seized and concealed the ballot box for a sufficiently long time to permit tampering, and then substituted a box different from the official one. The District Court, Northern Illinois, concluded from this behavior that "rank and file members of the union" would be denied the right to vote as surely as if the doors of the union had been barred against them while the balloting was conducted inside the hall." The court rejected "the suggestion that plaintiffs must . . . await the completion of the election and the counting of the purported ballots and then seek a remedy under Title IV."[10]

The reach of 101 (a) (1) was settled by the United States Supreme Court which ruled, *Calhoon* v. *Harvey*,[11] that disqualification of candidates for union office because they did not meet standards of eligibility specified in the constitution

> was not a discrimination against their right to nominate, since the same qualifications were required equally by all members. Whether the eligibility requirements set by the union's constitution and by-laws were reasonable and valid is a question separate and distinct from whether the right to nominate on an equal basis given by Section 101 (a) (1) was violated.

Mr. Justice Black, writing for the majority, noted that Title IV "sets up a statutory scheme governing the election of union officers," and allows unions to fix "reasonable qualifications uniformly imposed" for candidates for office. Section 402, as amplified by 29 CFR[1°] 452 issued in December 1959, the court noted, sets up an exclusive method for protecting Title IV rights. It allows union members to file complaints with the Secretary of Labor, who may, if he finds that a violation which may have affected the outcome of the election has occurred, file a suit in the appropriate United States district court.

The dispute had its origin in the Marine Engineers Beneficial Association whose requirements for district office were 180 days of sea time on vessels under contract with the union, self-nomination, and five consecutive years of membership. Only those who had previously served as full-time union officers could nominate themselves as candidates for district president. It was the position of the union, as well as the government, which submitted a memorandum as *amicus curiae*, that Section 101 (a) (1) requires only that a union apply its rules to all members without arbitrary distinctions or classifications. The government feared that if challenges to eligibility standards could be made under Title I it would produce "an undesirable overlapping of remedies and would frustrate the purpose of Congress to center in the Secretary control over litigation involving the substantive rules under which union elections are conducted."[13] The Second Circuit Court of Appeals had found that the restrictions which the union rules imposed violated the provisions on equal rights to nominate. This view was held erroneous in the above decision by the Supreme Court.

The view in *Calhoon* did not undermine the utility of the equal vote provision. Taking cognizance of the view of the Supreme Court, the Second Circuit,[14] held:

As long as no claim is made that the provision of the constitution and by-laws are being applied in such a way as to deny equality in voting, there is nothing in Section 101 which authorizes consideration of these documents.

The decision was given in an appeal of members of Local 802 Musicians, in New York, who favored the registering of voters in the local union election in person, during September of the same year. The heads of the local favored the use of a mail ballot which had been adopted by a membership referendum. The proposal for individual registering was adopted at a membership meeting and was ruled invalid by the international executive board when it was brought before it by a challenge from the local officers. The sponsors of the resolutions endorsing registration then appealed to the courts.

The dispute was between the full-time musicians who believed the registering requirement would reduce the number of part-time musicians who would be available to register as many were likely to be out of the city during the month of September. In its decision, the court noted that the "guaranty of the equal right to vote is surely not a general commission for the federal courts to review the constitution and by-laws of the union." It happens that the part-time musicians are a majority of members in Local 802.

The rights which such members should exercise raises a difficult problem. A number of unions limit the rights of part-time workers, and the courts upheld such restrictions as reasonable.[15] In the case of the part-time musicians, they constitute a majority in some of the locals, and they have the same responsibilities to the organization as those working full time. A court could reasonably make this distinction. In the Typographical Union, the multiple job holder is unusual and is, in fact, not welcome. The part-time musician is numerically important, and his exclusion would seriously weaken the union. Differences in treatment appear justified.

Giving so-called associated members unequal rights to vote, nominate or participate in union meetings violated the equal rights provision of LMRDA. In contrast to Calhoon, the "essence of the claimed wrong . . . is unequal treatment of nominators, not plaintiffs right to be nominated."[16] The United Scenic Artists Local Union No. 829, Painters, had granted associate members inferior status in voting, the right to nominate candidates for local office, and to participate in union meetings. When the District Court of Southern New York refused to dismiss, the complaint was discontinued, and the union abolished the discriminatory rules.

In Bookbinders Union Local 25 the members were divided into an A group of skilled journeymen and apprentices and a B group of lower skilled workers. The latter were excluded from voting for the three top officers. Suit to end the difference was started in the District Court of Southern New York. The court held "that such distinctions may not indefinitely affect a discrimination in the right of a member to exercise the right given to all other members in election of those who will represent his interests."[17] Furthermore, the court observed that the class are "full fledged members under the statute in a class reserved for unskilled and semi-skilled workers. . . . We think the disqualification is manifestly unreasonable and operates to deprive a large segment of the local of proper representation and voice in the matter which vitally affect their material and economic interests."

A union's discrimination in the nominating and voting rights accorded to members "illegally infringed their Section 101 (a) (1) right to nominate the vote."[18] A member of the Brotherhood of Railroad Trainmen was ruled off the ballot because he had not transferred to the lodge holding jurisdiction of the job upon which he was employed. The Third Circuit Court found that the rule on transfer had not been strictly observed, and that many members had not transferred to the proper lodge when their job assignments had been changed. In fact, that the disqualified candidate had been allowed to hold office in the lodge which now disqualified him as a candidate because of improper affiliation indicated to the court that the controversy was triggered by the discriminatory practices of the union.

Blatant irregularities and miscounting of ballots of a referendum on the removal of the headquarters of the International Printing Pressmen's and Assistants' Union, it was held, "resulted in substantial dilution of the plaintiffs' equal rights within the union," and was grounds for setting the referendum aside.[19] The proposal, favored by the internal officers, carried by a narrow margin, but a subsequent investigation disclosed serious violations of the law and the constitution of the organization. The illegal votes were counted by the board of electors and were included in the published tabulation of the final results.

Allowing only part of the members to vote on a proposal as to whether a separate local or over-the-road drivers should be established was held to be a violation of the equal-right to vote provision.[20] The issue arose in Local 327, Teamsters, which had a membership of about 5,000, 2,000 of whom were drivers of over-the-road trucks and were called "freighters." A request from some of the freighters for a separate charter was twice submitted to a vote of the local membership and defeated. Although the international president could, on his authority, issue a charter, he was evidently anxious to ascertain the extent of the wishes among this special group.

The decision of the court was based upon a literal interpretation of the equal-rights provision. To be effective as well as equitable, the rights and interests of minorities as well as majorities must be considered. Such a requirement has to be carried out if the statutory obligation of fair representation is to be met. The danger of neglecting the needs of a minority of members is frequently present, and the attempt to ascertain their wishes in a limited advisory vote which is not binding on the officers does not appear to contradict the equal-rights requirement.

Unions have enacted differing provisions with respect to the member's right to transfer from one local to another of the same international union. For example, paid-up members of the International Typographical Union have the right to change from one local to another without limitation. On the other hand, the International Alliance of Theatrical Stage Employees of the United States and Canada restricts severely the movement of members among local unions without the acquiescence of the local union to which a member in good standing wishes to transfer. These may be regarded as the extremes, and most unions' rules on this point fall somewhat in between the two. The restraints are generally influenced by availability of jobs, and by the fact that a "visiting" member may be liable for higher financial contributions and receive fewer or no fraternal benefits. The refusal of a local union of Iron Workers to accept a paid-up member from another jurisdiction who was employed in the local's area for some time was held to be in violation of the equal-rights provision of Section 101.[21] Under the decision of the New Jersey District Court of the United States, the petitioning member had the right to vote, attend meetings of the local, and to participate in the local's deliberations. However, the local refused to perform the ministerial function of swearing the petitioners in as members, and the federal courts could not under the equal-rights provision compel the local to do so. The dilemma was solved by the New Jersey courts which found the position of the Union "an unreasonable exercise of the discretion allowed under the constitution," and ordered the member's acceptance into the local union.

Even when the rights of transfer between local unions are expressly granted by the International constitution, the Southern New York District Court held that a local union did not violate the Act when it denied admittance to members of other locals in the same district who had procured clearance cards from the original locals, as the members intended to work within the district.[22] The dispute arose in Painters District Council No. 9, to which the original local and the one denying admission were affiliated. It appears that the transfer was an attempt to colonize within Local 1011 which had rejected the application. It was part of the campaign to win control of the district council, but the court's decision was based on the fact that the applicants were not "traveling 'members in search of employment or employed', the mandate . . . of the Brotherhood Constitution was unapplicable."

However, the Ninth Circuit directed Local Union 357, International Brotherhood of Electrical Workers, to accept several traveling members because there was nothing in the constitution of the International Union which grants a local union autonomy to refuse to accept a traveling member's card when he has complied with Article XXV of the union's constitution governing transfers. This article imposes an obligation that "travelers" receive a traveling card from their home local and that the local to which the traveler wishes to transfer includes the type of membership for which the traveling card was issued.

The International favored a liberal transfer policy, and in this case, the Vice-President in the district urged the acceptance of travelers from other local unions of the International. He did not order the local to comply with his suggestion "because of repeated holdings of the International Convention that the admission of travelers is a matter of local autonomy."[23] Given the desire of the officers to follow the views of the convention, the appellate court held that exhaustion of internal remedies was unnecessary as appeals to the union would be "futile." The appellate court rejected the views of the International Convention, and based its decision on the union's constitution, that if members comply "fully with the provisions of Article XXV, they are entitled to the rights and privileges guaranteed by Section 101 (a) (1)."

Denial of admission of a member suspended for a limited duration into the union after the expulsion had expired constituted a denial of equal rights in violation of Section 101 (a) (1).[24] The difference between a suspension and an expulsion has not always been observed in union disciplinary decisions. In fact, the majority of unions require that suspended members re-apply for admission, and in some instances there is no requirement for automatic reinstatement. A member of the Hotel and Restaurant Workers Union, in Philadelphia, had been suspended, and at the expiration of the term of his suspension the union refused to readmit him to membership. The court ordered his readmission to good standing because "suspension cannot be equated with expulsion. Suspension," said the court, "is a temporary cessation of rights and benefits, whereas expulsion is a disfranchisement, a severing of connections between the expelled members and the organization."

Refusal to accept members of a local union which had merged with another organization because of their refusal to sign a non-communist oath was held illegal and impermissible by the Second Circuit Court of Appeals.[25] The requirement, the signing of the "oath," was held to be "an unreasonable substantive ground for expelling a member from his union. Although the right to expel a member for engaging in subversive activities was not questioned, the appellate court feared that a compulsory oath may "place substantial restriction on the political activities of those who sign it conscientiously."

The reclassification of membership by a union did not violate the member's rights under Section 101 (a) (1) even though it affected the member's assessments, voting rights and priority.[26] Under the laws of the International Typographical Union, a member employed full-time in another occupation is classified as "not-at-trade." As a result, the member lost his seniority rights and was compelled to pay two assessments for the old age and mortuary funds, or double the amount of other members. He sued, charging violations of Section 101 (a) (1), and of other provisions of the LMRDA.

The Court of Appeals Tenth Circuit ruled the "classification was fairly applied to plaintiff. No showing is made of any improper motivations, of any discrimination, or of any intent to punish the plaintiff by depriving him of privileges. The Union simply enforced their rule pertaining to members having full-time employment outside the printing trade. The concurrence of the above circumstances—the regulation's reasonableness, its fair application, and plaintiff's outside employment—convinces us that the reclassification did not amount to discipline." The member had not been given a trial, and he raised the question whether he could be penalized without a hearing.

The court found that in the above situation a trial was unnecessary as his reclassification did not amount to discipline.

The court said:

> In this situation he would be unable to show that the regulation did not apply to him, and, in light of the union's initial decision to reclassify him and our conclusion that the scheme is reasonable, it can hardly be urged that he would successfully assert that for some reason it should not be applied to him . . . We conclude that where a reasonable regulation is applied in a fair and just manner to one who, by self-admission, is covered by it, such application does not come within the statutory phrase "otherwise disciplined".

This is an important decision in that it recognizes the difference between union regulations directed at members who are few and whom the union does not seek to attract. It would seem that they are in a different position from the part-time musician or retail clerk who may comprise a large proportion of the membership or the branch members of the Operating Engineers.

The issue raised in one case was one of unequal voting districts established by the Brotherhood of Railroad Trainmen for its general grievance committee. The mandate in *Calhoon*, in addition to the specific language of Title IV, meant that the reapportionment of the grievance committee could be attacked only by a suit under Title IV.[27] The complaint in this suit was that the general grievance committee was made up of local grievance chairmen each of whom had an equal vote, regardless of the number of members he represented. The complainant sought to have the court reorganize the grievance committee so that it would reflect the theory of one man, one vote. The court refused to take action on the complaint.

The right to vote in a referendum is predicated on the assumption that the proposals submitted will be clearly and unambiguously stated so that the voter can comprehend and decide the matter or matters before him. The International Association of Machinists, after its 1960 convention, submitted forty-seven amendments to its members to be voted in one group or as one question. This mode of submission was challenged in the courts.

In setting the ballot aside, the court held that the form of submission constituted "an abuse of power." Moreover, the court added, "where such confusing language is used, in addition to the grouping of such large number of amendments and such diverse matters into one proposition for amendment, there is additional reason to hold the action of the International organization and its officers as erroneous and arbitrary and as such illegal."[28]

Failure to hold a strike vote by secret ballot did not violate the equal rights provisions of Section 101.[29] A group of members of the independent Peninsula Shipbuilders Association, Newport News, Virginia, filed suit because the vote taken on the calling of a strike, defeated in a referendum, was not by secret ballot. A proposal to increase dues was submitted at the same time and was also defeated, but the contract with the employer was approved. The members were not denied the right to vote, and they exercised their judgment in the making of a choice on each of the proposals. There was no provision in the union constitution and by-laws that a vote on the contract was to be by secret ballot, and so the complaint was dismissed.

Acting under the "equal rights" provision, the United States District Court of Massachusetts enjoined the effort of the International Brotherhood of Telephone Workers from denying to six members of Local 2 the right to serve as delegates to the union's convention. In enjoining the officers of the international union, the court noted that the complaining members had been elected as delegates to the union's convention in 1969 and that two of them had also been elected to local office. No complaints of the election had been filed with the Secretary of Labor, and it was probable that the protesting members would prevail on the merits of their position.[30]

A different result followed the protest of the Rank and File Committee against the Amalgamated Clothing Workers of America on the ground that the constitution and by-laws vested excessive power in the officers so that the exercise of Title I rights was discouraged. The court rejected the Committee's claims that holding the election under the supervision of the joint board would effectively undermine the opportunity to run a fair election. Nor did the court find need to invalidate a by-law which forbade candidates to attend meetings at which refreshments were served. It also rejected the claim that required written and printed campaign material to be presented to the Board of Directors because no claim of censorship had been made.[31]

Section 101 (a) (1) has been utilized for challenging inequitable conduct and denial of equal rights. It has played a more restricted role in establishing democratic procedures than Title IV. The section is, however, by no means redundant. On the basis of the decisions of the courts the section is effective against discriminatory treatment of members in the electoral activities of the organization. It has been successfully invoked in cases where the vote has been mishandled or miscounted. Denying some members a vote has also been challenged under this title, but the members were disqualified not by the mandate of the constitution and by-laws, which might have made the issue one for a Title IV suit, but by fiat of the officers. As no basis for differentiation between members existed, the denial came under the ban of Section 101 (a) (1). The experience tends to indicate that although this section can be applied only in more special situations than Title IV, it is useful in protecting the democratic rights of union members.

4

Freedom of Speech, Press, and Assembly

Congress declared in Section 101 (a) (2):

Every member of any labor organization shall have the right
to meet and assemble freely with other members; and to
express any views, arguments, or opinions; and to express at
meetings of the labor organization his views, upon candidates in an election of the labor organization or upon any
business properly before the meeting, subject to the
organization's established and reasonable rules pertaining to
the conduct of meetings: *Provided*, That nothing herein shall
be construed to impair the right of a labor organization to
adopt and enforce reasonable rules as to the responsibility of
every member toward the organization as an institution and
to his refraining from conduct that would interfere with its
performance of its legal or contractual obligations.

Section 101 (a) encountered some Congressional opposition on
the ground that these rights were adequately defended by the
states. Although the state courts generally showed sympathy with

the petitions for relief of aggrieved members who had been penalized by their unions, there were a number of organizations which prohibited the meeting of members for the discussion of union business outside of the union hall or the circulation of printed material without the permission of the officers. Moreover, the courts in different jurisdictions did not follow uniform policies with respect to the rights of members. Prohibition of meetings outside of the union hall, denial of the right of members to establish opposition groups, and restriction upon publication and circulation of materials critical of incumbent officers, tended, it was believed, to inhibit the development of democratic processes which could check abuses and promote the policies favored by the members.

The issue of whether a union can punish a member who had been found guilty of libeling an officer, or whether such conduct was protected by the "bill of rights for union members" arose in *Salzhandler* v. *Caput*.[1] The Court of Appeals Second Circuit held that members of labor unions could not be penalized for statements on matters affecting the union irrespective of truth or falsity or whether the statement was libelous or not. The case arose in District Council No. 9, Painters, the scene of almost 50 years of factional warfare.[2] Attacks upon the leaders have never been restrained, and the Salzhandler episode might be regarded as a skirmish in an interminable factional battle.

Solomon Salzhandler, the financial secretary of Local 442, charged Isadore Webman, another officer of the local, with having stolen funds from a former business agent who had jointly with Webman been elected as delegates to two labor conventions. The charges were made in a leaflet circulated among the members, and in which Webman was denounced as a "robber." Webman filed charges, and Salzhandler was tried, found guilty and removed from office. He filed suit in the Southern New York District Court which found that Salzhandler had been guilty of libel, and that his removal from his part-time office was justified. The Court of Appeals Second Circuit reversed and noted:

The trial board in the instant case consisted of union officials, not judges. It was a group to which the delicate problems of truth or falsehood, privilege, and "fair" comment were not familiar. Its procedure is peculiarly unsuited for drawing the fine line between criticism and defamation.

Based on the view that union officials are not judges, the opinion adds:

> It is wholly immaterial to Salzhandler's cause of action under LMRDA whether he spoke truthfully or not, and accordingly Judge Wham's views on whether Salzhandler's statements were true are beside the point. Here Salzhandler's charges against Webman related to the handling of union funds; they concerned the way the union was managed. The Congress has decided that it is in the public interest that unions be democratically governed and toward that end discussion should be free and untrammeled and the reprisals within the union for the expression of views should be prohibited.
>
> It follows that although libelous statements may be made the basis of civil suit between those concerned, the union may not subject a member to any disciplinary action on the finding by its governing board that such statements are libelous.[3]

Much of the above is in line with the state decisions. However, the sweep appears too broad, and within the context of the situation in which Salzhandler arose, unnecessary. The record shows no evidence for the accusation. It was not made in anger during a debate or during a political campaign. It might be argued that the level of political debate within the local has always been bitter and unrestrained, and that the members know how to interpret accusations of the kind made. However, the charges were calculated, they were embodied in a leaflet, and history tells us that the attack upon union officers has been a favored method for undermining an organization. One need only glance at the findings of the LaFollette Committee of the United States Senate, as well as other investigations, to become aware of that tactic.[4]

A union, moreover, cannot discipline a member for exercising his right to speak, even if he speaks with malice.[5] A member of the Seafarers International Union attacked the shipping rules and the attitude of his union towards other maritime organizations. In voiding the verdict of the union tribunal, the Second Circuit said "the *Salzhandler* rationale that union tribunals are not competent to apply technical doctrines limiting free speech is equally applicable to trial committee's additional finding that Cole spoke with malice." Moreover, the court added that "neither habitual opposition to incumbent officers nor errors in fact nor both combined result in the loss of free speech protection when the occasion of its invocation is directly related to union conduct and concern."

The two decisions have been accepted by the Federal District and Appellate Courts. Even if the statements attacking a proposed union constitution are false, "their dissemination to Union members would not justify expulsion as a matter of law."[6] Union constitutions have included prohibitions on circulating inaccurate statements about the organization, its policies or officials. In this case, members of the Boilermakers' Union opposed the adoption of a new constitution and issued a leaflet critical of the document. They were tried and expelled on the charge that the leaflet contained false information, but a political document cannot be held to standards of accuracy that prevail in personal relations. Strict construction of the meaning of accuracy would have an inhibiting effect upon union discussion, and the Court of Appeals struck down the penalty.

Even when a union offers a defendant in a disciplinary proceeding "procedural requisites of a full and fair hearing," the verdict of the union tribunal will be voided if "the substance of a full and fair hearing was not afforded to the plaintiff . . ."[7] The Massachusetts District Court found an absence of substantial evidence in support of the charges, and they "were only a pretext and the real purpose of the board was to get rid of Leonard because he was an opponent and critic of the union officers and their policies."

A member who advised his colleagues, in a leaflet, not to pay a tax because it was illegal could not be expelled because, in the view of the Second Circuit "a rule which subjects a member to expulsion for complaining of a tax which he reasonably believes to be illegal is not a reasonable rule."[8] The American Federation of Musicians, Local 802 New York, had devised a tax to substitute for the one declared illegal by Judge Levet of the U.S. District Court Southern District of New York. A member, Farowitz, advised other members of the local, in a leaflet, not to pay the new tax on the ground that it was illegal. He was brought up on charges, found guilty of damaging the union, and expelled. The court did not rule on the issue of a member's liability to pay dues and stated that each case must be judged on the facts.

In virtually all unions, failure to pay dues for a specified period of time places a member in bad standing with the possibilities of suspension and expulsion if the arrearage goes beyond a given time. A musicians' organization could also face a serious problem by mass abstention from dues payment as many of its members are employed on limited single engagements. Evidently, the courts refuse to consider potential harm, and examine actual damage of the act.

Picketing of a union office and displaying signs critical of the union officials cannot be grounds for union discipline, for the right of members "to criticise is limited only insofar as it interferes with the performance of the union's legal or contractual obligations." In setting aside the union verdict, the United States District Court of Eastern Pennsylvania observed: "Sensitivity to personnel criticism is a luxury not available to any holder of elective office, whether it be in public or private life."[9]

However, the right to attack and to criticize is not unlimited, for the union, Congress recognized, must be able to defend itself against those who might hamper the organization from carrying on its duties. It therefore added a proviso to Section 101 (a) (2) which declares: "That nothing herein shall be construed to impair the right of a labor organization to adopt reasonable rules as to the responsibility of every member toward the organization as an institution and to his refraining from conduct that would interfere with its performance of its legal or contractual obligations."

Mere claim that a specific act falls within the proviso is insufficient. It must be shown that the organization was injured by the act for which the member was penalized, or that the act was not protected. When a member of a local of the Operating Engineers was penalized for calling the union's support of a softball team a "racket," the union failed to sustain its claim that his behavior could be penalized under the proviso. The United States District Court for Rhode Island found no evidence that the statement affected the union as an institution and set the penalty aside.[10] A much broader restriction upon the proviso was imposed by the Second Circuit in a case involving a member of the Upholsterers' Union who had been disciplined for charging financial malfeasance in the handling of health and welfare funds. The court held "fiscal misconduct was not within the proviso," and, moreover, the charge of mishandling funds made against the union rather than the officers did not render protected speech unprotected.[11]

However, the United States District Court for Eastern Missouri found that the promotion of a dual union was grounds for expulsion and that the decision of the union had the sanction of the proviso. In agreeing with the union's action, the court said: "When local officers encourage local members to break away from the national organization and form an independent union, it clearly undermines the responsibility of local members to the national organization, and threatens the enforcement of contractual obligations."[12]

The above view was rejected by the Fifth Circuit[13] which based itself on an inapposite precedent by the Sixth Circuit Court of Appeals.[14] The Sixth Circuit did not reach the issue of dual unionism, but limited itself to denying the union the right to fine its member for filing a decertification petition with the National Labor Relations Board. It upheld the charge that the union committed an unfair labor practice "in the face of the strong policy which allows union members unimpeded access to the Board."

This decision is in line with long-time precedents, that union members cannot be penalized by their organizations for appealing to a government agency for relief or for testifying before it.[15] The right of the member to approach the government transcends any right a union may have. In this case, however, Lowdermilk, an employee of Eastern Airlines and a member of Machinists' Local 702, had been compelled to join under a union shop agreement. He subsequently became a member and an officer of a rival organization and supported the rival union in a bargaining election on another airline against the Machinists. He was brought up on charges of dual unionism and fined $500.00. He refused to pay, and the union sued to compel him to do so.

The Fifth Circuit upheld the right to levy the fine, but basing itself on *Salzhandler*[16] ruled that the defendant's activity was protected speech. The court claimed the "IAM did not choose to expel him or to bar him from meetings and the like, defensive actions which would have protected the IAM. Rather, IAM sought to compel his allegiance by the imposition of a fine." Furthermore, the fine "exceeded the authority of the union under the circumstances here which involve compulsory membership under a union shop agreement coupled with the free speech overtones which are inherent in undertaking stemming from dissatisfaction with one union and action seeking to displace that with another."

The court misconceived the problem facing the union, how it could prevent Lowdermilk from undermining its position. Expulsion would not bar Lowdermilk from contact with other members, as he would inevitably meet them at his work, for a member, under a union shop contract, can only be discharged for failure to pay dues. Consequently, the only avenue of defense of the union is a fine to discourage active sponsorship of the rival organization. The free speech section was designed to protect members who want to reform the union and not, as in this instance, to destroy it. The attachment of the proviso was for the purpose of allowing unions to protect themselves, and if they cannot punish the promotion of a rival union by one of its members, the section is a dead letter.

A union can, however, try a member for making statements discreditable to the organization. The union's views, though, must be supported by adequate proof that the written or spoken words were such as to reflect discredit upon it or injure it in some other way. When a local union of Operating Engineers charged that a member's article contained false and derogatory statements about the union, the District Court of Southern California would not enjoin the trial.[17] However, the court reserved the right to review the proceedings of the union tribunal. The member was tried, found guilty and expelled from the union. The verdict was, however, set aside.[18] A member, said the court, had a right "to express views, arguments or opinions wherever and whenever he chooses." These rights extend beyond the union hall and their exercise must be "free of reprisal from the union or any of its members."

Reversing the penalty imposed upon a member of the Carpenters' Union, the District Court of Minnesota ruled: "If the underlying topic of conversation concerns union affairs, the arguments, questions, or accusations relating thereto are protected."[19] The penalty followed a question by a member of the right of the union to try a member for belonging to the Communist Party. A member objecting to the reading of the minutes could not be penalized for improper conduct.[20] The member had been fined one dollar which he refused to pay. His dues were refused and he was removed from his job. The fine and suspension were voided by the District Court of Eastern Louisiana, and he was awarded back pay for the wages lost. He was, however, denied attorney's fees and damages.

The rights guaranteed in Section 101 (a) (2), said the Second Circuit, "encompasses the right to assemble, consult and decide matters of concern to the local union without the inhibiting presence and control by the international union."[21] The decision was in a dispute within an independent union, and the international union sought to have a representative present at the business meeting of the local. The court held the international representative could be barred. The court conceded that the international could have imposed a trusteeship upon the local.

But the defendants have pointedly chosen not to establish a

trusteeship according to the procedures set in Article XVII of the Constitution and Title III of the LMRDA, and in the absence of such recourse, the autonomy of the local should be our primary concern.

The logic is difficult to follow, for the international union could not injure the organization by having its representative present at the business meeting.

A dispute between the employer and a local of the International Association of Machinists led to an unauthorized strike and the discharge of a number of the leaders. After the ending of the walkout, revocation of the discharge of a number was agreed upon and the remaining cases were submitted to arbitration. The arbitrator reduced the penalties in a number of instances, but upheld the discharge of five leaders. A movement to challenge the arbitration in the courts was started, but the local union leadership refused to agree. Under New York law no arbitration was possible without the approval of the representative union. A petition signed by a considerable number requested the calling of a special meeting because the chairman of the regular meeting, a leader of the local, had refused to recognize the dissidents and permit presentation of their case for court review of the arbitration. The dissidents then sued in the United States District Court of Western New York on the ground that their rights under 101 (a) (2) had been violated. Their case was dismissed, and on appeal the majority of the Court of Appeals Second Circuit held that neither the refusal to call a special meeting nor the refusal of a motion at the regular meeting constituted denial of free speech within the meaning of the statute.[22]

Section 101 (a) (2) declares that every "member of any labor organization shall have the right to meet and assemble freely with other members; . . ." This provision was directed at the prohibitions found in union constitutions against members assembling for the discussion of union business without the presence or consent of union officers. In other words, the rights guaranteed are unrestricted as to time and place. The union restrictions are a carryover from the time when union members faced the danger of being blacklisted and when company agents might be anxious to learn the organization's plans and programs. Unions, Congress believed, do not require such protection.

Nevertheless, on occasion, unions have tried to continue enforcement of these restrictions. Expulsion for meeting with other members for discussing the reform of the union constituted, said the District Court of Puerto Rico, a deprivation of the members' "equal rights and freedom of speech and assembly provided by the Act..."[23] Members of a union will be protected against threats by officers of their organization because they had joined together in a meeting and discussed an application to the international for another charter.[24] Under those circumstances, said the District Court of Eastern Michigan, the plaintiffs were not obliged to avail themselves of the internal remedies available to them.

While the right of members to meet away from the union hall free from the inhibiting presence of officers is protected, the exclusion of dissident members presenting proof of their good standing will be enjoined.[25] A district council which tried to prevent members from attending meetings was also directed not to issue union membership cards to nonmembers or to allow them "to participate in union meetings."

The attempt to penalize supporters of an opposition slate in election for union office by the head of District 50, United Mine Workers of America, was held to violate the LMRDA. The United States District Court of the District of Columbia ordered those staff members who had been demoted or transferred against their will reinstated, and directed that the head of the organization cease threatening to interfere with, coerce, or penalize the opposition candidates in the exercise of any LMRDA rights.[26]

The attempt of a union to try a group of members for publishing an article critical of several union officers was enjoined by the district court because the publication was protected by 101 (a) (2), the free speech provision. The contention of the union that it could proceed against the complainants under the proviso in 101 (a) (2), which allows a union to enforce reasonable rules as to the responsibility of its members to the organization as an institution, and to prevent interference with its contractual obligations, was rejected by the court. It ruled that the union had no power to discipline its members for publishing the article in question.

The court also rejected the union's argument that the plaintiffs were obligated to exhaust their union remedies, holding the article is clearly protected by Section 101 (a) (2). It also denied the need for the complaining member to exhaust his union remedies as a union tribunal had no option in this case but to bar prosecution on the charge. It also found that the threatened injury to the plaintiffs was immediate and of a nature so that damages would be inadequate relief.[27]

Claiming they were to be tried on vague charges, the supporters of Miners for Democracy asked the United States District Court to prohibit the trial. Three opponents of the officers of District 50, United Mine Workers of America, were charged with violating Article X, Section 10 of the District constitution which prohibits "members resorting to dishonest or questionable practices to secure the election or defeat of any candidate for district office. . . ." In enjoining disciplinary proceedings against the accused, the District Court held the clause under which they were charged could not stand a due process test. The provision, said the court, failed to provide an ascertainable standard of conduct and was, therefore, so vague as to violate the first essential of due process. In the opinion of the court, the provision under which the members were charged "can have no other effect but to suppress the free exercise of criticism and electioneering" guaranteed by the LMRDA, because it allowed officers to file charges against members opposing them for conduct during an election campaign. It found the article in the District constitution inconsistent with the rights of union members under Section 101 (a) (1) and (2) and permanently enjoined the proceedings against them. The District officers appealed, and the Appellate Court found "that the successive attempts by the District Executive Board to use the broad powers of Article X, Section 10 against their opponents while the election was being challenged before the Secretary of Labor was a 'studied evasion' or disregard of prior orders enjoining such practices." In addition, the Appellate Court held the district officers violated Section 101 (a) (5) and denied the complainants "a full and fair hearing."

In *Reyes* v. *Laborers Union*, the District Court rejected the complaint of a member that he had been denied his Section 101 (a) (2) rights. In reviewing disciplinary proceedings of a union, the court ruled it need not look any further than whether the standards enunciated in Section 101 (a) (5) had been followed. If the union proceedings had for their purpose the denial of rights guaranteed by the act, the court could examine proceedings and surrounding circumstances in order to determine whether the charges brought were legitimate.[28]

In examining the circumstances surrounding the trial, the court was satisfied that substantial evidence had been adduced to show that the incident upon which the charge was brought was not feigned and that the proceedings brought against the plaintiff were for legitimate reasons and not for the purpose of denying him LMRDA rights. The court noted that the right to free speech under LMRDA was broader than that guaranteed by the United States Constitution, but does not give members a license to threaten elected union officials with physical harm.[29]

While the rights of members will be protected against violations by officers or other members, the obligation to maintain decorum and obey reasonable rules is recognized. The claim that the officers had abused their positions during a business meeting by refusing to grant a member the floor was rejected when it was shown that the plaintiff had been disorderly at the meeting.[30] In another instance, the District Court for the Eastern District of Pennsylvania ruled that a proposal that had been twice rejected by the membership could be ruled out of order without such decision violating a member's right to freedom of speech.[31] To the charge that the presiding officer spoke harshly, the court said: "Not every ungentlemanly remark made by a local union's president to a member is a denial of a Section 101 right."

Provisions protecting freedom of speech, said the District Court of New Jersey, cannot be successfully invoked in defense of disorderly, riotous and abusive conduct at a union meeting. Those who are properly tried, found guilty and suspended cannot claim that the penalties violated the guarantees of free speech to union members.

> All that a union member is entitled to in any controversy between him and the union is a fair hearing.... In determining whether the plaintiffs in the present case were afforded a "fair hearing", the court is neither authorized nor required to weigh the evidence presented to the disciplinary body or to substitute its judgment for that of the union body respecting the creditability of witnesses or the weight of evidence.[32]

The experience under the LMRDA has not been much different from the time when aggrieved members were forced to appeal to the state courts. The latter had, when warranted, allowed compensatory and punitive damages, but generally not counsel fees. Many were convinced that the paucity of cases under Title I was because the federal courts followed the precedents of the state tribunals in not awarding counsel fees to attorneys of members who prevailed in their attempt to vindicate their Title I rights by suing under Section 102.[33]

The Third Circuit Court of Appeals found that counsel fees could be awarded, and that it was discretionary with the district courts. It found it "untenable to assert that in establishing the bill of rights under the Act Congress intended to have those rights diminished by the unescapable fact that the aggrieved union member would be unable to finance litigation and would have no hope of remuneration even if he could some way or other proceed with his suit.[34] The majority of the panel held that district courts have the discretionary power to award counsel fees to union members who pursued their rights under Title I.

This view was sustained by the Supreme Court.[35] Mr. Justice Brennan, writing the majority opinion, said that "federal courts in the exercise of their equitable powers may award attorney's fees when the interests of justice so require." "Thus it is unquestioned that a federal court may award counsel fees to a successful party when his opponent has acted 'in bad faith, vexatiously, wantonly, or for oppressive reasons.' "

He found the payment of fees by the union justified by the fact that the plaintiff, Cole,

> by vindicating his own rights of free speech guaranteed by Section 101 (a) (2) LMRDA . . . necessarily rendered a substantial service to his union as an institution and to all of its members. When a union member is disciplined for the exercise of any of the rights protected by Title I, the rights of all members of the union are threatened. And, by vindicating his own right the successful litigant dispels the "chill" cast upon the rights of others. Indeed, to the extent that such law suits contribute to the preservation of union democracy, they frequently prove beneficial "not only in the immediate impact of the results achieved but in their implication for the future conduct of the union's affairs."

Mr. Justice Brennan noted that placing the burden upon the union places the "costs of litigation" upon those who benefit from them. "We may therefore conclude," he said, "that an award of counsel fees to a successful plaintiff in an action under Section 102 of LMRDA falls squarely within the traditional equitable powers of the federal courts to award such fees whenever 'overriding considerations indicate the need for such recovery.' "

The Supreme Court found nothing in the legislative history which argued for a different conclusion. Mr. Justice Brennan found "no suggestion anywhere in the legislative history that even a single member of Congress was opposed to such relief or desired the words 'such relief as may be appropriate' to restrict the equity powers of the federal courts. On the contrary, there are expressions by sponsors and other supporters of the Act indicating that Section 102 was intended to afford the courts a wide latitude to grant relief according to the necessities of the case."

The above cases involved union members. A somewhat different problem arises when a union member, who is also an employee of the organization, is penalized for violating a union rule. Employees of unions are of two kinds: those who are members of the organization and others—accountants, lawyers, and officeworkers who may not be connected with the union in an official sense. They can be suspended and discharged, and they cannot appeal to the courts under the LMRDA. However, business agents, business managers, representatives, organizers, and others require membership in the union in order to be eligible for appointment. The question that can arise is whether the penalty for alleged misconduct is not in fact a reprisal for the member-officer's support of a policy not endorsed by the higher echelons of the organization. If the penalized officer has been elected by his constituents, the issue might be even more difficult to resolve. What are the rights of subordinate officers in a union?

Union staff members have recognized the ambiguity of their positions and have established independent labor organizations to bargain with their union employer and to handle grievances arising in employment. A union, in a broad sense, can provide the protection furnished by a civil service.

The distinction between officers and members has been recognized. In several cases, the issue was the removal of union officials because of the restriction in Section 504 which prohibits office holding by a member of the Communist Party or anyone convicted for enumerated crimes for five years after the termination of membership or the conviction or termination of a prison term.[36] In *Jackson* v. *The Martin Co.*, it was said the removal of an officer of a union because of criminal conviction was not disciplined within the meaning of Section 101.[37] In two cases, each involving a separate local of the Teamsters' Union, the Second Circuit Court and the District Court of Eastern Pennsylvania found the disqualifications were in harmony with the purpose of the LMRDA, and, moreover, officers were not protected in their employment.[38]

The removal from office of a member who is barred under the statute does not present a problem, but the issues are not as clear when the cause of removal is inefficient performance, refusal to obey orders of superiors, or even for differences over union policy. The courts have taken the view that Section 101 "secures safeguards against improper disciplinary action against union members, as members, but not as officers or employees of the union."[39] On this ground, the U.S. District Court for Southern District of New York held a union could discharge a Vice-President who had encouraged an unauthorized strike. He was also disqualified from running for office. In a similar case, the Maryland District Court found his ineligibility a direct consequence of his violations as an officer, and "is part of the punishment imposed for his dereliction of duty."[40] It might be noted that the court allowed the union to penalize a member officer by restricting his right to run for office, which is a prerogative related to membership. As the violation was not for inefficiency, but consisted of an act or actions which violated the union management agreement and the rules of the union, the officer could be penalized as a member.

The removal of an officer or employee from his position does not require a trial, said the District Court of Kansas in upholding the removal of a business agent for misconduct.[41] A business agent who complained to the court because he had been removed from his job was told that at most the act was an unfair labor practice, and, therefore, no relief could be obtained under the LMRDA.[42]

The distinction between the rights of members and officers has been most sharply drawn by the Third Circuit in *Sheridan* v. *Carpenters*.[43] A business agent who had been removed from office was denied reinstatement because in neither the "Bill of Rights" provision of Title I, nor under Section 609 proscribing disciplinary sanctions against union members, is plaintiff's status protected by the Act. It is the union-member relationship, not the union-officer or union-employee relationship, that is protected. Sheridan's claim that when he had a member of his local arrested, which was the cause of his removal as business agent, he was acting in his capacity as a member, was rejected. In commenting on Sheridan's claim the court said:

What plaintiff overlooks, however, is the fact officer's conduct whether in his individual official capacity, affects the confidence reposed in him by the union membership, and his effectiveness as an officer. Thus, a meaningful distinction cannot be drawn on the basis of the capacity in which plaintiff was acting when he had Burke arrested. The facts in this instant case illustrate quite clearly the invalidity of such distinctions.

In many instances, it is difficult to separate the acts of the officer from those of a member. However, unless officers can be controlled, the reforms contemplated by the LMRDA might well be frustrated. A problem arises here, as was noted above in *Sheridan*, as to whether sanctions were imposed upon an officer in his capacity as an officer. Sanctions against an officer are usually imposed in terms of the office, although sometimes membership is also affected. It is, therefore, necessary to examine whether the penalties were imposed for acts which are protected or for those which are related to employment. An officer of a local union could not, said the Second Circuit, be penalized for circulating documentary materials dealing with union affairs for his rights are derived from his membership in the union.[44]

The case of Franklin Nix presents several unusual aspects. Nix was a staff employee of the International Association of Machinists (IAM), and also a member of Fulton Lodge No. 2. He was active in the organization of the IAM Representatives Association, and was dismissed from his job because of these activities. Nix was also brought up on charges of misconduct for sending out a letter critical of the International, and was found guilty and expelled from the union. He appealed to the courts for injunctive relief and damages for his expulsion. The court agreed with Nix and ordered him reinstated, dismissal of charges against him, and that they be expunged from the union records. The court enjoined the release or publication of these records.

The union's defense was that Nix's remedy was through the National Labor Relations Act, but the union also brought him up on charges and acted upon them. This fact was noted by the Appellate Court which considered the appeal, that Nix was expelled for impugning the reputation of a union official, an action that is protected by 101 (a) (2). In its opinion, the Appellate Court noted:

> From this judicial evolution of the scope of the LMRDA free speech protection, a general rule is perceivable: a union member has the statutory right to express any views, arguments or opinions inside or outside of a union meeting, subject only to three general limitations: (1) reasonable union rules relating to the conduct of union meetings; (2) reasonable rules relating to the responsibility to the union as an institution; and (3) reasonable rules requiring members to refrain from conduct which would interfere with the union's performance of its legal or contractural obligations.

The Appellate Court found that the first restriction was not relevant in the case, and with regard to the other two restrictions, "the trial court has the responsibility to weigh institutional versus individual interests, and in this case correctly concluded that Nix's statements did not infringe upon either limitation."[45]

In another case involving an employee, a business agent of the Laborers' Union was removed from his job for allowing a project to pay its laborers less than the union rate. His dismissal, the Third Circuit Court noted, concerned the union-officer relationship unprotected by the LMRDA. However, he was also barred from holding office for five years, and that part of his penalty, the Appellate Court ruled, affected his status as a member. As no irregularities were found in the trial the penalty was undisturbed.[46]

The Sixth Circuit agreed with the above approach in *Barbour* v. *Sheet Metal Workers International Association*.[47] The Court of Appeals for the Sixth Circuit ruled that the removal of a union officer from his job and expulsion from the union after being found guilty of conduct in violation of the union constitution did not violate the provisions of Section 101 of the LMRDA. Robert Barbour, the President of Sheet Metal Workers, Local No. 292, had been found guilty by a union tribunal on four counts of acts of misconduct relating to his office, and one count of circulating a letter slandering the officers. On appeal to the International Executive Council, the charge of slander had been set aside, but his expulsion on the other four had been upheld.

Barbour had refused to submit to the local membership for a vote the question whether he should be a full-time paid officer. He was also charged with refusing to recognize the trusteeship imposed by the International and held valid by the District Court, and refusing to surrender records and monies to it. He staged a sit-in at the union office, and drilled the local union's safe and scattered its contents. In contrast to the trial judge, the Circuit Court found no "support for the inference that Barbour's libeling of the International Officers was of importance in his expulsion." On the contrary, it found the emphasis of the union's appellate tribunal "was on Barbour's interference with the operation of the local and the trusteeship imposed by the parent International."

The court would not interfere with the removal of two officers of Local 653, International Union of Operating Engineers, Mobile, Alabama. They had been found guilty of creating dissension, slandering officers, and misuse of funds and property. On appeal to the international executive board of the union, the verdict on the first two charges was revoked and the other charges were upheld. They appealed to the courts and the union showed that the funds and property had not been efficiently handled, that a union car had been put in the name of one of the defendants, and that funds had not been deposited in the bank as required. The court, while absolving the appellants of wrongdoing, found the union's action did not warrant the court's interference.[48]

The right of discharge of a member-officer from his job because of inefficiency or misconduct has been conceded. The courts, however, appear to have taken a different view on the dismissal of member-officers or member-employees because of differences between the discharged and their superiors over union policy or the support of candidates. There are two conflicting issues in this type of situation. The first is whether an officer-member enjoys all the rights to free speech, the right to support candidates of his choice and the other rights granted under the "bill of rights." Obviously, when stated in this form, the answer must be in the affirmative. The other question is whether officers chosen in a democratic election have the right to insist that the policies they have been assigned to execute must be supported by those employed by the organization.

In *King* v. *Grand Lodge International Association of Machinists*, the Ninth Circuit ruled the LMRDA forbade discipline of officers for exercising their rights to freedom of speech or to engage in political activities.[49] A group of Grand Lodge representatives supported an opposition candidate for the office of Secretary-Treasurer. Following the election, in which the incumbent was reelected, the group which had supported the opposition candidate was relieved of its posts. They sued, on the ground their dismissal constituted a denial of the right to express opinion, and they were reinstated as the Appellate Court could find "nothing in the legislative history to indicate that Congress wished to preserve an unrestricted power in the union to discipline officer members." The court also believed that to allow for dismissal of union officers for exercising their rights would mean that the "members thus exposed to reprisal would be those whose uninhibited exercise of freedom of speech and assembly is most important to effective democracy in union government."

The court recognized that it might be desirable to avoid conflicts among officers, and it suggested a union could adopt a principle of political neutrality. However, although statutes like the Hatch Act prohibit political activity by those on civil service, certain government appointees participate in politics and are usually obliged to leave their offices at the election of the opposition party. It is a difficult issue but democracy does not mean permanent tenure, and a union administration, similar to one in government, is entitled to have its followers in the posts of power, influence and administration. Nevertheless, following *King*, the U.S. District Court for the District of Columbia held in a dispute within the Retail Clerks International Association:

To withhold even partially the full rights of free expression from such members by allowing their superiors to discipline them in the name of policy or otherwise because they have unsuccessfully opposed those in authority would effectively weaken the ideal of union democracy.[50]

In fact, says the court, a successful candidate for union office must retain his defeated rival as the executor of policy. In the Retail Clerks' case, the two officers involved had been candidates for high office in the preceding election, one for international President, the highest office in the union, the other for Vice President. The court followed King in noting that plaintiffs were acquainted with the politics and policies of the union.

The use of the word "discipline" in this context tends to distort the meaning of the process. The defeated candidates ran on a platform, and they were rejected. If the successful incumbents believed that they were not in sufficient sympathy with the program that gained the members' approval, or that the posts in question should be filled by their own followers, the displacement could be regarded as an incident common in the politics "of competition" which is the essence of union and other forms of democracy.

The Fifth Circuit Court of Appeals in a Per Curiam opinion saw the issue differently, in *Wambles* v. *Teamsters*.[51] The newly elected business manager of Local 991, Teamsters, was charged with having dismissed employees of the local who had supported his rival in an election. The court held that employees were not protected by the free speech rights of Section 101 (a) (2). To give these rights to such officeholders would, in the view of the court, "give such officer a lifetime job except on dismissal for cause." The court noted that those elected rely on appointed officers to carry out the policies of the organization. To tie the hands of an elected official "by not allowing him to discharge without cause or for any reason those who must serve under him would so restrict the elected officers in the discharge of their duties that elections could be meaningless." As the dismissed officials worked against the candidate who was elected, it "would create an intolerable situation for the elected official in implementing his programs on which he was elected." Finally, the court declared: "The elected official has the right to the personal loyalty and loyalty to his programs from those working under him."

George v. *Bricklayers*[52] raised the same questions, and their resolution was more difficult. George, a member of the international staff was relieved of his job because of differences with the international on the question of local membership approval of agreements with the contractors. He was ordered reinstated by the U.S. District Court for the Eastern District of Wisconsin because officer-members are not excluded in the protection of the right of free expression for union members. The differences were over the right of local unions to ratify contracts negotiated by bargaining committees, and it was feared by the international officers that the policy advocated by George and others would increase the number of rejections. The court is saying that the union must retain a member on its payroll who may use his position to promote a policy that elected officers regard as harmful to the welfare of the organization.[53] This is not a trivial problem, but may seriously involve the entire union, the industry and the membership.

In another dispute over the dismissal of an international representative, and member of the International Machinists Association, Samuel E. Sewell, the Fifth Circuit upheld the union's right to discharge an employee. Sewell had been reprimanded for laxity in filing his reports. On December 22, 1966, President Siemiller of the International Association of Machinists noted that Sewell was opposed to the proposal for eliminating from the constitution a requirement that amendments to the union constitution be submitted to the local unions for ratification, which the heads of the union favored. He said that he had discussed his views with members but not with local lodges. He was subsequently discharged from his union office, and he sued for relief charging a violation of Section 101 (a) (1) and (2).

The cases were dismissed by the District Court, and Sewell appealed. The Fifth Circuit Court agreed that the Alabama statute of limitations of one year for tort actions effectively barred relief. However, "even if Sewell's complaint was not barred . . . we are of the opinion he should be denied relief." It concurred in the view that a member who is a union employee is entitled to the guarantees of Title I.

> This conclusion, however, does not permit an employee who accepts employment for the performance of certain specified duties to take the largesse and fees of the union, on one hand, and on the other, to completely subvert the purposes of his employment by engaging in activities diametrically opposed to the performance of his specified duties. . . . To permit an individual to accept union employment, to receive union pay, and to enjoy the prestige of a union position while spending his employer's time opposing the plans and policies he was employed to execute would in our judgment be unreasonable. . . . To hold that union has no right to discharge an employee for insubordination under the facts in the case would, we believe, seriously detract from effective leadership.[54]

The District Court of Western Michigan dismissed the complaint of a business agent of Operating Engineers Local 324, Michigan, who charged that he had been discharged from his job in violation of Sections 101 (a) (1) and (2). His membership was unaffected. The local has six branches and 1,200 members and has been headed by a president-business manager.

In the defense of the discharge, the union claimed that Wheeler J. Witte was responsible for considerable dissatisfaction among the members, that he did not clear his expenses with the business manager as he was requested to do, was drunk during business sessions, took time off for deer hunting not in his vacation schedule, sought to obtain unemployment compensation benefits while on vacation, did not promote a training program as directed, and failed in his organizing efforts. The court considered the allegations and rejected three. On the others, the court held that as far as lack of organizing success is concerned, it is "enough that Myers believed Witte to be responsible for the failure of a business agent to [perform] such a duty satisfactorily would be enough for discharge. So long as the belief was genuinely held by Myers that Witte was responsible we need go no further."[55]

The court recognized that there could be legitimate differences on the value of a training program, but Myers could demand that such a program be put in operation and had the authority to dismiss those he held responsible for failure.

In *DeCampli* v. *Greeley*[56] the District Court, New Jersey ordered the reinstatement of two business agents who had opposed use of union funds for support of two other business agents under indictment for illegal union activities. The court believed that a business agent of Teamsters' Union 676 has a duty greater than the ordinary member to speak out against abuses. "A business agent," the court said, "is . . . a union official to whom the membership looks for guidance be he elected or appointed and be an officer or an employee . . . To reduce him to silence through fear of reprisal is tantamount to saying that the member who succeeds in becoming an official of the union forfeits membership rights guaranteed to him by LMRDA." The opinion stressed that officers possess the same rights as members and they cannot be abridged. In this instance, the act of protest was that of a member seeking to prevent improper use of union funds.

The distinction between a member and an employee or an officer is generally recognized by the courts. It appears blurred when they are confronted by the discharge because of differences in policies. Superficially, such a discharge is an infringement of the member's rights protected by section 101. However, the test is generally whether the individual suffered any impairment of his membership. Employment with the union is not a right under LMRDA, and a union "politician" should have the same right to reward his followers as any other. Moreover, democracy within the organizations of labor is likely to generate differences, and those who are chosen to lead and to administer the union have a right to insist that only those who support their programs should hold appointive office. This is the affirmation and not a denial of democracy.

5

Dues, Assessments, and Initiation Fees[1]

Section 101 (a) (3) provides that changes in the contributions required of members in the union, and those who are seeking to join the organization, can only be made after membership approval. Congress did not set down criteria for levels of dues or other fees. Section 101 (a) (3) provides:

Except in the case of a federation of national and international labor organizations, the rates of dues and initiation fees payable by members of any labor organization in effect on the date of enactment of this Act shall not be increased, and no general or special assessments shall be levied upon such members, except—

(A) in the case of a local organization, (i) by majority vote by secret ballot of the members in good standing voting at a general or special membership meeting, after reasonable notice of the intention to vote upon such question, or (ii) by majority vote of the members in good standing voting in a membership referendum conducted by secret ballot; or

(B) in the case of a labor organization, other than a local

labor organization or a federation of national or international labor organizations, (i) by majority vote of the delegates voting at a regular convention, or at a special convention of such labor organization held upon not less than thirty days' written notice to the principal office of each local or constituent labor organization entitled to such notice, or (ii) by majority vote of the members in good standing of such labor organization voting in a membership referendum conducted by secret ballot, or (iii) by majority vote of the members of the executive or similar governing body of such labor organization pursuant to express authority contained in the constitution and bylaws of such labor organization: *Provided*, that such action on the part of the executive board or similar governing body shall be effective only until the next regular convention of such labor organization.

Within limits, unions can decide their own scale of contributions. There have, nevertheless, been a number of challenges to increases in dues or assessments. Although initiation fees are included in the general restrictions, it is not likely that they would be a frequent issue as national and international officers are likely to favor low initiation fees so as not to discourage the inflow of members. The pressure for high entrance fees usually emanates from those already in the union.

Past experience indicates that members are highly sensitive to dues increases, and that there are at least some political risks in sponsoring them. Members' attitudes towards dues and assessments are similar to those of taxpayers to increases in rates, and no more effective method for stimulating dissatisfaction among the membership exists. Even as strong a leader as John L. Lewis found himself confronted with a full sized rebellion in the anthracite coal fields, in the 1920s, as a result of the union levying an assessment even though it had been approved by the general membership. There are some, but relatively few, instances when a ruthless leadership was able to force an increase in dues or assessments, but such incidents are rare.

Unions follow a variety of methods in regulating their systems of contributions. Locals might be free to set the rate at will, the international being concerned only with the payment of the regular or per capita tax. Uniform dues charged by all locals is followed by a number, and the requirement of minimum or limitation on maximum charges is also in vogue. Another group of unions prescribes a range which locals can adopt. As a rule dues will be uniform for all members, or uniform for a class in those cases where a union recruits both skilled and semiskilled workers. Variations based on earnings within one of the frameworks described above are also used.[2]

Dues are either paid by mail, to the union steward, directly by the union member at the union office, or by voluntary checkoff, under which the dues payments are regularly withheld by the employer from the member's earnings and transferred to the union. The latter method gained popularity in the organizations of the CIO because of the role of coal miners in the early years of its history. A number of craft unions opposed this method of collection on the theory that the member loses contact with the union and the payment is not a conscious act. However, the opposition is all but gone, for the checkoff is a great convenience and prevents members from withholding their dues either through carelessness or design.

The local, the initial recipient of the dues, is generally obligated to pay a per capita tax on each member each month.[3] The amount is stated in the constitution and by-laws, and can be changed only by a convention or a membership referendum depending upon the method of voting used. Unions occasionally levy extra taxes designated as assessments, but they are seldom a regular feature of the financial plan.

It is obvious that in those instances in which uniform dues are charged by all local unions, the dues could only be changed by a convention or by a referendum vote of the membership. The question arose as to whether an increase in the minimum rate had to be approved by the local union in addition to the union's convention. If the statute were to be interpreted as also requiring the approval of the local before an increase could be instituted, it would mean that the vote of the convention or a referendum of the membership could be negated by the vote of the local union as far as the latter were concerned. However, the court held the action "of international union taken at its convention in increasing minimum dues payable by members of local unions is valid and authorized under Section 101 (a) (3) (B) of LMRDA."[4]

The challenge in *Ranes* was based upon the failure of the officers to submit the question of raising the minimum dues from $2.00 to $3.00 per member per month to the local membership. The dues were increased by delegates to the convention elected in accordance with the union constitution and by-laws and the statute. If the local union could have unilaterally maintained the first amount it would have exercised power which is normally lodged in the international, the determining of the schedule of dues that can be charged by local unions. A local can only modify its dues when it has discretion to do so under the union constitution. In this instance, it was compelled by the law of the international to charge at least the minimum, and it could not change it downward and conform to the union constitution.

A challenge to the dues increase voted by the United Automobile Workers' special convention was rejected by the court on the ground that the increase met the statutory requirements of Section 101 (a) (3). Two members who opposed the increased dues first charged before the National Labor Relations Board that they had been forced to pay increased contributions in violation of the Labor Management Relations Act, Section 302 (a) (1). The court disagreed. Nor would it accept the argument that there had been any irregularities in the making of the increase by the special convention. Local unions had been advised that dues increases would be considered at the special convention, and that met all the statutory requirements. The complaint was dismissed as the increase was lawful.[5]

In upholding the change, the court said:

Traditionally, international unions have exercised primary jurisdiction over the affairs of their affiliated unions, including the control of the local dues structure sufficient to insure the financial health of the union structure. Many international unions exercise control in the latter sphere of interest by the device of prescribing the minimum rate of dues which each of their locals shall collect from its members.

Although the question was not unambiguously stated, the U.S. Court, Eastern District of Pennsylvania refused to set the dues increase aside because the local union had met the requirement of notice and voting.[6] Local 20 announced a proposal would be submitted for a reduction of dues from seven dollars per member per month to five dollars. At the same time, the members were asked to approve a checkoff of dues by the employer of ten cents per hour, which amounted to more than the scheduled decrease. However, the members reduced the amount checked off to five cents an hour. On the ground that the proposal was incorrectly stated as a dues decrease, the changes were challenged in the court. While criticizing the wording of the issue on the ballot, Judge Francis L. Van Dusen dismissed the case.

The issue was misstated as to the effect of the two changes. The members were, however, aware that they were not only approving the decrease of two dollars in the monthly dues, but their reduction of the amount checked off from ten cents to five cents per hour indicated that they recognized the effect of this contribution. As they could have rejected one or both proposals, which were uncomplicated and the effect of which were easily ascertainable, the court allowed the changes to stand.

However, in another case the Appellate Court upheld the voiding of dues increase because it was linked with another question on the amount of the increase that was to be asked in the negotiations with the contractors for a new contract. The seventeen local unions of 8,000 carpenters involved in the proceedings were members of the Cuyahoga, Lake, Geauga, and Ashtabula District Council of Carpenters. A question was submitted on a referendum whether the agreement to be negotiated shall include an increase in wages and fringe benefits of at least one dollar an hour and a 2 percent gross wage assessment. The presentation of this kind of package placed the voters in a dilemma, and a group of members protested the ballot. The Appel-

late Court agreed that the method of presentation was improper
as the joining of a wage increase to the wage assessment "precluded a vote solely on the issue of wage assessment." The vote
was set aside.[7]

However, the attempt of Sugar Council, International
Longshoremen's Association, in Brooklyn, New York, to impose
a per capita tax upon its affiliated locals was struck down until the
council had been given the express power to impose such a
contribution.[8] In 1963, the convention of the union empowered
the Executive Council to set up "councils to coordinate the activities of local unions in the same craft or branch of the industry."
Under this power the Sugar Council was established. Local 1476,
with members on the sugar docks, was compelled to affiliate with
it. After the Sugar Council had negotiated an agreement for its
locals, it sought to impose an increase in dues to be paid to the
Council.

The increase was challenged by Local 1476, and the United
States District Court found that the union "constitution discloses
no power delegated to councils . . . to increase dues of its members
. . . The statute requires 'express authority' in the constitution in
order to clothe the Executive Council with the power to increase
dues." The collection of the dues was restrained as having been
imposed without compliance with Section 103 (a) (3).

The defect was cured by the special convention of the Sugar
Council to which Local 1476 refused to send delegates. Those
present unanimously voted to require every member employed
under contract with an affiliated union of the council to pay two
dollars per month. The levy, labeled a per capita tax, was upheld
because under the statute "delegates voting at a regular convention or at a special convention" have the authority to increase
dues.[9] The Appellate Court found: "The special convention followed the Executive Council's action and it created a proper basis,
so far as Section 101 (a) (3) is concerned, for collecting the dues
from Local 1476."

One can argue that the method of levying the contribution
made it dues rather than a per capita tax. While the tax is based
upon membership, and is defined as payment per member per

month, it is normally not made by the member except in those
instances in which it is described as international dues. A per
capita tax is based upon membership, but the responsibility for
payment is the local's and not, normally, the member's. There is
no ineluctable relation between the member and the per capita
tax. A local union's per capita tax may rise without affecting the
contribution of the members. If the increase is small or even
large, it might be absorbed from other funds. Moreover, the
member normally has no responsibility for payment of per capita
taxes. These rest upon the local, although they are calculated on
the basis of membership. Members are often not aware of these
taxes, although they can affect the level of dues if they are greatly
increased.

For example, the International Plater Printers, Die Sinkers and
Engravers Union of North America stipulates with regard to this
issue that per capita tax paid to the national organization by local
units—"The revenue of the International Union shall be derived
as follows: From charters for local unions, $7.50 per charter;
from necessary supplies at prices to be fixed by law. Defense fund
$1.50 quarterly per member; per capita tax, 75 cents per
member, shall be made quarterly to the secretary-treasurer, stating the number of members, and the amount so forwarded to the
order of the international union."[10]

Many unions do not have as detailed a description, but a typical
statement of per capita payments is "per capita tax paid to the
national organizations by local units—$1.25 per member per
month." The burden of paying the per capita tax rests on the local
union,[11] and not upon the individual member under union constitutions. In *Randazzo*, the council placed the new tax upon the
members each of whom was responsible for its payment.

The difference between per capita taxes and dues was clearly
visible in a challenge to an increase in the former by the International Association of Machinists.[12] The per capita increase,
enacted at the 1964 convention and ratified in a membership
referendum, was challenged by a number of members on the
ground that the increases had not been made in conformity with
Section 101 (a) (3). The court noted that the change had governed

only per capita and no change had been made governing minimum dues paid "by members to the local." The court found that the increase in per capita was paid in many locals without any increase in local dues. "It is clear," said the court, "that there is a distinction between 'per capita taxes' and 'dues', but whether the former fall within the ambit in 'the rates of dues' . . . payable by members is a question which must be answered in the light of the factual situation in each case." The court held in this case the per capita increase was not a dues increase within the meaning of LMRDA.

The U.S. Court of Appeals for the First Circuit held the increase "in per capita tax paid by local union to international union is an increase in rates of dues . . . payable by members whose adoption must conform to referendum procedure of Section 101 (a) (3) (B)."[13]

However, the court also found another basis upon which the increase could be voided. "The notified membership meetings employed in this case were not the same as and did not constitute a membership referendum within the meaning of the statute." What was given out as the vote for and against the proposition was the membership of the local so that a local whose majority voted to approve would have its total potential vote registered in this manner; those voting for the opposite result would also have their full vote registered in opposition. The court rejected this method: "Where a specific procedure is set forth in the statute that procedure must be followed." Finally, the court held the dues increase which a convention of the union had voted could be applied prospectively but not retroactively.

The distinction between per capita taxes and dues was made by the United States District Court of Eastern Louisiana in *Steib* v. *Longshoremen*.[14] In the vote on ratification of a contract, a six cents increase in per capita was included. It was to be divided between the district, the international and the local, each receiving two cents. The courts held that the amount to be given to the international and the district were increases in per capita and could be imposed without a vote, but the portion going to the local union was dues and had to be approved by a vote of the membership by secret ballot.

A standing vote of the membership is not a secret ballot within the meaning of the statute, and increases in dues made by this method are void.[15] The local had voted an increase in per capita taxes to the district which the court found had been legally adopted, but the increase in dues was voided for failure to adopt the change in conformity with Section 101 (a) (3). Nor could a local union cancel a dues exemption of members of more than 20 years without submitting the change to a vote of the membership by a secret ballot.[16]

Several suits were part of a campaign by a number of orchestra leaders to reduce the influence of the American Federation of Musicians. The Federation had levied a surcharge on miscellaneous out-of-town engagements to equal 10 percent of the minimum wage prevailing in the jurisdiction in which the engagement was performed. This amount was transmitted to the International, which divided it in accordance with a specified formula. This surcharge was held a violation of Section 302 of the Taft Hartley Act, in that leaders who were employers were compelled to make these contributions.[17]

Sixty-four percent of the revenue of the Federation was derived from the surcharge. The 1963 convention abolished the surcharge, and, under rule 11, allowed local unions to levy a tax on members of traveling orchestras up to 4 percent earned on performing in the local's jurisdiction. A charge of equal amount was to be imposed upon the local membership. The tax was challenged as illegal on the ground that the plaintiff had not been given an opportunity to vote upon it.

The U.S. District Court for the Southern District, New York, said that work dues equivalents imposed by local unions upon traveling members "was binding upon every local, as well as every member of the Federation." To the argument of the plaintiff that he was not given an opportunity to vote upon the proposal, the court noted that the legal requirement is that a majority of members voting must approve, but it does not limit the application of the charge to those who voted. "The statute merely defines the manner in which a local may lawfully increase dues and says nothing to whom the increase may apply." The work dues equivalent was held to be a service charge upon traveling members—" 'for the services, protection and accommodation furnished to the traveling members by the locals in whose jurisdiction they perform.' "[18]

An attack upon the percentage of earnings method of calculating dues also came from a group of members of Local 110, Chicago. This local had levied a tax of 2 percent on basic scale earnings of each member and leader as payments of dues. The levy was challenged on the ground that it was not dues, but assessments that were being levied under this provision. The court rejected this interpretation on the ground that the operation of the LMRDA cannot be governed "by the varying semantic practices of local unions." The test of the nature of a levy by a union must be in terms of its purpose and not by the statement in the union constitution or by-laws. Dues, said the court, are for general purposes, while assessments are directed towards special ends. The court's interpretation[19] was in harmony with long-time practice. A number of unions have arranged their dues contributions on a percentage of earnings basis, and such arrangements do not transform the levy into assessments.

The right of the union to enforce the work dues equivalent was also challenged on the ground that it had not been legally adopted at the convention. Under the union constitution, voting is conducted on a voice vote basis, unless a roll call vote is requested by ten delegates or one delegate representing five locals. It did not appear to the presiding officer that Resolution No. 11, containing the proposal for the dues equivalents, received the required approval on a voice vote. A regular request was then made that each local "cast as many votes as has members, as per book of the Treasurer . . ." This voting method was followed, and the vote for adoption carried by 158,069 2/3 to 113,742.[20]

The dues change was challenged in the United States District Court, and Judge Levet "was forced to declare the action" of the convention "to be void." He found the roll call vote did not meet the statutory requirement for the adoption of a dues proposal. In upholding the decision of the District Court,[21] the Circuit Court read the mandate of a majority literally, "that the simple, unambiguous requirements set forth . . . were intended to mean just what they appear on their face to mean, and that in this way the Congress intended to prevent future skulduggery of every possible character and description in the fertile field of increasing dues, initiation fees and assessments, even if no particular abuses of weighed voting for such increases had been proved."

The decision was based upon a disregard of trade union experience. The delegates to a union convention are likely to have among them local leaders, politicians, and officers of the local and regional unions. It is not easy to pack a convention, and many of the delegates are neither naive nor incapable of ordinary counting. Delegate lists and the numbers of votes allocated to each local are usually distributed among the participants at the convention. Denying the larger locals a vote in proportion to their membership does not promote democracy, but centralism because the smaller locals are normally more dependent for assistance upon the central organization. The experience of the French unions, which allowed for equal voting of locals, shows that the locals are likely to be less responsible and that the basic support of the militant syndicalists, who controlled the French Federation of Labor in the first decade of the century, came from the undemocratic system of equal voting.

The Supreme Court took another view of the matter when it reviewed the decision. Writing for a unanimous court, Mr. Justice Byron R. White said, "Where the 'vote' cast at a convention is weighed according to the number of people the delegate represents, that vote we think, is a vote of a delegate. We believe the majority vote so determined in favor of a dues increase is approved by majority vote of the delegates voting at a convention."

Historically, some unions have followed a custom of allowing a rebate of a percentage of dues on condition that a member attend the monthly meeting. A member of the Denver, Colorado, Mailers' Union No. 8 failed to attend the regular monthly meeting and was denied the dollar rebate for attendance. When he failed to pay the full amount of his dues, he was denied a vote in the union election. He charged that the dollar was an illegal fine, but the court found it was a proper form of regulation and not a fine subject to 101 (a) (5).[22]

In the event of an illegal increase of dues, the monies collected would have to be returned to all members who paid the improper charges. The Associated Food Distributors, Local 138, was ordered to refund the monies to all who paid even though "some members did not protest seasonably and some members did not intervene in court action, the statutory violations being patent, inexcusable and not three years old when complaint was filed."[23]

Members protesting a dues increase may be requested to exhaust their internal remedies before seeking injunctive relief against an assessment.

Automatic dues increases provided in by-laws enacted before the LMRDA cannot be used to justify dues increases, since without membership approval as required by statute, they are void. The rules of District Court No. 16, Painters, provided that after the council negotiated a raise of wages, a specified increase in dues to be paid by the members of the affiliated locals would be imposed.[24] The procedure was followed and subsequently challenged by one of the locals. The trial court concluded that, as the rule was adopted prior to the enactment of LMRDA, the members should be allowed to vote on the continuance of the automatic increases.

The most interesting result of this survey is the fact that few cases that have come before the courts involve attempts to change the member contributions by illegal means, or by failure to meet the standards spelled out in Section 101 (a)(3). This result should not be surprising. Students are aware of the resistance of union members to increases in contributions. Members are aware of the costs of belonging to the union, and they are seldom enthusiastic about an increase in their contributions. The challenge in most of the cases that have been brought before the courts was whether the procedure followed in making changes conformed to the requirements of the statute. The attempt to deceive was present in two instances, although the court found in *Brooks* v. *Local Union No. 30* that the members were aware of the nature of the proposal. In *King* v. *Randazzo*, the objection to the dues increase came from one local. The challenge in the musicians' cases was from members who were band and orchestra leaders and opposed the levy on other grounds, and who believed that it might be killed by a technical deficiency. All and all, the results can be said to be in harmony with expectations.

6

Protection of the Right to Sue

Section 101 (a) (4) declares:

No labor organization shall limit the right of any member thereof to institute an action in any court, or in a proceeding before any administrative agency, irrespective of whether or not the labor organization or its officers are named as defendants or respondents in such action or proceeding, or the right of any member of a labor organization to appear as a witness in any judicial, administrative, or legislative proceeding or to petition any legislature or to communicate with any legislature: *Provided*, That any such member may be required to exhaust reasonable hearing procedures (but not to exceed a four-month lapse of time) within such organization, before instituting legal or administrative proceedings against such organizations or any officer thereof.

Holding that the statute does not impose "upon the union member an absolute duty to exhaust union remedies before applying to the federal courts," Chief Judge Lumbard, of the Second Circuit, declared: "The act provides that a member 'may be required' not 'must be required' to exhaust internal procedures, and the legislative intention was not to formulate a new and absolute exhaustion doctrine, but to preserve the doctrine that had developed and continues to be developed by the courts. The proviso, therefore, does not bar immediate judicial relief if warranted by the facts in the particular case."[1]

The rule that exhaustion of internal remedies is not absolute has a long history and a statement of the principle and conditions under which it is effective is found in the writing of two legal authorities who discussed the issue in separate studies in the middle 1890s.

One writer notes:

> Where the expulsion . . . was without jurisdiction, as where it was founded on a charge on which the lodge had no jurisdiction to try him, his expulsion is null and void, and it is not incumbent on him to have it reversed in the higher judiciatory of the society. If when he has appealed to a superior tribunal, the member is practically deprived of the benefit of such remedy, by evasion, intentional delays, or other unjust procedure on the part of such tribunal, he may resort to the courts, alleging and proving such evasion, delays, or other unjust procedure, as an excuse for not having exhausted his remedy in the society. But it must clearly appear in such a case that the appellate tribunal is acting in bad faith and in practical disregard of the member's right of appeal.[2]

With few exceptions, the state courts followed the rules elaborated in suits by members of fraternal societies in cases brought by members of unions. The views of the state courts on the requirement to exhaust internal remedies have been summarized in a dissenting opinion by a member of the California Supreme Court:

> Where the provisions of the constitution and bylaws as to suspension and expulsion are not complied with, as where no

written charges are preferred against him as required by the
constitution and bylaws, or where the decision for expulsion
is contrary to the constitution and bylaws of the union, or the
offense with which the member is charged is not a ground for
expulsion, or where the expulsion is void for lack of authority or jurisdiction in the body or person conducting the trial
or rendering the decision for suspension or expulsion, or is
otherwise irregular, the requirement that the internal
remedies within the union must first be exhausted will not be
insisted upon as a condition to grant equitable relief for
reinstatement, as in all these cases the action of expulsion or
suspension is not the authorized action of the union, and the
member's duty to exhaust first the internal remedies within
the union is generally understood as contemplating an action
of the union which is authorized under its constitution and
bylaws. In other words, the rule as to exhaustion of internal
remedies presupposes a legal and regular proceeding for
suspension and expulsion.[3]

Both the issue of exhaustion of union remedies and the right of
a union member to appeal to the courts arose in *McCraw* v. *United
Association*.[4] James R. McCraw was a member of Plumbers and
Pipe Fitters Local 43 and charged the union business agent with
discrimination in making job assignments. When the union denied the charges, he filed a complaint with the National Labor
Relations Board, which found it without merit and dismissed it.
The business agent brought charges against McCraw for violating
a union rule that members must first exhaust their internal
remedies before appealing to a government body. Found guilty
and fined, McCraw refused to pay his fine which led the union to
suspend him.

McCraw appealed to the courts and brought suit under
LMRDA, alleging that the fine was illegal and that denial of his
right to participate in union meetings and benefits was also in
violation of LMRDA. The District Court held that McCraw's
rights under Section 101 (a)(4) had been violated because he had
exhausted his internal remedies before going to the National

Labor Relations Board and that his fine and suspension were void. The court then directed that he be reinstated with full membership conditional upon payment of his back dues.

Generally, the federal courts have followed the traditional rules with respect to the requirement that members exhaust their union remedies before appealing for relief. In *Ryan* v. *Electrical Workers, IBEW*,[5] the issue was whether a union could fine its members for appealing directly to the courts without exhausting their union remedies.

A unit within Local 134, Chicago, rejected in August 1963, contract proposals and asked the head of the union for permission to strike. Permission was denied on the ground that arbitration of differences was required. Three members unsuccessfully sought to enjoin the arbitration proceedings, and when the court rejected the plea for a restraining order, the three were expelled for violating Article XXVII, Section I, of the union's constitution, which provides for automatic expulsion of any member who initiates court proceedings against the organization before exhausting his internal remedies. The three appealed their expulsion citing the fact that if they had utilized the available union remedies before bringing suit, the arbitration would have ended and a new contract signed before they could have obtained relief.

The men now appealed to the District Court alleging that Article XXVII, Section 1, was invalid and could not serve as a basis for an expulsion, since it violated Section 101 (a) (4). The District Court agreed, holding that the section had "no force and effect to the extent that it provides for the expulsion of a member because he brings a suit in court." The court also found that the four months requirement for pursuit of internal remedies, specified in Section 101 (a) (4), was not "an unvarying jurisdictional limitation," and whether it was necessary to exhaust internal means was a question for the courts to decide and not the union. The union provision was held to be offensive to Section 101 (a) (4), for it "provides for expulsion even if a member brought suit as a necessary step to determining whether he had an 'exceptional case' lying beyond the reach of the exhaustion remedy provision."

The decision was affirmed on appeal. The union conceded that the courts have discretion to decide whether exhaustion is required. In the particular case, the court had dismissed the suit as premature, and the union argued that the expelled were obligated to pursue their union remedies. The Appellate Court disagreed. Such a claim, the court held, is "too chancy a gamble for the member and effectively blocks access to the courts by placing the member in the dilemma of swallowing the grievance about which he wishes to sue (and against which the court might grant immediate and necessary relief), or suing upon the speculation that he will be safe from expulsion by the court's discretion being exercised in his favor."

The Appellate Court did not believe that Congress had intended to put the union member to such a hazard. "The right of free access to the courts is too precious a right to be curbed by the risky prediction that the judge's discretion may, like a lucky roll of dice, turn up in favor of the suitor." It therefore declared Article XXVII, Section 1, inconsistent with Section 101 (a) (4) of the LMRDA, and of no force or effect.[6]

The Supreme Court interpreted Section 101 (a) (4) as "not a grant of authority to unions more firmly to police their members but a statement of policy that the public tribunals whose aid is invoked may in their discretion stay their hands for four months, while the aggrieved person seeks relief within the union."[7]

Edwin L. Holder, a member of Marine and Shipbuilding Workers Local 22, complained that the president of the union violated the International constitution. Rejected by the local members, Holder went to the National Labor Relations Board without exhausting his union remedies. He charged that he had been discriminated against by Local 22, but the National Labor Relations Board found the charges baseless and dismissed them. Because he did not exhaust union remedies before appealing to a government body, Holder was expelled from Local 22.

Holder now appealed to the Board on the ground that he had been penalized unlawfully by Local 22. The board agreed, but the

Appellate Court refused to enforce the Board's order that the union reinstate him. The decision was based on Section 8 (b) (1) (A) of the National Labor Relations Act, which allows a union "to prescribe its own rules with respect to the acquisition and retention of membership therein." The Appellate Court concluded that the expulsion of a union member for complaining to the government was illegal, but it believed the union should be given "a fair opportunity to correct its own before the injured member should have recourse to the Board."

The Supreme Court reversed the ruling of the Appellate Court and directed the enforcement of the NLRB order:[8]

> We conclude that unions were authorized to have hearing procedures for processing grievances of members provided those procedures did not consume more than four months of time; but a court or agency might consider whether a particular procedure was "reasonable" and entertain the complaint even though those procedures had not been "exhausted." We also conclude . . . that where the complaint or grievance does not concern an internal union matter, but touches a part of the public domain covered by the act, failure to resort to any intra-union grievance procedure is not grounds for expulsion from a union.

The Supreme Court recognized that Section 8 (b) (1) (A) gives a union freedom for self-regulation in instances where its own internal affairs are concerned, but public policy is affected when a member is penalized for filing an unfair labor practice complaint. It concluded that the restriction in the constitution of the International was against the policy of allowing complaints to be made to the NLRB without pressure or coercion of the people who make them.

The Supreme Court held "that there should be as great a freedom to ask the Board for relief as there is to petition any other department of government for a redress of grievances. Any coercion used to discourage, retard, or defeat access is beyond the legitimate interests of a labor organization. The overriding public interests makes unimpeded access to the Board the only healthy alternative, except and unless plainly internal affairs of the union are involved."

As Holder's charge originally affected both the union and the employer, the Supreme Court held the issues cannot be examined in an internal union proceeding. There was, therefore, no justification for insisting upon exhaustion of internal remedies inadequate for dealing with the problems affecting the employer, employee, and the union. While unions can design their own rules as they relate to acquisition and retention of membership, they lack the power "to penalize a member who invokes the protection of the act for a matter that is in the public domain and beyond the internal affairs of the union."

Following the above case, the Ninth Circuit Court of Appeals held that the right of a member to sue in any court is unlimited and cannot be infringed. In upholding the voiding of a fine assessed against a member of the Operating Engineers Union who sought to enjoin an election for local union officers, the court noted: "Section 411 (a) (4) speaks of—'an action in any court.' The word 'action' is in no way limited, and there is nothing in the Act which distinguishes between suits involving member as opposed to employee rights, between internal as opposed to external union problems, or between suits brought in good faith as opposed to those brought in bad faith." In the view of the Circuit Court "there are no exceptions to the law forbidding labor unions from disciplining their members for bringing actions, then the attempts to discipline Burroughs in this case were illegal regardless of the faith or lack of good faith."[9]

However, a member who appeals to the courts before exhausting his internal remedies runs the risk of punishment if his petition for relief has been rejected by the courts before he has utilized the tribunals of his organization.

The issue arose in the case of Charles Buresch, a member of the International Brotherhood of Electrical Workers (IBEW). Buresch had been a member of Local 28, Baltimore, when its members went out on strike in defiance of the directive of the

International President. After a controversy lasting for some time, the charter of Local 28 was revoked. The decision was successfully challenged in the United States District Court, but was subsequently reversed by the Fourth Circuit Court of Appeals.[10]

Local 24 was chartered in the jurisdiction formerly allocated to Local 28. A number of members denied admission to Local 24 sued in the United States District Court, and the International President agreed that all former members of Local 28 could retain their membership in the International Brotherhood of Electrical Workers. By obtaining travel cards from locals outside of Baltimore, the former members of Local 28 would be able to seek employment in the jurisdiction of Local 24. The proposal was accepted by those bringing the suit, and in May 1963, the District Court dismissed the suit with prejudice.

Buresch, who had obtained a travel card from one of IBEW locals in Oregon, had been employed in the jurisdiction of Local 24. His application to transfer to the Baltimore local had been rejected, and he finally sought assistance from the National Labor Relations Board, which dismissed his petitions. He then filed suit in the United States District Court on the ground that his rights as a member had been infringed by the local's refusal to accept him. The union's motion for dismissal of the complaint was approved by the court. When Buresch failed to appeal the court's decision, he was brought up on charges of violating Article XXVII, Section (1) (1), of the IBEW constitution, which forbids members from resorting to the courts without first exhausting their internal remedies for "at least a four month period." He was tried on the above charges, found guilty, and fined $800.

In answer to the claim that the "penal" provisions of a union constitution must be strictly applied against the union, the court held the rule applied to substantive aspects of a union's constitution,[11] and as long as the member is granted "due process" the union's verdict will stand.

Buresch did not appeal to the union tribunals, nor did he pay the fine. After six months he was expelled from the union. The court refused to intervene as it found by an examination of the entire trial board transcript that plaintiff was afforded a "full and fair hearing." He was given ample notice of the charges against him; given details as to time and place of his alleged violation, and the name of the complaining party against him; afforded an opportunity to cross-examine the witnesses against him which he did; advised of his right to present witnesses on his behalf which he did not; advised of his right to have a fellow IBEW member, of his choice, assist him, which he refused; advised on his right to have counsel outside the hearing room for consultation, which right he chose to forego; and advised of his rights to appeal which he refused to follow.[12]

Finally, the court concluded:

The internal procedures established by the IBEW Constitution for the presentation of grievances by union members is not unreasonable nor calculated to prevent a fair hearing and resolution of such problems. To allow the plaintiff to forego the opportunity of permitting the union to resolve such internal union affairs would defeat the clear legislative intent of the statute. As the defendants contend, to allow plaintiff to present his grievances directly to the courts in the first instance without prior exhaustion of internal procedures established by the IBEW and its local unions under the Constitution would be unwarranted where such procedures are not unreasonable.[13]

7

Safeguards Against Improper Discipline

In seeking to protect the rights of members of labor organizations, Congress declared certain acts immune to punishment. As a result, the exercise of free speech, press, or assemblage could not be made a cause of discipline. However, unions retained their power to make and enforce proper rules. As noted above, violations of union rules can be penalized. Congress has required that union tribunals must provide a member on trial for violation of union rules with a full and fair hearing.

Section 101 (a) (5) reads: "No member of any labor organization may be fined, suspended, expelled, or otherwise disciplined except for nonpayment of dues by such organization or by any officer thereof unless such member has been (A) served with written specific charges; (B) given a reasonable time to prepare his defense; (C) afforded a full and fair hearing." Provisions in union constitutions inconsistent with the section are "of no force or effect."

A District Court has held, moreover, that "even where Section 101 (a) (5) has not been violated or is inapplicable, proof that a union member was disciplined . . . because he exercised his right to engage in intra-union political activity guaranteed by Section 101 (a) (1), and Section 101 (a) (2), entitles him to relief under the LMRDA."[1]

The court noted: A union member is, under the provisions of the LMRDA, free to criticize union officials openly, and even to libel and slander them, without being subject to union discipline;

> ... if plaintiff did in fact accuse defendants of a conspiracy to bribe officials, the truth or falsity of the accusation in no way affects plaintiff's right of free speech. If defendants, in the face of such unfavorable criticism, conspired to expel plaintiff, they unlawfully disciplined plaintiff in violation of Section 609 and Section 101 (a) (2), even if plaintiff's accusations were false and malicious. Thus, for plaintiff to recover in this action, he need only prove that defendants reacted improperly to his accusations,—not that defendants were in fact guilty of accusations.

It was the court's view that the conspiracy theory "cognizable under Section 609 of the LMRDA makes doubly secure the protection of the members in the exercise of their rights."

The court would not intervene when no proof of wage loss or other damage was shown. A member of the Carpenter's Union sought to have a reprimand imposed by the executive board expunged from the record. Relief was denied because of the absence of a claim "of lost wages or other actual damage resulting from the reprimand."[2] The court said that a reprimand was not "otherwise disciplined," and directed that the complainant first exhaust his union remedies. However, union members could seek remedies against injustice, even if they had not been punished.[3]

Joseph Tirino and several other members sought a declaratory judgment against Local 164, Bartenders, that the charges against them were not sufficiently specific; they sought an order enjoining the local from violating their rights under LMRDA. The local sought dismissal of the suit on the ground that the plaintiffs had not been disciplined, but the court held that suits under Section 101 (a) (5) are not automatically barred because they seek to enjoin prospective violations of Section 101. In rejecting the union's contention that the issues involve employment and not union rights, the court said that interference with a member's employment opportunities may constitute "discipline" within the meaning of Section 101 (a) (5), and in this case if proof was adduced that "acts were committed on the basis of a predetermination that the plaintiffs had engaged in a wildcat strike."

A union cannot revoke the charter of a local union without proper notice and a hearing because such revocation constitutes "otherwise disciplined" in violation of their rights under LMRDA. The revocation of the charter was taken, according to the union, for administrative and not disciplinary reasons, as Local 2263, Carpenters, was a small local and it was held desirable by the International that the members be distributed among other locals in the area. Motives, said the court, are not relevant because the purpose of the Section 101 (a) (5) is to assure certain procedural safeguards to the members. Moreover, the court believed that the transfer would mean loss of certain membership rights such as running for office within the year as one-year membership in a local is a requirement for candidacy. As Local 2263 had fewer members than the local to which members were likely to transfer, their influence on the selection of leaders would be diminished. Revocation of the charter was therefore discipline within the meaning of Section 101 (a) (5). The status quo was reestablished, with the Brotherhood being granted the right to begin new revocation proceedings on condition that notice and a hearing would be provided and the action be in conformity to the union constitution.[4]

The rights of a member under Section 101 (a) (5) were sustained when he was charged with being unruly and disrespectful, and was found guilty and fined, without receiving notice or trial.[5] The fine was ordered remitted to the member. In another case involving several members of the Carpenters Union, Local 845, the court set aside a summary penalty of debarment from attending meetings for three months because the accused had not been given charges, allowed a reasonable time to prepare a defense, and afforded a full and fair hearing. The union argued that it had the right to insist upon obedience to reasonable rules as the responsibility of each member to the union. However, the District Court of Eastern Pennsylvania held that union rules "cannot dispense or bypass procedural safeguards as embodied in Section 101 (a) (5)."[6]

In the case of *Jacques* v. *Local No. 1418, International Longshoremen's Association*,[7] the member was notified to appear, which he did, and was tried for misconduct and subsequently notified that he had been expelled. He sought to appeal, but was unable to get in touch with the Appellate body. Jacques lived in New Orleans and the President and district Secretary of the union, who were authorized to hear appeals, resided in Galveston, Texas; they did not respond to his efforts to have them hear his appeal. When Jacques brought suit to have his expulsion invalidated, the union claimed he had not exhausted his internal remedies. The court disagreed, and held that the requirement of exhaustion of internal remedies "is not an absolute one and each case involving union member's rights must be considered on its merits."

Jacques had only been given seven days' notice before trial, and Local 1418's by-laws required twenty days. Moreover, the union had failed to comply with its by-laws that charges must be in writing, and must specify "the circumstances and acts upon which the charges are based, together with the time and place as nearly as can be ascertained." The court noted: "We do not expect union officials to frame their charges and specifications technically as formal legal pleadings. However, we do require that they be so drafted as to inform a member with reasonable particularity of the charges, as required by the by-laws." The court did not order reinstatement, but directed the holding of a new trial within sixty days from the date of judgment. Jacques' request for attorney's fees was denied.

Courts are required to enforce union constitutions and by-laws only to the extent that they affect rights under the LMRDA. As a result, the District Court of Southern District of Texas found that a member of the Carpenters' Union had been properly disciplined when he received "written notice of charges" which informed him "of the specific union by-laws he was charged with having violated and the time and place that the violation occurred." The member, William Null, who was tried on such charges three weeks later, was not deprived of his right to be served with specific charges.[8]

Null, a steward on a construction job, failed to inspect the credentials of workers employed on the project and had failed to obtain the signature of each member on the steward's report as required by the council by-laws. Charges were brought against Null, and the trial committee voted to remove him as steward and to reprimand him for failure to carry out his duties. The penalty was upheld by the General President. Null's appeal to the courts was based upon the failure of the union tribunal to follow the procedures required in the constitution.

The court found that the union had not carried out all the requirements of its constitution during Null's trial, but it noted that "the courts are not given jurisdiction to enforce compliance with any and all provisions of a labor organization's constitution and by-laws. The courts have only to do with such constitution and by-laws insofar as they are related to or connected with the question as to whether a union member has been denied rights given him by the Labor-Management Reporting and Disclosure Act . . . In the present case, the plaintiff does not claim that any of his rights under the act, have been violated." The union's failure to abide by all the procedures, the court held, did not impair the safeguards he had under Section 101 (a) (5).

In setting aside a penalty imposed by Local 768, IBEW, the District Court noted the rule under which the member was tried was unclear: "A charge is not specific," said the court, "if it specifies the violation of a rule which itself is not sufficiently specific . . . A union should not discipline its members for violation of a rule unless the rule establishes a clear line between what is permitted and what is not."[9] Because the union's by-laws did not meet this standard, the penalty imposed under it was set aside.

Gleason v. *Restaurant Employees' Union* also involved the absence of specific charges. James Gleason, business agent of Local 11, Hotel and Restaurant Employees, was charged and was found guilty of violating the constitution of the union and expelled. His expulsion was upheld by the union appellate tribunals, and he appealed to the courts. The District Court, Southern New York, found the

> circumstances surrounding an alleged disciplinary infraction by a union member, and the time and place as nearly as can be ascertained constitute the minimal information that the union should disclose to the accused in order to afford him a reasonable opportunity to prepare his defense.

Furthermore, the court found, "absence of specific identification of individuals presumably harmed by the accused."[10]

The requirement of specificity is not met when a union notifies its members that he is to appear before the executive board to answer charges for violating a clause in the union constitution. A letter of notification, the United States District Court of Western Missouri held, was not sufficient statutory notice. The requirement of "specific charges" is not satisfied by reference in the notice to a section of the union constitution without any statement of the factual basis of the charges. "No technical formalities should be imposed on those, often laymen, who must comply with Section 411 (a) (5) (A), but some factual assertion, no matter how informal, is necessary to allow an accused member to prepare his case."[11]

A member must be tried for violating a specific rule prohibiting the charged offense, and not one which does not cover the violation. D. R. Allen, a member at large of the International Alliance of Theatrical Stage Employees and Motion Picture Operators sought to transfer to Local 506, Anniston, Alabama, but the local refused to accept him. He nevertheless found a job as a projectionist in 506's jurisdiction, and when he refused to leave it, at the orders of Local 506, he was brought up on charges and expelled as a member-at-large. He sued for reinstatement, but the District Court refused to order him reinstated.

On appeal, the decision of the District Court was reversed because Allen had not received a full and fair hearing, inasmuch as he had been convicted on a constitutional provision which requires a member of one local to leave the jurisdiction of another when ordered to do so by the latter. As Allen was a member-at-large, the court ruled the provision applied to members of locals, and not to members-at-large. The accused should have been tried on a different provision in the union constitution, the Fifth Circuit ruled, the one requiring a member of a dissolved local to work in the community in which it held jurisdiction, unless permission had been given the member to work elsewhere. "Fair play," said the court, "entitles an accused to rely on the written charge against him in preparing his defense, limits the trial to proof in support of the charge and bars him being found guilty of an offense with which he is not charged."[12]

Holding, therefore, that the plaintiff was improperly expelled and deprived of some of his rights, the Circuit Court remanded the issue to the District Court with instructions that he be reinstated as a member-at-large, with the right of the International to try him under the proper provision of the union constitution. The International was held liable for the acts of Local 506, but the court refused to order the plaintiff admitted to membership of the Anniston local.

Under the same principle, the Fourth Circuit ruled that "a union cannot discipline its members except for offenses defined in its constitution and bylaws, and the courts lack power to recognize implied offenses . . ."[13] A member of the Avisco Local suspected of election fraud refused to take a lie-detector test and as a result was brought up on charges, found guilty, and suspended from the union. The court found that the member had not been tried for complicity in an election fraud, but for noncooperation in declining to execute a release in advance of a polygraph test. The union could act against the debasement of its election, but not against the refusal to take a lie-detector test.

Labor organizations prohibit assaults upon officers engaged in carrying out their official duties. Violations are punishable under the constitution and by-laws. Such a rule is essential because a business agent or representative may be compelled to take a position opposed by some members in the allocation of jobs, settlement of disputes with the employer, or upon a general policy of the union. Such protection is necessary so that the officer is not intimidated or physically injured in carrying out his duties. An assault in which the union is concerned is related to the carrying out of official duties in the union hall, office, or on the job.

International Brotherhood of Boilermakers v. *Braswell* followed a dispute over job assignments between Herman B. Wise, business manager of Local 112, Boilermakers, Mobile, Alabama and E. T. Braswell. When Wise left the hall, he was struck by George Hardeman, a member. E. T. Braswell was standing at the edge of the encounter and intervened in behalf of Hardeman. The police were called, and when Wise pointed to Braswell, the latter struck Wise and broke his jaw. Braswell was brought up on charges, convicted, and expelled by the local. His appeals were rejected by the union appellate tribunals.

Braswell was tried and convicted for violating two provisions of the union constitution. One of these, Article XII, Section I, reads: "(1) It shall be a violation of three by-laws for any member through the use of force or violence to restrain, coerce or intimidate, or attempt to restrain, coerce or intimidate any official of this International Brotherhood of Subordinate Lodge to prevent or attempt to prevent him from properly discharging the duties of his office."

He was also charged under Article XIII, Section 1, a more general clause which prohibits attempts to "create dissension among the members;" or "who works against the harmony of the International Brotherhood or Subordinate District Lodge;" or advocates secession or dualism, or supports an organization hostile to the Brotherhood "shall upon conviction be punished by expulsion from the International Brotherhood."

The trial court granted a jury trial to determine the relief to be allowed. The Court of Appeals ruled it to be proper, holding that "Congress contemplated the entire range of remedies both legal and equitable." Because Braswell sought only money damages, the court held that his cause of action was legal. Stating that the District Court's decision that the Section 101 (a) (5) rights were violated, the Appellate Court said:

[the] act charged to Braswell was a blow struck in anger, and nothing more. However reprehensible this act may be, it did not constitute a violation of the provisions in the charges. Article XIII, Section 1 of the constitution on its face is directed at threats to the union as an organization and to the effective carrying out of the union's aims. Braswell's fist was not such a threat. Article XII, Section 1 of the bylaws proscribes the use of force and violence where the purpose of such force is to prevent an officer of the union "from properly discharging the duties of his office." There is no evidence that Braswell was motivated by that purpose.[14]

The Appellate Court also upheld the award of punitive damages on the ground that Section 102 allows a court to grant such relief "as may be appropriate." While punitive damages are not "strictly speaking . . . in the nature of relief," the award of damages in appropriate cases serves "as a deterrent to those abuses which Congress ought to prevent."

Following the decision, George Hardeman, who had been expelled on the same charges and whose appeal had been by the union, filed suit in the U.S. District Court of Alabama, charging a violation of 101 (a) (5). The District Court ruled that he had been illegally expelled. The jury awarded $152,000 compensatory and punitive damages. Basing itself on *Braswell*, the Fifth Circuit Court of Appeals upheld the verdict and the damages assessed.[15]

The construction of the court seems unduly narrow. Neither Hardeman, nor Braswell for that matter, was aroused by a personal act, nor did they appear in the union office on business unrelated to the business of the organization. Their complaint and problem was the administration of the hiring list, an activity the union performed. Dissatisfaction with the manner in which Wise performed his duties could be transmitted to the International Union and/or the National Labor Relations Board. Does the assault upon an officer disrupt the union? If such acts are successful, they destroy the organization's ability to function as an impartial agency for the allocation of jobs. Without a thorough examination it is difficult to determine if Wise acted improperly in the distribution of work. Many factors are involved, including the amount of work that had been performed by particular members. In any event, a member could appeal to the union or the board, and, if the discrimination in work assignments was the result of internal union disputes, to the United States District Court.

Hardeman chose not to use any of the remedies available to him. Instead, he had determined to prevent the recurrence of the alleged discriminatory act by using his fists. The position of the Fifth Circuit in Braswell and even more in Hardeman does not appear to be valid.

The Supreme Court granted review to consider two questions: (1) Whether a federal court considering an expulsion of a member by a union can apply a standard of review whereby the court substitutes its factual findings and interpretation of the union's constitution and by-laws for those of the union; and (2) whether the National Labor Relations Act preempts the action brought under Section 102 of the LMRDA as the expelled member did not seek restoration of his membership, but damages for failure to refer him to employers. On the theory that Hardeman's suit was based on loss of employment, the union argued that the National Labor Relations Board was the proper forum for his appeal. The argument was rejected by the Supreme Court on the ground that Hardeman's complaint was based on an alleged violation of Section 101 (a) (5). The fact that he did not seek reinstatement in the union was held to have no bearing on the issue.

The Supreme Court decided that federal courts are limited in their review of union disciplinary proceedings, and that neither Section 101 (a) (5) nor its legislative history permits the courts to substitute their interpretation of union rules for those of the union in order to determine the scope of offenses warranting discipline of a union member. Section 101 (a) (5) requires written charges to be served on a union member prior to disciplinary action; federal courts have the authority to determine whether the charges are sufficiently specific and whether an opportunity has been given to present his defense, but not to scrutinize the union regulations to determine whether particular conduct may be punished. In the particular case, the Supreme Court noted, notice had been given, and it included the specific charges for which Hardeman would be tried by the union tribunal.

The Supreme Court ruled that the "full and fair hearing" of Section 101 (a) (5) (C) requires that some evidence be presented to support the charges. To set higher standards would lead to a breakdown of the authority of labor organizations to manage their internal affairs; lower standards would render Section 101 (a) (5) (C) meaningless.

In the above case, there was a physical assault on a union official by a member of the local union. In *Kelsey* v. *Local 8*[16] the charge upon which complainant was convicted by the union was making threats to an officer. Joseph P. Kelsey was chosen Vice-President of Local 8, International Alliance of Theatrical Stage Employees Local 8, and later that year Raimound Sinker was chosen Secretary-Treasurer in charge of assigning jobs. Believing that he had not been treated fairly in job assignments, Kelsey became embroiled in an argument with Sinker. The latter charged that he was threatened, a charge which Kelsey denied. Kelsey was tried and eventually found guilty. Although the penalty did not include denial of assignment to certain jobs, Kelsey claimed that he had been denied assignment as head of the carpentry department at Convention Hall since his altercation with Sinker. When he received no relief from the International Union, he appealed to the courts.

The U.S. District Court, Eastern Pennsylvania, enjoined the

union from discriminating against or disciplining Kelsey, and awarded him $1,941.25 in damages for wages he would have earned had he worked on jobs in 1967 that were available as head carpenter at Convention Hall. In setting aside the union's penalty, the Appellate Court said: that "where legal significance and the right to impinge on substantial individual rights are concerned, the characterization of what is or is not a threat has been held to involve considerations of the intent of the speaker, all of the circumstances in which the statement was made and even the reasonableness of the interpretation by the person addressed or allegedly threatened."

The court said that weighing of factors to determine whether or not to discipline a member whose conduct might be protected by LMRDA is not solely within the discretion of the union. A member is protected in making those statements which concern union business unless they fall within the proviso that they are contrary to his responsibility toward the organization as an institution. Kelsey's statements to Sinker regarding the allocation of jobs concerned union business. As the court found no evidence that Kelsey had threatened Sinker, his conviction and its affirmance by the International Union were held to be void and in contravention of Section 101 (a) (2).

The removal of a business agent from office and his expulsion from the Plumbers' Union for physically and verbally assaulting a national representative were upheld as not being in conflict with his rights under LMRDA and the union's constitution.[17] A national representative of the Plumbers' Union was sent to settle a jurisdictional dispute involving Local 211. While in conference with the contractor's representatives, the national representative of the union was abused and assaulted by the Local 211 business agent. The latter was brought up on charges and expelled. He sued, charging conspiracy and asking the restoration of his office and damages and salary lost. He was denied relief by the District Court and appealed. The Fifth Circuit found that he had been expelled in accordance with the constitution of the union, that his trial had been fair and there was substantial evidence to support the findings. "A member charged with encouraging a strike in violation of an agreement cannot be convicted without a full and fair hearing."

Boilermakers Local 802 voted that unless a contract was reached with the Sun Drydock Company facilities in Chester, Pennsylvania, by January 4, 1967, a strike would be called. Prior to the beginning of the first shift on the assigned date, the local officers announced a tentative agreement and requested that work continue. On the theory that the agreement was not the kind visualized by the membership, James S. Falcone urged that a strike be called. His suggestion was followed.

Charged with violating the constitution and with jeopardizing the agreement and causing a loss of a day's pay to 1,100 members, Falcone was urged to plead guilty at an informal hearing in exchange for a mild penalty but he refused. He was then given a regular trial and suspended from the union for five years. Following an unsuccessful appeal to the International, he complained to the courts claiming that his rights to free speech, advocating a strike, had been violated, and that he had been denied a "full and fair" trial. The trial court would not examine his claim that his right to free speech had been impaired on the basis of lack of jurisdiction. It held, moreover, that he had received a full and fair hearing, and that the "informal discussion" was an attempt at an amicable settlement which in no way affected his trial. The trial court found:

> The disciplining of a union member found guilty of instigating a strike in violation of the union's commitment to an employer to maintain work without interruption during the negotiations for a new contract and pending its ratification was merely the enforcement by the union of reasonable rules dealing with the responsibility of each member to the union, and was not an interference with the member's right of free speech.

Falcone appealed, and the Appellate Court reversed the decision of the trial court on the ground that one member of the union trial body had made up his mind on Falcone's guilt. As a result he was deprived of a full and fair hearing and therefore "warrants overturning the action of the union trial body."[18]

In another case, involving the charge of instigating an unauthorized strike, the Court of Appeals overruled the voiding of the penalty against a local officer for having instigated the walkout and said: The courts should "avoid overzealous intervention in the internal affairs of unions with its concomitant atrophic effect on the ability of the organization to function as a disciplined unit, being careful not to subject the union's interpretation of its own industrial jurisprudence to the 'removed, untutored, and possibly antipathetic judgment of a court.' "

Frederick E. Lewis, President of Local 403, State, County, Municipal Workers, was charged with encouraging and causing a number of work stoppages in violation of the union constitution and the collective bargaining agreement. He was expelled from the union, and his expulsion was upheld by the appellate tribunals of the organization. The District Court, Eastern District of Pennsylvania, held his removal from office was not reviewable but his expulsion from the union violated Section 101 (a) (5) and was "illegal, arbitrary and unjustified, and in violation of due process of law." He was ordered reinstated as a member of Local 403, and the union appealed.[19]

The Appellate Court held that it was proper for federal courts to review how the expulsion of an officer was effected. However, it also held that the District Court erred when it overturned the verdict of the union tribunal, on the ground that its decision was not based on "substantial" evidence. There was no intent, said the court, "to adopt standards of review equivalent to the substantial evidence test . . ." A court may not substitute its judgment for that of the union trial board or reexamine the evidence so as to determine if it would have reached the same conclusion. There must be some evidence to support the charges, and on that basis the verdict that Lewis played a role in calling and directing the strikes is not unreasonable.

To reach a contrary conclusion required the court below to exercise an authority of review greatly in excess of its limited and circumscribed power . . . No reviewing court has such prerogative . . . Once the court determines that the findings of the union's tribunal were "not without any foundation in the evidence," that the proof adduced related to appropriate charges, and that procedural due process was observed, the action of the union tribunal must be upheld.

This means presentation of charges, adequate notice to prepare a defense, the right to present witnesses and to examine adverse witnesses, and all the other procedural observances, which are necessary for a fair trial. A member charged with belonging to the Communist Party when he joined the Carpenters' Union and falsifying this fact on his application was expelled, but was denied an opportunity to confront hostile witnesses. He appealed to the courts, and he was ordered reinstated, but without prejudice to the union's holding a hearing in conformity of Section 101 (a) (5).[20] The court restricted the issues to the consideration of whether the accused, Anderson, had falsified his application for membership.

Anderson was again tried. This time the procedural requirements were observed. He was found guilty, and the court found no basis for reversing the decision.

The jurisdiction with which the court is clothed in this proceeding requires that it recognize that if there is sufficient evidence in the record, which, if believed, affords a basis for the findings of the Committee, it is not for the Court to set aside the findings even if perchance they run counter to the Court's own appraisal of the testimony; that is, the Court is not required and should not attempt to determine whether it would have arrived at the same conclusion as did the Trial Committee. The Court cannot substitute its judgment for that of the Committee, and if there is valid evidence sufficient to sustain the Committee's conclusions, the Court should affirm.[21]

A union's finding of guilt supported by evidence at the trial has to be accepted, as a court cannot substitute its judgment for that of the union. However, the fairness of the union's hearing procedures must be tested by the evidence and circumstances presented to the court. A case arose as a result of the suspension of John Burke, an official of Local No. 6, Boilermakers, who had been indefinitely suspended from the union for taking contracts from the printer and withholding them from the members and thereby postponing the signing of an agreement. He claimed his action was in the interest of the union, but he was not authorized to take it. The court found the trial had been fair and that he had been convicted on four of the five charges lodged against him. The claim, by Burke, that officers had unduly influenced the verdict, was held unproven by the court which ruled that the penalty imposed was not "so gross, arbitrary or unfair" that it constituted a violation of due process or Section 101 (a) (5).[22]

A member who fails to maintain his dues and is automatically expelled from the union cannot gain reinstatement on the ground that he has been denied rights under Section 101 (a) (5). Herbert Schuchardt was expelled from Carpenters' Local 2834 in January 1965. His expulsion was stayed while his appeal was pending before the general President. Schuchardt refused to pay dues before January 1965, and by November 1966, he was delinquent for a period making his expulsion from the union automatic. He appealed to the District Court, which denied relief, holding he had been expelled for non-payment of dues. He appealed.

The Appellate Court held that, as the union constitution protected the accused's membership while his appeal was pending, he was obligated to pay his dues as also required by the constitution. In fact, Schuchardt

> remained a member of the union, was entitled to all the rights and owed all the obligations of union membership. The filing of appellant's judicial action did not and could not deny him his continued right to have the order of the local remain ineffective to accomplish expulsion. Nor did the fil-

ing of the action relieve appellant of the obligation to pay dues to remain in good standing.

His failure to pay and automatic expulsion in fact constituted a resignation from the union.[23]

8

Collective Bargaining and Title I

Federal courts have retained jurisdiction of a Section 101 (a) (5) suit even when elements of the case were, perhaps, subject to the National Labor Board's jurisdiction. It has been held that the LMRDA added a new protection for union members to those already available under the National Labor Relations Board and other federal statutes. If it can be shown that a member's rights under 101 (a) (5) have been violated through collusion with the employer, or by failure to take action on behalf of the member, then the statute can be invoked.[1]

A few cases in this area have arisen in a variety of contexts. Usually they charge that the union, in cooperation with the employer, has arbitrarily penalized the member for opposition to the officers or a policy, or that an act ostensibly dictated by a collective bargaining agreement is a disguised form of union discipline. The cases have involved claims that the seniority system has been unfairly administered, that the union was in collusion with the employer in permitting a discharge of a member, that the enforcement of an arbitration agreement was carried out by violating the due process of the member, or that the denial of the hiring hall was a means to effect a member's expulsion from the union.

The courts have long recognized that procedures which had developed under collective bargaining contracts were designed to meet the changing problems of particular industries and firms. On occasion, a union may be forced by the logic of events to accept decisions on the allocation of jobs, changes in the rules, or imposition of penalties which are not motivated by malice or a desire to inflict harm, but are compelled by the needs or the power of the employer. Only the facts can determine the character and the motivation of the disputed action. Another question involved is whether the union is a party to the action, or whether it is merely a passive spectator inhibited from defensive action by the collective bargaining agreement.

The union may be allowed, under a bargaining agreement, to review all or some penalties imposed for infractions of rules. Such an arrangement is designed to diminish disputes between the management and the union so that non-merited penalties will be challenged at an early stage of the grievance procedure, and mitigated or reversed if such decision appears to be warranted. Under this type of arrangement, the aggrieved member, even before he has presented a formal grievance, is given his day in court. Should it appear that the penalty is not arbitrary or excessive, the union may decide not to contest it by further appeals. In a sense, however, the union acquiesces in every penalty imposed by the employer which it does not challenge. However, the duty of fair representation requires that it question those penalties which are unfair, inequitable, or too severe.

In one of the early cases in which a worker charged that the employer and the union had entered into a conspiracy to deprive him of employment and union membership, the court held that there was "nothing in the act to indicate jurisdiction in this court for an action by an employee against an employer to review a justification on non-jurisdiction for a discharge."[2]

In another suit, the charge that discrimination in the use of the union hiring hall and allocation of jobs constituted a violation of Title I rights was dismissed for lack of jurisdiction.[3] The court also rejected a suit under Section 101 (a) (5) by a union member who based her charges on the claim that the union had refused to refer her to employment. These violations, the Eighth Circuit Court held, were "a routine allegation of an unfair labor practice and a violation of 8 (b) 2."[4]

A remedy for improper discipline under Title I can only be invoked upon a showing that such discipline was imposed because of union membership.[5] In a discharge of a member of an independent union from his job with the Newport Shipbuilding and Dry Dock Company, the court ruled that if the member proves "that the company acted at the behest of the union, he states a cause of action against the union. The Act does not allow the union to achieve indirectly what it is prohibited to do directly."[6]

Duncan had been an opponent of the leadership and protested the preceding election to the Secretary of Labor. It was Duncan's belief that the discharge was the result of collusion between the union and the employer, for union membership was linked to employment by the particular company, since the union did not recruit outside of that firm. The court ruled that the instigation of a discharge by the union so as to rid itself of a dissident member fell within the "more general prohibition that the union cannot, without notice, without time to prepare a defense and without a hearing 'otherwise discipline' a member." The ruling of the District Court dismissing the suit under the LMRDA with respect to the company was upheld by the Appellate Court. The court, however, did not uphold the District Court's dismissal of the suit with regard to the union. Duncan, said the Appellate Court,

> seeks to prove that the union schemed with the company to effect discharge from employment, in circumstances where discharge would necessarily terminate union membership. Thereby, the complainant also charges, the union wrongfully "expelled" Duncan from its ranks. It does not matter that expulsion was accomplished by company action. If Duncan proves that the company acted at the behest of the union, he has stated a cause of action against the union.

In another case, the National Maritime Union denied shipping rights to three members who had a number of years earlier been convicted of narcotics possession. While the Court of Appeals Second Circuit acknowledged that interference of employment opportunity of members may constitute discipline under Title 101 (a) (5), it held that a union's refusal to register a seaman and to refer him for employment, "was pursuant to the terms of a collective bargaining agreement and in compliance with the declared policy of the shipowners that they will not hire seamen known to have a narcotics conviction" and did not amount to discipline.[7]

In a case involving the International Longshoremen's and Warehousemen's Association, two members were removed from the hiring list, deregistered and denied access to the hiring hall which supplied longshoremen for the San Francisco Bay Area docks. The action followed a hearing before the Joint Port Labor Committee. Suing under Section 101 (a) (5), in part, they claimed that their exclusion from the docks and employment was in fact expulsion from the union without a hearing.

The court rejected this claim on the ground that the issue was loss of employment and not union status. Deregistration cannot, said the court, be described as being "effectively expelled." The argument made was that "deregistration" was covered by the proviso of "otherwise disciplined." It was conceded that the union might initiate a complaint with the Port Committee against one of its members. If, then, the representatives of the Pacific Maritime Association expresses no opposition, "there is the possibility for arbitrary and unfair conduct by the union against one of its members." Nevertheless, the court said that Section 101 (a) (5) does not indicate that "Congress intended to write the procedural guarantees into grievance machinery set up under a union collective bargaining agreement simply because the union participated in the grievance machinery and there was the possibility of abusing that power." It also called attention to the fact that nowhere in Section 101 are there provisions or references to collective bargaining agreements. Summary judgment was granted to the union on the ground that Section 101 (a) (5) did not apply to grievances of the kind that were challenged.[8]

However, the allegation that there was a conspiracy between the union and the employer group to deregister the aggrieved longshoremen stated a cause of action under the Labor-Management Relations Act, and this part of the complaint was not dismissed.

A union may not aggressively seek sanctions against a member, but instead may take advantage of an opportunity to punish by refusing to defend him against an unjustified suspension or dismissal by the employer. Is the sanction merited, or is the union using the occasion to punish someone who has expressed opposition to officers or policies?

A member of the Teamsters' Union discharged by the Brink's office in Jersey City complained that the union's refusal to demand his reinstatement was a violation of his rights under Section 101 (a) (5). His argument was rejected by the court, which noted that it was "quite clear from a reading of Title I that its intent was to protect a union member from the violation of his rights, as against the union only, and only as specified in Title I. . . . Nowhere in Title I is there any mention whatever of a union member's democratic rights thereunder save in Section 104." The court added that the latter section only gives the member a right to a copy of the collective bargaining agreement, but does not give the right to sue under the agreement.[9]

The role of the union was completely passive in the above instance. A union may in fact be more active in the disciplining of employees. Cooperation with the employer may be based on a desire to assist in the carrying out of the collective bargaining agreement and not to punish a member for behavior within the union. In *Scovile* v. *Watson*, the union cooperated with the employer and refused to challenge a discharge for excessive absences from work. Prior to the dismissal, the business agent of the local union had proposed that grievances arising from disciplinary penalties for excessive absences from work not be arbitrated in the future. Following the adoption of the proposal, an employee of a chemical plant in Elkhart, Indiana, and a member of Oil, Chemical and Atomic Workers was discharged on the ground that her frequent absence from work justified her dismissal. When the union refused to appeal her discharge, she complained to the court that her rights under Title I had been violated. She also charged that her freedom of speech had been breached when she was denied an opportunity to present a motion revoking the resolution against arbitrating disciplinary penalties for excessive absences.

While granting the claim that refusal to arbitrate a grievance under a union-management contract might be considered improper discipline, the court held that the resolution adopted on refusal to arbitrate grievances arising from discharge for excessive absences cannot be so regarded,[10] "the action taken by the union was prospective and applied to the entire membership, and not to the plaintiff alone." As for denial of free speech by refusing to entertain a motion, the Appellate Court said that "the exercise of the right at union meetings must accommodate itself to the union's correlative right to conduct its meetings in an orderly fashion and in accordance with its previously established rules." Acquiescing in the discharge of a member of the union by the grievance committee of a New York local of the Retail Clerks Union which reviewed disciplinary discharges by the employer was, in the opinion of the District Court, "in accordance with fair procedure." The union's removal of the plaintiff from his position, after fair investigation and a hearing before the grievance committee and the executive board, was equivalent to a discharge for fair cause.[11]

Gross was employed by Food Fair Stores and was a member of Retail Clerks Local 1,500, New York City. According to the union secretary,[12] he had a record of grievances and transfers and demotions, and as such it was "determined that the employer had just cause for discharging Gross."[13] Although the union did not contest the discharge, it played no other role in the action. As a matter of fact, the employer announced that Gross would be discharged, regardless of the view of the executive board. The union's dereliction, if there were any, would have lain in that refusal. No evidence was presented at the trial that animus existed against Gross on the part of the officers or that he engaged in any activity which would encourage the officers to discriminate against him. The only basis upon which the union's action can be attacked is that it was a product of venality, but that was neither stated nor implied. The court found "that action by a union affecting the relationship of a union member and his employer are not within the usual interpretation of the relationship described within the term 'other disciplinary action' in Title I, Section 101 (a) (5) of the Labor Management Reporting and Disclosure Act of 1959."[14]

Rekant v. *Meat Cutters* is similar to Gross except that the work had been granted to an unemployed member by those with jobs in accordance with the union's work sharing program. When the member who had been given employment failed to perform his duties satisfactorily, his job allotment was cancelled by Meat Cutters Local 446, Philadelphia. He sued, claiming unfair discipline under Section 101 (a) (5). It was the opinion of the Third Circuit Court of Appeals that the rescinding of the resolution allowing the unemployed worker to share in the available work touched the union-member relationship. However, the court believed that the rescinding of the resolution was a result of failure to take the jobs offered and unsatisfactory performance. "Viewing the rescinding resolution in the light of its actual effect on appellee," the Appellate Court found, "he was not 'otherwise disciplined' within the meaning of Section 101 (a) (5). At most the rescinding resolution was an implied and indirect reprimand or censure of appellee for his behavior."[15]

Inequitable job assignments by a local union operating a hiring hall cannot be challenged by a Title I suit in the federal courts. A member sued Millwrights, Machinery and Erectors Local 1693, Chicago, Illinois, because jobs had been given to out-of-town members and not to the complainant. The charges, the court said, were "not sufficient to state a cause of action under the Bill of Rights section of the Act, since the subject was unrelated to the guarantees protected by this section. The Bill of Rights section applies only to questions relating to the internal political and civil rights which exist between the union and its members."[16]

Business agents' practices of extortion, job discrimination and bribery for preference in work assignments were also held to be abuses that could not be reached by Title I because a federal court lacked jurisdiction to entertain a suit brought by union members under the Bill of Rights provision of the Act.[17]

In several instances complaints to the courts have been made by members that their rights have been violated when they have been excluded from a local union by the International without a trial. In these instances, a recalcitrant local, after notice and trial, has had its charter revoked by the parent organization. Another local union would be established in the same jurisdiction to which the leaders of the opposition to the decision of the International union would be denied admission.

A situation of this kind arose as a result of a jurisdictional dispute between two New Jersey locals of the United Association of Journeymen and Apprentice Plumbing Pipe Fitting Industry of the United States and Canada, when the International union ruled that Local 14 must withdraw from a job in the Jersey City, New Jersey, area on which its members were employed. The local refused to obey the order, and unsuccessfully sought to prevent the carrying out of the decision in the New Jersey courts. After the charges against the International had been dismissed, the charter of Local 14 was revoked and Local 69 chartered in its place. The charter of Local 69 covered the same Jersey City jurisdiction as had formerly been held by Local 14.[18] The funds of Local 14 were transferred to Local 69, and members of the former were told they could transfer to the latter without payment of additional initiation fees. All former members, except nine officers and leaders in the fight over jurisdiction, were admitted to membership in Local 69. The nine sued for admission claiming they had been expelled improperly from the union.

Judge Reynier J. Wortendyke, of the United States District Court of New Jersey, ruled

where such revocation is part of a scheme to discriminate against certain members of the local, accomplished by their exclusion from membership in a new but essentially successor local, to membership in which all other members of the former local are automatically admitted, the conclusion is inescapable that those who are thus excluded from union benefits have been, in effect, expelled from their union without a hearing upon specific charges as required by the Bill of Rights.

This view is similar to those views stated in the state courts.[19] Calabrese is, however, a civil liberties case in the sense that the plaintiff and his associates were penalized for bringing suit in the New Jersey courts. The dispute initially arose over differences on work assignments. It was a clear violation of Section 101 (a) (5) in that the members were separated from their organization without a charge, hearing, or trial,[20] and the court ordered their admittance to the Local 69 on the same terms as other members.

More difficult is the situation in which the decline of jobs, the combining of departments or firms require the merging, dovetailing, or "sandwiching" of seniority lists. Some workers may lose their favorable seniority positions or jobs. Not unusual is a feeling of grievance or a conviction that the union has not provided some of its members "fair representation." Such disputes have been brought, over the years, to both the state and federal courts, and changes in work assignments on the New York division of the New York Central railroad brought a Section 101 (a) (5) suit from a group of aggrieved members.

An agreement was made between Lodge No. 1,085, Brotherhood of Railroad Carmen, and the New York Central Railroad Company to merge the seniority rosters so that the "seniority dates" employees held at the New Haven Yard would be preserved for them and inserted upon their transfer to the Grand Central terminal in New York City on a roster with those already working at the latter facility. Some of those employed at the terminal were adversely affected by the change as those employed at the New Haven yards who had greater seniority were placed ahead of those with lesser seniority at the Grand Central terminal. The changes were challenged in the United States District Court on several grounds, among them one that the changes were a reprisal against critics of the manner in which the Lodge's finances had been handled.[21]

The charge was made that the employer aided the union in carrying out this illegal objective. The court dismissed this part of the complaint because the court had "consistently held" that the LMRDA "regulates only the relationship between the union and its members and not that between an employer and his employees." The changes were carried out in accordance with the rules of the union and the agreement between the Brotherhood of Railroad Carmen and the carrier. The court therefore dismissed the case.

Does the denial of the right of union members to ratify an agreement made with the employer on their behalf violate the LMRDA? The dispute between Local 4, American Federation of Musicians, and employees of the Cleveland Symphony Orchestra antedated the enactment of the statute. Since 1918, Local 4 has negotiated the contract for the symphony musicians with the Musical Arts Association. The members of the orchestra could advise, but not ratify the contract. A campaign for the right of ratification began in 1954. It was regularly rejected by the local's leadership, the last time being in 1962. Suit to compel ratification was started in the courts on the grounds that denial was a violation of "the bill of rights." The petition of the symphony musicians was rejected by the court, which found that the contracts had been made in accordance with the local constitution and by-laws. There was no "deprivation of legal rights of the symphony musicians as a result of not permitting them to approve or reject the contract made on their behalf by the bargaining agent authorized and directed to act on them in accordance with the union by-laws."[22]

An attempt by a union, the American Guild of Variety Artists, to compel a member, Gene Detroy, to compensate an employer for a breach of contract and also place the member who refused to pay the claimed damages on the union unfair list was held to be a violation of Section 101 (a) (5). The District Court rejected the suit because the plaintiff had failed to exhaust his union remedies. However, the Court of Appeals[23] ruled that the statute did not impose "upon the union member an absolute duty to exhaust union remedies before applying to the federal courts."

A more important question was the right of the union to enforce an arbitration award under the special circumstances prevailing in the entertainment industry.

Members of the American Guild of Variety Artists (AGVA) do not depend upon the single employer or booking agent, nor do the latter depend upon a particular performer or groups of employees for long periods of time. AGVA requires that employers and performers subscribe to an Artist Engagement Contract which governs the specific terms of each engagement. One of the provisions, Rule 11, specifies that all contracts must be "pay or play," and noncancellable. This means that the party who breaks the contract must pay to the other the amount that would have been earned if the contract had been carried out. Thus, if the employer cancelled the contract before the expiration date, he would be compelled to compensate the performer for the full amount he would have earned had he been allowed to complete the full term of his engagement. Conversely, if the performer left the engagement before he had fulfilled the run of the contract, he would be, under the "pay or play" principle, obligated to pay his employer the amount he would have earned had he carried out the contract.

Gene Detroy, a member of AGVA, withdrew a week before his contract had expired in an engagement at the Dunes Hotel, Las Vegas, Nevada. As a result, the union required him to recompense the owner of the hotel with the salary he would have earned, $1,250. Detroy protested, and the controversy was submitted to arbitration. Detroy agreed to the procedure and attended the hearing. The arbitrators held unanimously that Detroy had breached his contract, and the Dunes Hotel was entitled to recover. The verdict was not contested in the California courts, the state in which the arbitration had been held. After Detroy had refused to accept the arbitration award, he was put on the "unfair list," and the union tried to have the amount of the award withheld from Detroy's salary when he was employed elsewhere. Detroy petitioned for an injunction against the union's unfair list and its attempt to garner the amount charged against him. The petition was brought under Section 101 (a) (5), on the ground that he had been convicted without charges, a trial, and a full and fair hearing.

The union, in the view of the Court of Appeals, had failed to provide written charges, and a proper hearing. It did not regard the arbitration hearing as "the type of hearing demanded by Section 101 (a) (5)." In the proceedings, the union as an institution had no quarrel with Detroy. His penalties were imposed for violating the contract between the union and management, and not the union constitution as it affects membership. The sanctions that were imposed were required by the union-management agreement and are unusual only in the fact that the union member is required to pay money damages to a third party, the employer. As employment is on a temporary basis, no other sanctions could be imposed upon a "defaulting" performer except to compel him to deposit a given sum with which to compensate the employer for losses sustained in the event of failure to carry out contractual engagements.

Contract violations can take on a number of forms but the breaking of an engagement is peculiar to industries in which employment is for short spans of time. As already indicated, the problem could be solved by a bond or a cash deposit by the entertainer. Otherwise, the employer would be subjected to a penalty while the entertainer could escape by refusing to pay. The mutuality of obligations inherent in a contract of employment would under those circumstances be absent, as far as this clause is concerned, since an employer would be penalized for a breach of an agreement while a worker could escape it.

The union does not in fact impose discipline as an institution upon such a worker any more than it does when it accepts the penalizing of its members by the employer for the infraction of a work rule. It is true that Detroy's penalty was imposed when he was no longer an employee of the Dunes night club and could not be effected without the cooperation of the union.[24] The court obviously used this fact as the peg upon which to hang the decision. Nevertheless, the decision shows a lack of appreciation of the peculiar problems facing an industry. Moreover, Detroy did have his day in court. He was able to present his case before an impartial body which found that he wilfully left his employment without cause. It cannot, therefore, be argued that the union's action was capricious.

The same question arose in the discharge of a worker who refused to return to his former job after he had been on a leave of absence. He insisted upon his right to another position, but an arbitration award upheld the view of the company that he had to return to the job he had held at the time of taking his leave of absence. In refusing to dismiss the complaint, the court held that the "cases do not signify that acquiescence in an employee's discharge constitutes 'discipline' but rather that activity which is really 'discipline' is not made less so because it involves the employee's status as an employee and not as a union member."[25] The complainant failed to establish that the union which held the contract had engaged in disciplining him under Section 101 (a) (5). The District Court noted: "The union can discipline a member by failure to pursue a grievance as well as by fine or suspension. But there must be some basis for the charge that the union's activity constituted discipline. The word alone—discipline—is conclusory and cannot avert dismissal where it is not supported by specific allegations which would indicate how the union's activity was directed toward plaintiff's membership . . ." The case was dismissed with respect to LMRDA.

Although the Bill of Rights has not caused a flood of complaints to the federal courts, it has had an important effect upon the behavior of unions in matters connected with the rights of members. The most obvious result is the equalization of treatment of union members in disputes over certain rights. The federal law is uniform throughout the country. In addition, certain practices, such as excluding groups of members from full participation in the life of the union by limiting voting or office-holding to a particular group in the organization, have been outlawed as violations of Title I. These provisions could not be successfully challenged under the common law, since membership was accepted on the limited basis provided in the constitution.

The free speech section has given the membership protection of their rights to express opinions and assemble for any purpose without interference by the officers of the union. While the dictum that libel of an officer and persumably a fellow member is not an offense against the union might be criticized on some grounds, it means that any expression of opinion, unless it can be shown to fall under the proviso, cannot be attacked in a union tribunal. The view of the courts is that if the subject of discussion is union business it is protected. The burden is, therefore, upon the union to show that the speech adversely affected the union as an organization.

Another effect of the free speech section is the ending of the prohibition on the discussion of union business outside the union hall. These prohibitions go back to the time when labor organizations feared that information on union intentions might be carried back to the employer. The implicit view of the courts today is that labor organizations can tolerate such disclosure and that the benefits from free discussion override the possible harmful effects that might follow if a hostile employer gains possession of such information. Title I has also wiped out the prohibitions upon the circulating of printed materials which discuss union business among the members. Some unions had outright prohibitions upon such distribution. Others required permission from an official of the International. Both rules have become invalid and unenforceable.

The prohibition upon union members' assembling for the discussion of union business without authorization of the officers of the organization has also been invalidated. The basis for such provision was originally to protect against the leaking of information which might be of assistance to an adversary. It can, however, be used to suppress the dissident and to prevent the formation of an opposition, and Congress had this aspect in view when it prohibited such by-laws.

The McClellan Committee hearings did not muster much evidence to show that there had been widespread abuses in the levying of dues and assessments by the standard labor organizations. International unions generally prescribed that notice must be given if dues are increased or assessments imposed. Violations could be protested to the officers of the organization. Congress believed, nevertheless, that no burden would be imposed upon the labor organizations by prescribing minimum standards, adequate notice and a secret ballot. There have been relatively few cases, and only a limited number of these involved an attempt to evade the requirements of the statute.

More significant still is Title I, Section (a) (5), which specifies that a union member charged with violating his obligations must be served with written charges, given adequate time to prepare his defense, and be "afforded a full and fair hearing." Under a ruling of the United States Supreme Court, a member who prevails in a Title I suit may be awarded counsel fees. It has provided union members with another forum for complaint and their right to review cannot be questioned. A member may be required to exhaust reasonable hearing procedures, not to exceed a four months' lapse of time. This provision places a time limit upon the union's appellate procedures. The appealing member must be apprised of the verdict of the union tribunal within that period, and the union cannot use a multiple appellate procedure to prolong a decision thereby frustrating access to the federal courts. The number of cases in this area has not been large, considering the millions who belong to unions, because the state courts have been willing to hear the members' complaints of harsh and arbitrary actions of the union or its officers against the members.

9

Reporting and Disclosure

The reporting and disclosure provisions of Title II, with the exception of Section 203, have for their purpose the protection of the finances and other assets of labor organizations. Little objection was offered to their enactment except that some of the witnesses believed that small local unions should be exempted because the requirements would place an undue burden upon their part-time officers.[1] The problem of protecting union funds is not a recent one, nor one limited to the United States. Whenever large sums are entrusted to an individual, protection of the funds by bonding is essential. The membership of unions was not always aware of this need, and, for a time, unions had no defense against dishonest officers because as unincorporated associations they had no standing in court.

A student of the labor movement of the nineteenth century observed, in 1906: "As in so many other labor organizations the Iron Molders Union has not been free from defaulting officials. As far back as 1878, the defalcation of a president made necessary a call for a convention."[2] As this worthy was not bonded, the only penalty that could be imposed upon him was expulsion from the union. The member who followed him in office stole four times as much as his predecessor—$19,864.46, of which only $6,000 was recovered from a surety company.

Nor was peculation of union funds peculiar to iron molders. The evidence indicates the opposite is true. "The bonding of officials has gradually come to be regarded by the unions as a fundamental administrative principle. Defalcations have frequently occurred, and bonding is the only available method for idemnification to the organizations and their members."[3] The embezzlement was not conducted by a minor official in desperate need of a few extra dollars, but by the heads of the union. The Grand Secretary-Treasurer of the Brotherhood of Locomotive Engineers stole, in the early 1870s, the insurance funds. His example was imitated by the chief finance officers of two other railroad unions. In 1885, the Secretary-Treasurer of the trainmen was expelled for dishonesty and misappropriation of funds, and three successive finance officers of the Switchmen's union, the rival of the trainmen, were guilty of the same practice.[4] In 1887, the Secretary-Treasurer of the Switchmen's Union of North America absconded with $9,000, and his replacement improved upon his performance by embezzling $32,527 from the union treasury. The third appointment may be regarded as an improvement, or the union may have increased its vigilance for he was ousted from office after he misappropriated $2,689.[5]

Eventually, embezzlement of union funds became a crime, but the prosecution of wrongdoers was dependent upon a complaint from the organization which was victimized. Unions were reluctant to prosecute because of sentiment for the wayward officer or the fear of the unfavorable reaction of the members or the public. As a result, there has been a tendency to avoid publicizing such misdeeds, if partial or complete restitution of the diverted funds was made. Unions have also developed their own system of protecting their funds. Auditors are elected or appointed to check the assets of subordinate units. Requirements that the members of the local union elect auditing committees at periodic intervals are also found in many union constitutions. In some instances, outside accountants may be required, as aids to the rank and file committee. In addition, many unions require that financial secretaries and treasurers be bonded,

It is a matter of statistical probability and experience that some finance officers of unions will betray their trust and misappropriate funds entrusted to them by the organization. The reluctance to advertise these misdeeds, as already mentioned, accounts for the paucity of knowledge regarding this problem, prior to the enactment of the LMRDA. It may therefore be useful to describe the little information obtained from the records of eight unions to give some idea of the magnitude of the problem.

In 1936, the Bakery and Confectionary Workers International Union of America informed its members: "The numerous reports of shortages impel us to address again a word of caution and advice to local trustees."[6] In seven years, thirty locals had reported shortages which ranged from $1.83 to $3,815. All but $727.57 was recovered from surety companies.

More detailed information is available on the Bricklayers' Union. After payments of losses by surety companies and settlements by defaulters, the new shortage, in 1930, was $2,360 spread over thirteen locals. The gross amount of losses was not given. In the following year, thirty-three local unions reported shortages in their funds, with net losses put at $22,000. In 1945, losses of $23,000 were incurred by ten locals. The International Brotherhood of Electrical Workers did not give its loss experience, but announced, in 1948, a reduction of premiums by its bonding department based on lower losses in the preceding five years.

The United Cement, Lime and Gypsum Workers International informed its members of the need to audit the accounts of its finance officers periodically. At the same time, the members were told that, in 1941, four local officers had defaulted for amounts ranging from $11.18 to $1,030. Most of the money was recovered, but one local which had failed to bond its officers lost more than $300. In subsequent years, shortages were reported in nine of ten locals and the total amounts diverted ranged between $3,000 and $5,000. The annual shortages in the Molders' and Machinists' Unions were higher, and both of these organizations operated their own fidelity departments, so that the net losses to the locals were only a fraction of the gross amount.

Between January 1946 and 1950, the Painters' Union experienced 101 known instances of diversion of funds by local officers amounting to more than $100,000. Of these, fifty-five were for less than $500; nineteen for sums between $500-$1,000; eighteen between $1,000-$2,000; five for $2,000-$3,000; and four involving more than $5,000. The Brotherhood of Maintenance of Way Employees reported six claims amounting to $22,689 for losses incurred by its local lodges in 1947. The number of claims rose in the following year, and the total losses were above $3,000. In 1949, claims had dropped to three, and losses to slightly more than $1,300.

The Brotherhood of Railway and Steamship Clerks reported its losses at four-year intervals. In 1943, the union reported ninety-seven instances of shortages amounting to over $40,000. In the next four years, the number of diversions dropped by two, and the total amount to somewhat over $28,000. If the losses are reduced to an annual basis, they are within the range of the other organizations. It might be noted that the data represents the experience of local unions, and that neither regional nor national officers are listed in the data. As this experience is different from the information on the unions in the nineteenth century, as well as the evidence adduced since the enactment of Landrum-Griffin law, it might be reasonably assumed that in some instances at least their accounts were not submitted to rigorous examination.

The need for reporting is obvious, and the information that has been accumulated as a result of the labor reform law shows that misappropriation is not limited to the officers of the above eight unions. As already noted, in some instances the shortage may have been a temporary "borrowing" or "intermingling" of personal and organization funds, and the sudden arrival of the auditor made it impossible to put the books in order. Greater honesty is the only means of correction, but the outstanding student of labor corruption believes that honesty is not enough.[7] Dr. Hutchinson believes that the personal philosophy of the officers, and even more of the labor organization involved, will affect the honesty of those holding office. The difficulty is that he limited himself to examining organized and collusive industrial racketeering. However, racketeering is influenced by the character of the industry and whether collusive arrangements requiring the assistance of the union officers are necessary. Virtue is sometimes the result of the absence of opportunity to be sinful. If we examine the sources of embezzlement, the picture changes, and we find that unions of all kinds and outlooks are victimized by faithless officers. An efficient auditing system may be a more effective method of curbing embezzlement than the most advanced philosophy.[8]

Title II requires that every labor organization adopt a constitution and by-laws, and file a copy of the document with the Secretary of Labor together with a report to be signed by the principal officers. The report must contain information on dues, transfer fees, rules governing admission of members, their qualifications, the use of funds, the disciplinary and appellate procedures, and the rules for bargaining with employers and acceptance of contracts. Changes made in the above provisions must be reported.

In addition, every labor organization must file annually a report listing its assets, receipts, expenditures and liabilities at the beginning and end of the fiscal year. Sources of receipts must be listed, as must be salary payments to each officer and to each employee who, during the fiscal year, received more than $10,000 from a labor organization or any other labor organization affiliated with it. Allowances and reimbursed expenses must be reported. Table 2 gives the number of unions submitting such reports.

Efforts to simplify the reporting requirements have been made by the Office of Labor-Management and Welfare-Pension Reports. Labor organizations with $30,000 or more of annual income and those in trusteeship submit their reports on the four page LM-2. Others use the one page LM-3. About 25 percent of the organizations use the LM-2 form.

Unions are also required to report any loan in excess of $250, together with its purpose, the security given for it, and the arrangement for repayment. Direct and indirect loans to business must be reported, along with the security given and the arrangements for repayment. The information required to be contained in the report to the Department of Labor must be available to

Table 2.
Labor Unions Submitting Annual Financial Reports
by Fiscal Year Ending June 30[1]

Year	Number
1960	52,078
1961	49,785
1962	52,237
1963	53,843
1964	52,237
1965	56,475
1966	57,950
1967	53,902
1968	55,899
1969	56,054
1970	50,968
1971	49,345
1972[2]	59,908

[1] Figures have been compiled from the annual *Summary of Operations*, and by the Department of Labor's Officer—W.P. who administers the LMRDA.

[2] Postal unions were included and 11,704 postal unions registered.

members. They can enforce this right, for just cause, by a suit in the District Court of the United States. The court may allow a reasonable counsel fee in such suits.

Section 202 (a) requires that every officer and employee of a labor organization, exclusive of those performing clerical and custodial duties, must file a report listing securities owned by himself, spouse or minor child, or income or other things of monetary value received from employers whose employees the union represents or is seeking to represent. Direct or indirect business transactions with employers whose employees are represented by the union or whom the union seeks to represent must also be reported, except for those which are payments for work performed or goods purchased.

The Secretary of Labor was given authority under Section 208 to "prescribe by general rules simplified reports for labor organizations . . . for whom he finds that by virtue of their size a detailed report would be unduly burdensome." The Secretary has the power to revoke, after a hearing, the use of the simple form. The Department of Labor's power to investigate is authorized under Section 601, which gives the Secretary the authority to conduct such an investigation ". . . enter such places and inspect such records and accounts and question such persons as he may deem necessary to determine the facts relative thereto."

The power to inspect financial reports was delegated to the Office of Labor-Management and Welfare-Pension Reports by the Secretary of Labor. The Office routinely audits the reports submitted by the Internationals. A sampling of subordinate bodies and local unions is also audited monthly. Under the Act, the Secretary has the right to subpoena documents he regards as relevant to his investigation. When the Truck Drivers Local 229, Teamsters, refused to comply with a subpoena, the District Court for Eastern Michigan supported the local's contention that the Secretary is required to show "probable cause" for his investigation. The decision was overturned by the Sixth Circuit Court of Appeals, which said that "it might hamper the Secretary in the performance of his duties with respect to investigations which were imposed upon him by the Act." With such a requirement, each investigation would likely be met by a lawsuit in which the Secretary would be obliged to prove a probable violation of the Act, or enforcement of subpoenas would be denied. Even if successful in his proof, the investigation by the Secretary might be delayed for months or years while the matter was being litigated. The Secretary could not very well perform his statutory duty and determine whether the Act was being violated or about to be violated without making an investigation. Requiring the Secretary to first establish a probable violation of the Act, as a condition precedent to making an investigation, would have effectively stripped him of the power to investigate and prevented him from determining whether the Act was being violated or about to be violated.[9]

By the end of fiscal 1972, fifty-two suits had been filed by or against the Secretary of Labor. In ten of these instances the reports were submitted prior to the trials. In the overwhelming number of cases in which violations were disclosed, the Office of Labor-Management and Welfare-Pension Reports was able to achieve correction by voluntary measures. In fiscal 1961, the first full year, more than 1,900 violations by labor organizations were uncovered but virtually all of them were corrected by voluntary compliance.[10]

The Office provided technical assistance and, from the beginning of its operations, sought to simplify and consolidate the reporting forms. By the end of fiscal 1962, the Office was able to reduce the size and the complexity of the financial reports required "while retaining all essential information."[11] The standard form used by organizations with annual receipts of $30,000 or more was condensed from nine to four pages, while the short form, authorized in the statute, was revised and simplified even further for the small unions. Some inadequacy in the reporting of 3,019 organizations was found, but 96 percent of these violations were found to be technical or without criminal intent. In such cases, LMWP took the necessary action to have the violation corrected and to prevent its recurrence.

Section 209 (a) penalizes the violation of the reporting requirements by a fine up to $10,000 or imprisonment for not more than one year, or both. Section 209 (b) provides that any person making a false statement or knowingly withholding a material fact in any document, report or information required is subject to a fine of not more than $10,000 or to imprisonment for one year, or to both. Willful concealment, or destruction of books, records, reports or statements required to be kept is made punishable by the same penalties as the other sections of 209. Those required to sign reports under Sections 201 and 203 are held "personally responsible for the filing of such reports and any statement contained therein which he knows to be false."

In addition, Section 501 (c) provides: "Any person who embezzles, steals, or unlawfully and willfully abstracts to his own use, or the use of another, any of the moneys, funds, securities, property, or other assets of a labor organization of which he is an officer, or by which he is employed, directly or indirectly, shall be fined not more than $10,000 or imprisoned for not more than five years or both."

According to the Office of Labor-Management and Welfare-Pension Reports, 888 persons were indicted for criminal violations of the statute in the period from September 14, 1959, to June 30, 1972 (see Table 3).[12] In this group, 669 were convicted, 66 acquitted, and the indictments or criminal information were dismissed against 71 others. About 98 percent of those indicted were charged with embezzlement of union funds, and/or violations of related provisions, such as making false entries in union records, willfully not keeping records, or failing to file reports.

In 339 instances in which information on the size of the amount diverted was available, the largest number fell in the class of $1,000 to $1,500. The median is higher; it is in the class of $2,000 to $2,500. Sixty, or slightly under 19 percent, misappropriated under $500. In some cases, it was a temporary comingling of union and personal monies with no intent to defraud.[13]

Substantial sums were also taken. Eight of those indicted were regional officers or Vice-Presidents of their organizations. A regional director of the United Automobile Workers and one each from the Steelworkers and Operating Engineers were caught mishandling union funds. A Vice-President of the International Longshoremen's Association was convicted of padding his expense account. His was nothing compared to the peculations of some of the other worthies. Only one member of the Brotherhood of Operative Potters was charged with misuse of funds, but he stole $35,000 belonging to the union. A Vice-President of the Teamsters had been charged with diverting $25,000. The largest amount, however, was embezzled by a Vice-President of the International and regional director, and the Secretary-Treasurer of District No. 3, International Union of Electrical, Radio and Machine Workers. The LMWP claimed the

TABLE 3. LMRDA Criminal

| | Fiscal | | | | | |
	1960	1961	1962	1963	1964	1965
Number of individuals indicted or charged in criminal informations	1	23	63	109	89	80
Number of individuals convicted[2]	1	15	23	75	67	87
Number of individuals acquitted	0	1	0	13	14	2
Number of individuals whose indictments were dismissed[3]	0	1	2	6	2	8

[1] Based upon records maintained by LMWP. The figures in each category should be interpreted as minimums, as the totals do not include all LMRDA criminal actions and LMWP does not maintain complete records on all LMRDA criminal actions investigated and prosecuted by the U.S. Department of Justice. All figures are subject to change.

[2] Four of these convictions were set aside on appeal. See *U.S.* v. *Brown,* 381 U.S.

Actions, Fiscal Years 1960-1972[1]

Years							Cumulative Sept. 14, 1959-
1966	1967	1968	1969	1970	1971	1972	June 30, 1972
72	71	61	60	86	90	77	888
64	58	58	41	51	67	55	669
3	2	3	2	3	8	15	66
12	1	4	3	21	6	3	71

437 (S. Ct. 1965], *U.S.* v. *Lynch,* 366 F. 2d 829 (3d Cir. 1966), *U.S.* v. *Greene,* 400 F. 2d 847 (6th Cir. 1968), *U.S.* v. *Spingola,* 464 F. 2d 909 (7th Cir. 1972).

[3] Figure does not include indictments which were dismissed after superseding indictments or criminal informations were filed.

illicit diversions amounted to $150,000 but the union claimed that perhaps twice that amount was misappropriated. A Vice-President of the United Textile Workers was also on the dishonor roll; he embezzled in the neighborhood of $35,000 before he was caught, indicted, and convicted. Table 4 gives a summary of the number of persons and amounts involved.

Table 4.

Number of Persons in Each Class and Amount
Misappropriated

Amount	Number
Under $500	21
$501 to $1,000	39
$1,001 to $1,500	59
$1,501 to $2,000	31
$2,001 to $2,500	32
$2,501 to $3,000	18
$3,001 to $3,500	19
$3,501 to $4,000	13
$4,001 to $4,500	16
$4,501 to $5,000	10
$5,001 to $5,500	10
$5,501 to $6,000	10
$6,001 to $10,000	18
Over $10,000	23

Embezzlement seems to be a solitary activity, although the LMWP uncovered some cooperative efforts to defraud the union. A group of Teamsters' officers was uncovered in the Kansas City area engaged in siphoning funds from the union treasury. Most of them ended up in prison as a result of the Office's efforts. A smaller group of Teamsters' officials in

California was also engaged in a joint effort to misappropriate union funds. The worst and, in a sense, an unprecedented attempt of a group of international officers of the Bakery and Confectionery Workers' International Union to loot the treasury was uncovered by the Office in its first years of activity.

This union was a founding member of the old American Federation of Labor, with an honorable record of service to its members and the labor movement. The organization had a socialist background. James Cross, its President, had graduated from Brookwood College, a residential labor school operating after World War I for more than two decades supported by the more liberal unions. During the convention of 1956, dissident delegates were assaulted, and in March 1957, Curtis Sims, the Secretary-Treasurer, made a series of charges against Cross and a Vice-President of the union, several of which concerned the mishandling of funds. Cross was exonerated by his executive board, and Sims was brought up on charges. In the meantime, the McClellan Committee summoned Cross and other officers to testify. The revelations were among the shabbiest that came from the hearings. The Bakery and Confectionery Workers' Union was brought up on charges and, when it refused to make amends, it was expelled from the AFL-CIO and a rival organization was established.

As a result of complaints from some of the locals, the LMWP investigated its finances. The investigation of the Bakery Union revealed that the President, Secretary-Treasurer, and several Vice-Presidents had conspired to divert $35,000 from the union treasury to their personal use. Cross, the Secretary-Treasurer, and three international Vice-Presidents were either convicted or pleaded guilty.[14]

Seventy-nine international unions, a trades council, a city central labor body, and a federal labor union are represented among the officers and employees who have been indicted for illegal diversion of union funds or for attempting to use their positions in the union for extorting monies from employers. Nine unions are represented by more than twenty persons on the list, and thirteen others have only one indictee affiliated with its organization. The nine with the largest number are: the Teamsters' Union with eighty-eight; laborers, fifty-six; carpenters, forty-eight; painters, thirty-six; auto workers, thirty-five; longshoremen (ILA), twenty-three; operating engineers, twenty-three; hotel and restaurant employees, twenty-two.

Table 5.

Number of Persons Indicted Per International Union	
Under 5	37
5 and less than 10	20
10 and less than 20	13
over 20	9

One of the major disclosures of embezzlement, extortion and shakedowns uncovered as a result of the LMWP's activities involved the construction of the $400 million pipeline from Houston, Texas to Linden, New Jersey. In the construction of a pipeline for any distance, work is inevitably carried on across the jurisdictions of a number of locals. Union dues are checked off by a particular union officer who is responsible for transmitting each local's share for the time work was carried on in its jurisdiction. Some local business agents diverted the temporary dues or "dobies" to their own pockets. While such diversions were difficult to detect and trace, the LMWP "by cross-checking employer records against union records," was able to obtain evidence and convictions of a number of union officials in the Detroit area. The LMWP believed that it was worthwhile looking into conditions in other locations where pipelines were being constructed, and it struck "pay dirt." In 1968 it found that more than $100,000 collected by checkoff from contractors had not been deposited in union treasuries. As a result seven were indicted, five convicted and two are awaiting trial. The indictees were from locals in Pennsylvania and Michigan.

At the same time, the activities of Peter W. Weber, President and business manager of Operating Engineers Local 825, Newark, New Jersey, and one of the more powerful officers in that union, were uncovered, Weber did not touch a "dime" of union funds, but in an old-fashioned type of shakedown funnelled several hundred thousands of dollars from a number of contractors to himself and several favorite associates. Weber also saw to it that certain contractors received jobs and others were stopped from working on that pipeline. Weber and several others were indicted, and Weber was convicted and sentenced to prison.

Weber was an effective bargainer, and he usually was able to win concessions.[15] Yet men such as Weber are a menace to the labor movement and its members. The monies paid to him could have been paid to his members in wages, because the contractor must regard payments made as a cost of doing business. All forms of corruption are in fact carried on at the expense of the members of the union, for the successful bidder could have paid the amounts that were extorted by Weber to the members of the union that were working on the pipeline job.

The ability of men such as Weber to go on and function springs from the inability of his union or the labor movement to discover the hard evidence against his kind of operation. Hence, the importance of the LMWP, which can investigate, subpoena witnesses and bank statements, and follow leads. As a result of such powers, the illicit activities of Weber, for one, were discovered, and the central character in the operation brought to book.

The Office of Labor-Management and Welfare-Pension Reports has joined the strike force set up by the United States Department of Justice to combat organized crime. Its investigation led to the indictment of three officials of the Teamsters' Union, Local 97, Newark, New Jersey, for expending more than $50,000 for non-union purposes. The first Vice-President of the Laundry Workers International Union was indicted for perjury for denying that he had accepted payoffs from outside sources. It was also instrumental in the indictment of William Presser, an International Vice-President of the Teamsters' Union, and President of the Ohio Conference of Teamsters. Presser pleaded guilty to violating the Labor Management Reporting and Disclosure Act, and subsequently was indicted on another charge, embezzling money from the union and changing records.

The strike force was also instrumental in uncovering diversion of hundreds of thousands of dollars from the Barbers' International Pension Fund by the union's President, assisted by several advisors. In 1972, the strike force found evidence which led to the indictment of three officers of Local 57, Providence, International Union of Operating Engineers, for embezzling more than $54,000 in union funds. In Newark, New Jersey, two long-term officers of the Amalgamated Meat Cutters and Food Store Employees Union were indicted for embezzling over $50,000 from the union treasury. In Pittsburgh, Pennsylvania, the former and present business managers were charged with conversion of $61,000 of Laborers' Local 1058 to the use of the head of the criminal syndicate in Western Pennsylvania.

"*Just cause*," Section 201 (c), requires that labor organizations make available the information contained in reports filed with the secretary to members,

> and every such labor organization and its officers shall be under a duty enforceable by suit by any member of such organization in any State court of competent jurisdiction of the district court of the United States for the district in which such labor organization maintains its office, to permit such member for just cause to examine any books, records, and accounts necessary to verify such report.

The court may, at its discretion, award those filing the suit reasonable attorney's fees and costs to be paid by the organization.

This provision arms members who believe that for "just cause" the report to the LMWP is incomplete, misleading or false. They can ask for the records and appeal to the courts if their request is rejected. This provision is in line with the belief of the sponsors of the reform legislation that providing the rank and file members with the needed information will stimulate reforms of union financial practices. The important issue is the definition of "just cause." The emphasis in two cases initiated in the state courts was that the duty to permit the member to verify the report "cannot arise until there has been a demand setting forth the cause and relating the books, records and accounts to be a specific report."[16] A similar view was expressed by a Wisconsin court, in which it was held that the union member must allege by a "written demand upon his union which sets forth (1) cause to examine; and (2) a statement linking records to a specific report."[17]

The obligation to allow for inspection of records has been more broadly conceived by the federal courts which have dealt with these issues.

> It is enough that a union member seeking inspection shows that the size and nature of certain expenditures were such as a reasonably prudent member having an interest in the proper management of the union would naturally be put upon inquiry, and in the course of making the inquiry has been denied access to the union's records.[18]

At the same time, the court said:

> The right to inspect is in the nature of a discovery action, quite different from full fledged suit at law for money damage, injunctive, or other relief. However, the member does not have unlimited rights to examine records and books of account. He must show just cause for making such an examination. He cannot make it solely to annoy and make trouble for the opposition without reasonable ground to believe that nothing relating to the records is wrong.[19]

On reargument, the court set aside the summary judgment because of a dispute over material facts and under the circumstances summary judgment cannot be granted.

A report listing "other disbursements" might be too vague to convey the character of the expenditure. The disbursements were not discussed "at union meetings, reported to or voted upon by the members of the union."[20]

The right of inspection is not limited to financial records. Union members have a right to inspect documents needed to verify financial reports

> where discrepancies were revealed in the figures recited as salaries for union officers, the salaries actually paid had not been authorized by the membership or in accordance with the constitution of the international union, and the reports failed to list the contingent liabilities of the union.[21]

The court held that a member is entitled to inspect and verify information and the "identity of employees who are covered by a collective bargaining agreement," if such information constitutes part of the collective bargaining agreement "and members are entitled to have a copy or to inspect such information. The court also found that just cause had been found for an inspection of referral system," particularly the "card file or index applications for employment." Finally, the court noted that "just cause" is established when a union member shows

> that there is reasonable ground to believe that such report is incomplete or inexact, or that it inadequately explains the information required to be submitted. It is not necessary that it be shown, or that the Court make findings and conclusions, that the labor organization or any of its officers has in fact violated any law or any provision of its Constitution or By-Laws.[22]

The right to inspect for just cause includes subsidiaries and corporations controlled by the union. A group of members challenged the accuracy of the annual report submitted by Longshoremen's Local 1419, charging that many items listed were incorrect. They claimed, moreover, that there had been extensive diversions of funds from the funeral home, drug store and recreational facilities the union controlled. The union was directed to make its accounts and those of its subsidiaries available for inspection. On appeal, the Fifth Circuit Court ruled that the records of subsidiary corporations controlled by unions could be inspected, if an inspection of union books and records would not yield all the information needed to establish the charges.[23]

The right to inspect was granted to a union member who sued in the California state courts claiming there were discrepancies between the report and actual expenditures. In support of his position, the member produced testimony of a former officer who alleged monies listed as allowances and expenses paid to him had not been received. The union insisted that the expenses had been paid. The court, nevertheless, directed that the accounts be made available for inspection. The decision was appealed. The Appellate Court found that inspection could be ordered either under state or federal law and that the member had shown adequate cause. The conflicting claims of the parties with regard to expenditures should be resolved by the trial court. To the argument that the inspection would impose a serious burden upon the union, as it would necessitate a union representative being present while it was taking place, the court agreed. Nevertheless, the court noted "the inspection is merely a preliminary step to determine whether abuses may exist, and it does not appear to interfere unreasonably with the union's policy in view of the broader public policy to be served by permitting the inspection."[24]

The request of a member of the Plumbers' Union that the organization allow him to inspect its records was rejected because the request was made in general terms and for records extending over a period of time. Thus, it was not possible for the court to identify whether the records had been denied or were of the kind to be disclosed under Section 201 (c).[25]

Ignoring a request for inspection by a member constitutes a waiver of the union's "right to advance notice . . ." Three members of Teamsters' Local 760 of Yakima, made up of fruit packers, sued the union and its Secretary-Treasurer after their letter requesting an opportunity to have their accountants examine the annual reports of 1962 and 1964, already submitted to the Secretary of Labor, was ignored.[26] As a result, suit to obtain the records was brought. In such a situation trial court may consider other facts not stated in the letter in determining whether just cause exists. It was held that, if the information requested was not clear, or discrepancies existed in the reports, or the expenses of the Secretary-Treasurer appeared excessive, these facts would be sufficient to establish just cause.

The court allowed the costs of examination, rejecting the view that Congress had intended that a member could exhaust his intra-union remedies when he was denied requested records. Section 201 (c) had been enacted, said the court, "for the specific purpose of allowing union members an opportunity to obtain information concerning the financial affairs of their union without the necessity of exhausting their intra-union remedies prior to instituting court proceedings."

On appeal, the allowing of the costs of examination was reversed. All other aspects of the case were allowed to stand. In its decision, the Court of Appeals noted: "Opinion as to what constitutes 'just cause' may differ. It is an amorphous concept. It may mean one thing to a union member, and something entirely different to a union officer. Yet the statutory requirement must be judged by the objective standard of the reasonable man." The court alluded to the fact that the statute does not specify who must make a "showing of just cause," or when and how it is to be made. Nevertheless, the court assumed the party seeking access to union records has the burden of showing he has just cause. However, Congress did not specify how the burden can be met. "Congress in its wisdom has not fixed any particular mode of demonstrating just cause, nor any particular time for doing it." The court concluded that it had never been "intended that the exercise of the right to inspection be restricted by requiring a demand with all the technical ritual of a formal pleading." The "just cause" standard is intended to prevent harassment of union officers, "not to pose any barrier to a union member's honest inquiry into the supporting records."

The court acknowledged that the union had a right to advance notice before an appeal is made to the courts. However, the right is not absolute. In the present case, the union ignored a written demand to inspect the records.

> Had it wished to exercise its right to have a showing of just cause, the union should have asked the demanding members to allege such cause. To completely ignore the members' demand is inconsistent with the purpose of the union's right to first consider the just cause allegation . . . It is an abnegative of the officer's position of high trust and solemn responsibility to disdainfully neglect an application of this kind from a member, unless convinced that it was without basis or merit. We conclude that any right the union had to be forewarned of the just cause for inspection was waived by the union after receiving the demand. We therefore conclude that, within the facts and circumstances of this case, the demand was sufficient.

The Appeals Court upheld the finding of the trial court that there was just cause and held that the standard for determining "whether there was just cause is necessarily minimal." It need not be shown beyond a reasonable doubt, nor by the weight of evidence. "It need not be enough to convince a reasonable man that some wrong has been done; it is enough if a reasonable union member would be put to further inquiry." The court alluded to the failure of the Secretary-Treasurer to reveal his salary, and the discrepancy between a statement and its supporting schedule on the amounts paid.

The court held that there may be strong support for the view that exhaustion of internal remedies is required, but it cannot apply "unless there is available from the union a remedy which is neither uncertain nor futile . . . 'where a union moves to dismiss the complaint, it should place before the court *facts* (italics in decision) establishing that union remedies are available to the plaintiff and the plaintiff has neglected to use them'."[27]

The reporting provisions have been in effect for fourteen years, and they reveal that diversions of funds and falsifying reports are not limited to unions whose officers have been on occasion charged with racketeering and corruption. Some of the largest defalcations have been committed by officers of the International Typographical Union and the International Union of Electrical Workers, organizations which have no record of being involved in systematic kickbacks or extortion or collusive arrangements with employers for the profit of the leaders of the union.

As noted by the McClellan Committee, the large majority of unions are honestly and conscientiously managed. When the requirement for reporting was introduced, there was some grumbling that the new rules would place a severe burden upon the unpaid officers so that competent members would be discouraged to serve. There is no evidence that such a result has followed. Moreover, the reporting requirements for small local unions have been simplified and place a very light burden upon those who are required to fill out the reports.

Few suits for the opportunity to inspect union records, permitted under Section 201 (c) with the approval of the courts, have been instituted. In general, the courts have been liberal in their interpretation of "just cause," and it appears that any act or circumstance which can arouse the suspicion or the question of a reasonable person would be held sufficient. The view of the courts appear to be consonant with the intent of Congress. Members of unions are not lawyers, nor do they normally have legal advice at their disposal. To place a burden of requiring some proof would tend to defeat the purpose of the provision. The courts have acted wisely in requiring only a minimum of reasons, the kind that would raise an inquiry in the mind of a reasonable man. Yet, few union members have availed themselves or felt the need to challenge the financial reports of their union officers.

The reporting and disclosure provisions have compelled all organizations to adopt constitutions and by-laws in which the responsibilities, obligations and rights of the members are defined. It has also compelled labor organizations to adopt a system of record keeping which allows for determining the disposition made of income and other assets during the last fiscal year.

Although the reports of all local unions cannot be audited annually, it is known that samples of reports are examined every year and that embezzlement of union funds is punishable as a federal crime. The enactment of the reporting provisions has improved the accounting procedures of local unions and has helped the central organizations to achieve uniformity of standards of financial management which many Secretary-Treasurers have advocated. Another important contribution of Title II is the prohibition of loans to the officers, employees or members in excess of $250 during the fiscal year. In some organizations, loans were made to members to purchase tools of the trade or to travel to a job, but such practices did not envisage the huge loans which some union officers made to themselves.

Experience with the reporting provisions shows that the Office of Labor-Management and Welfare-Pension Reports does not limit itself to auditing the accounts of local unions. In fact, the income and outgo of the Internationals are checked every year. It means that the speculations which several high officers of important unions were charged with by the McClellan Committee could not take place today. A President of an International Union, and several International Vice-Presidents have been convicted of misusing the funds of their organizations in this way.

Members who are suspicious of the reports submitted to the government have the right under the statute to request information from the officers. This provision was inserted to allow the member to investigate if he believes that financial irregularities may have taken place. This provision has not been utilized to any large extent, and it may be due to the lack of knowledge the average member has of the operations of a union, especially of a larger unit.

On the whole, the effect of the reporting provisions has been salutary. They have made possible the discovery of diversions of funds, by single persons and groups, which, under former conditions, would hardly have been revealed. Unions have benefited from these rules. In addition, the padding of expense accounts, the multiple charging which William E. Maloney, the one-time head of the International Union of Operating Engineers, had practiced would be a basis of prosecution today. The limitation on loans that can be made by unions is also a desirable change resulting from the reform legislation. The fear that there would be a flight from union offices has not materialized, and in fact there appears to have been an increase in candidacies, the result doubtless of other provisions of the reform legislation. Better accounting is another advantage. The long-overdue requirements can be regarded as a desirable and completely successful reform of considerable benefit to the unions and their members.

10

Trusteeships

A trusteeship is a method of supervision and control whereby a parent organization suspends the autonomy of a subordinate body—a local union or intermediate unit such as a district council. The international union or central body has been delegated authority, in many labor organizations, to intervene if a subordinate unit is unable to fend for itself, cannot administer its collective bargaining contracts, or when other conditions which tend to weaken the organization exist.

The trusteeship depends upon the existence of a sufficiently strong national union which is able to impose its control for a sufficiently long time so as to eliminate the cause of intervention.

Local unions and intermediate bodies—districts, joint and district councils, departments and conferences—are chartered by national and international unions. They are required to obey the constitution, by-laws, and rules enacted at conventions by the legislative bodies of the organization. Subordinate units which fail to follow the policies prescribed by the legislative and executive branches of the union may under appropriate circumstances be placed in receivership or trusteeship.

Trusteeships can be divided into two kinds: the benign and the disciplinary. The benign trusteeship is imposed upon the local union which has lost members because of competition of other organizations, but more often because of the departure of a plant in which its members were employed or some similar reason. In these circumstances, the International intervenes at the request of the affiliate, and may, depending on circumstances, keep the local afloat until it regains sufficient strength to function on its own, or it may act as a "receiver" and try to wind up the local's affairs.

The second kind of trusteeship, the "disciplinary," arises out of different conditions. The decree of trusteeship may be issued in opposition to the desires of the local leaders and members. A local may have failed to organize its jurisdiction, or the collective bargaining agreement may not have been administered fairly or effectively. Factional rivalries and arrogant, corrupt, or oppressive leadership may be other reasons. The refusal of a local to accept a jurisdictional decision, encouragement of wildcat strikes, resistance to a mandated merger, and the misuse of union funds may also lead to the imposition of a trusteeship.

Because the suspension of the autonomy of a subordinate unit has been regarded as discipline by the courts, notice and a hearing are required before the trusteeship is imposed.[1] However, if the parent union complies with the requirements of due process, the courts tend to allow it, at least temporarily, pending a hearing in which the trusteeship might be challenged on the ground that it violates the organization's constitution and by-laws. Once the trusteeship is allowed or is not challenged, it is not subject to any governmental supervision, although grave abuses by the trustee might be restricted by the courts, or the trusteeship might be cancelled as a result of abuse of the trustee's position.[2]

In the past, most organizations sought to use the trusteeship as a means of curing some evil, abuse, or inefficiency, and then to restore the autonomy of the subordinate unit. Other unions seldom invoked this remedy because of a belief that it was too drastic or because they were not confronted with situations which would warrant intervention. However, a number of organizations have used the trusteeship as a means of permanently placing locals under the control of the international union. Such an instance, however, while deplored in the press and by public officials, lacked the force necessary to convince Congress or the public of the need for reform in this area. Not until the McClellan Committee hearings were sufficiently serious and widespread abuses in the administration of trusteeships revealed. One of the more sordid episodes in the history of organized labor was the use of trusteeships by President James G. Cross of the Bakery and Confectionary Workers' International Union of America.

> The Committee finds that these thefts . . . were made possible under two Chicago trusteeships of the most arbitrary and capricious stripe . . . The Committee finds that the trustee-ship principle itself was thoroughly abused in practice. De-signed to safeguard union members' interests, trusteeships as applied by international officers of the bakers not only depredated the funds but despoiled all democratic rights of the rank and file.[3]

The McClellan Committee discovered that trusteeships had been imposed by the International Union of Operating En-gineers on twelve locals with 51,506 members, comprising about one-fifth of the total membership in the union. The Committee found that "even the merest semblance of their autonomy" was thereby destroyed. In addition, the Committee "found that the trusteed local's assets are seized and no elections are held. Added to the absolute nature of these trusteeships is the evil of their indeterminate duration. Of the IUOE locals now so saddled, 7 have been under trusteeship for at least 10 years, and 2 for as long as 29 years."[4]

To again quote the McClellan Committee: Officers of the Teamsters' Union

> have indiscriminately used the power of placing locals under trusteeship and kept these union entities in servitude when it served the interest of the union leadership to do so. When a local is under trusteeship, its members completely lose con-trol over their finances and the right to elect their own officials. Some 13 percent of all the locals in the Teamsters'

Union are under trusteeship, Teamster officials have admitted before the Committee that they do not know the reason why some were put under trusteeship or they remain in that state at the present time. Some of the locals have been under trusteeship for 15 years.[5]

While the Operating Engineers, Teamsters and the Bakery and Confectionary Workers' unions were singled out for gross abuses in their administration of trusteeships, the McClellan Committee also castigated the Allied Industrial Workers, the Meat Cutters and Butcher Workmen, and the Jewelry Workers Unions for their arbitrary use of the trusteeship procedure, for destroying the autonomy of local unions for frivolous or no reasons, for draining funds from the treasuries of local unions placed under a trustee, and for using the votes of the locals under trusteeship on behalf of favorite candidates. Although the McClellan Committee and Congress recognized that the abuse of trusteeships was practiced by only a few unions, it believed that the evil was sufficiently serious to warrant federal control.

Regulating Trusteeships

Title III, Section 301 (a), requires that a parent organization, usually an international union, imposing a trusteeship upon one of its subordinate bodies—a local union or district council—must file a report with the Secretary of Labor within thirty days of the imposition of the trusteeship and twice a year thereafter. In the report the parent body must give the reasons for imposing the trusteeship. In addition, information on the extent of the members' participation in elections and in the making of policy must be given, as well as a complete account of the financial resources of the trusteed local. During the period of the trusteeship, the parent body must file the annual financial reports required of other labor organizations. Violations of the above requirements are a misdemeanor, punishable by fines and imprisonment. Withholding of material facts or destruction of books and documents upon which the report is based is also prohibited.

Section 302 declares that trusteeships can be imposed only in accordance with the constitution and by-laws of the parent union, and only for the following purposes: To correct corruption of financial malpractices; assure the carrying out of the collective bargaining agreement or other duties of a bargaining representative; restore democratic procedures, or otherwise carry out the objectives of the parent organization. The language of the statute appears to be broad enough to allow for the suspension of autonomy of subordinate units where the situation appears to warrant such a step.

The McClellan Committee discovered that trusteed locals were used for political purposes by the parent organization, since delegates could be selected by the trustee, an appointed representative of the parent body, to represent the trusteed local at conventions. Thus the voting power of the local under control of the international union could be used to strengthen the position of incumbent officers. Section 303 (a) is designed to eliminate this kind of abuse. It prohibits counting the votes of delegates from a trusteed local union, unless the delegates have been chosen by secret ballot in an election in which all eligible members are allowed to participate.

The misuse of the funds of the trusteed local was shown in a number of instances in which members eventually appealed to the courts for protection against the rapacious conduct of the trustee. Such abuses were further documented by the McClellan Committee. Section 303 (a) was adopted to eliminate such conduct. It prohibits the transfer of funds from the treasury of a trusteed local, except for the payment of regular per capita and assessments. Funds cannot be transferred to any intermediate body or the international union from a local for any other purpose.

Section 304 (a) states that a trusteeship, established in conformity with the union constitution and by-laws and authorized or ratified after a "fair hearing" by a union tribunal holding such power, is valid for eighteen months. Such a trusteeship is not subject to attack "during such period except upon clear and convincing proof that the trusteeship was not established or maintained in good faith for a purpose allowable under section 302." At the expiration of eighteen months, the trusteeship is presumed invalid "unless the labor organization shall show by clear and convincing proof that the continuation of the trustee-ship is necessary for a purpose allowable under section 302."

Two methods of enforcement are available under Section 304 (a). A member can either institute a suit in a district court of the United States or make a written complaint to the Secretary of Labor alleging a violation of the provisions (except Section 301). The Secretary is directed to investigate the complaint and if he finds probable cause that such a violation has occurred and not remedied, he is directed to bring suit without disclosing the identity of the complainant. From the enactment of the statute to the end of fiscal year 1969, the Secretary instituted four suits.[6] From fiscal 1960 to fiscal 1972 inclusive, 2,263 trusteeships were reported by the Secretary of Labor. A low point was reached in 1966, but the number has risen since that year, with the changes thereafter not being significant.

Initial trusteeship reports totaled 592 through June 30, 1960. During the same time 285 were terminated (Table 6). About half of the trusteeships were eighteen months or more old and about one-fifth, more than ten years old. A preliminary study showed that more than 30 percent of the trusteeships was imposed to close out the business of locals which had lost their members because of plant closings or the local needed assistance to handle its affairs. Another 23 percent of the trusteeships was established because of threats of secession and internal dissension. Slightly under 10 percent was established because of financial malpractices.[7] As indicated above, the Secretary of Labor is au-thorized to bring suit against the parent body if he finds, after a member's complaint, that the trusteeship has not been estab-lished in accordance with the union's constitution and by-laws and for the reasons specified in the statute. During fiscal 1960, there were 144 investigations by the Secretary, and in 35 instances voluntary compliance was achieved. No basis for the other com-plaints was found. Between September 14, 1959, and June 30, 1961, 487 trusteeships were terminated.

Table 6.

Number of Trusteeships Established, Terminated, and Active for Fiscal Years 1959-1972 Ending June 30[1]

Year	Established	Terminated	Active
September 14, 1959	487		
1960	72	285	264
1961	127	213	188
1962	128	108	190
1963	124	99	196
1964	135	130	223
1965	145	135	226
1966	114	120	234
1967	130	77	287
1968	134	110	316
1969	144	153	307
1970	169	123	353
1971	165	140	378
1972	172	199	351

[1]Figures from compliance reports.

One of the complaints against a trusteeship involved a Tennessee local of the United Automobile Workers, established because the local union had segregated washroom facilities and drinking fountains in the union hall. The local had been warned on several occasions that the segregated practices violated the union constitution and by-laws. After the trusteeship had been in effect, a white member complained to the Secretary that the trusteeship was illegal. An investigation was made by the Bureau of Labor Management Reports (BLMR), which found that the trusteeship was established for the "purpose of 'carrying out the legitimate objects of such labor organization' within the meaning of the Act."[8]

By the end of fiscal 1963, the BLMR had initiated 262 investigations into trusteeships, having started its first suit to have a trusteeship lifted from a subordinate unit on June 28, 1963. The suit was directed at the American Guild of Variety Artists (AGVA), which had rejected efforts to obtain a voluntary termination of the trusteeship. The suit was settled in January 1964, when the District Court directed AGVA to lift its trusteeship over its Philadelphia branch and conduct an election for branch officers under the supervision of the Labor Department. The court's order was based on stipulation between the parties.

A second civil action was started in December 1964, for the purpose of ending the provisional status of six districts of the United Mine Workers of America, four of which had been imposed in 1939 and two in 1941. The international union denied that the districts were under trusteeship, claiming that they were placed in provisional status for achieving administrative and financial efficiency and that their status had been approved by every union convention from 1933 through 1964.[9] A supplemental complaint was filed in October 1965, contesting the legality of the trusteeship of District 17 in Charleston, West Virginia.

The court ruled that the United Mine Workers had violated Title III by imposing and maintaining trusteeship over the districts and their successors for more than eighteen months, and that the maintenance of the trusteeships was not necessary for a purpose allowable under Section 302.[10] The Secretary was directed to submit an order for the discontinuance of the trusteeships and the election of officers in the districts.

The union's defense was that there had been changes in the organization under which districts which had been autonomous units were changed into administrative arms of the international union. The District Court rejected the claim and pointed to the facts that the districts maintain their own bank accounts, conduct the activities of labor organizations and have the indicia of labor organizations.

By the end of fiscal 1966, there were only nineteen trusteeships—eighteen of them involving affiliates of the United Mine

Workers of America—which had been established prior to the enactment of the Labor-Management Reporting and Disclosure Act. During 1966, the Secretary filed a suit seeking an order directing the termination of a trusteeship of the International Longshoremen's Association (ILA) over Local 1368 in Brownsville, Texas, and the filing of required reports concerning the trusteeship. It was the first suit which charged a parent union with failure to file trusteeship reports. The Secretary charged that the ILA had not established the trusteeship in accordance with the Constitution and Rules of Order, nor for a purpose allowable under Section 302 of the act. Moreover, the Secretary asserted that the trusteeship had been in effect for more than eighteen months and was presumed invalid under 304 (c).

The trusteeship followed charges with the National Labor Relations Board by members of the all-black Local 1368 in Brownsville, Texas, that the division of work formula which gave 75 percent of the work to members of the all-white sister Local 1367 was inequitable. Shortly after the filing of the complaint the local was placed under a trusteeship by the ILA. The NLRB ruled the trusteeship was imposed as a retaliatory measure and that it be terminated, and that the division of work between the locals was illegal. The union appealed.

In November 1967, the court granted the Secretary's motion for a summary judgment and directed the holding of elections within ninety days under the Secretary's supervision. It also ordered the immediate termination of the trusteeship, as soon as the election of local officers was certified by the court, and that the union and the trustees file within sixty days the trusteeship reports and the annual financial reports for Local 1368 for every year, from 1963 to 1966 inclusive.

In another suit, the Secretary charged that the trustee appointed by the United Packinghouse Workers over two locals in Puerto Rico had failed to file the reports required, including the one on the locals' finances. In April 1968, the District Court, based upon a stipulation between the parties, directed the international and the trustee to file within fifteen days specified reports with regards to the trusteeships of Locals 962 and 1963.

The most complete information on trusteeships has been provided in a study by the Department of Labor which was required under Section 305 by Congress.

At the time the Secretary reported to Congress, at the end of the statutory three-year period, three-fourths of all national unions subject to the act had not reported that any subordinate unit had been under trusteeship since the passage of the Act. Twenty-three of the seventy parent organizations, which had reported trusteeships, had reported only a single one, and 11 percent reported only two trusteeships during this period. Only seven unions reported twenty or more trusteeships, with District 50, United Mine Workers of America reporting the largest number, 127 (Table 7).

The Teamsters terminated all but four trusteeships which had

Table 7.

Total Trusteeships by the Seven Unions Reporting
20 or More and the Number of Total Locals Reporting[1]

Parent Labor Organization	Number of Trusteed Locals or Intermediate Body
Carpenters	74
Steelworkers	80
District 50, UMWA	127
Teamsters	67
Automobile Workers	52
Hotel and Restaurant Employees	41
United Mine Workers of America	28

[1]*Union Trusteeships*, A Report to the Congress Upon the Operation of Title III of the Labor-Management Reporting and Disclosure Act, 1962.

been in existence for more than eighteen months; thirty-six had been in existence for more than five years, the oldest for more than nineteen years. The Bakery and Confectionary Workers terminated nineteen trusteeships, sixteen of which had been in existence for more than eighteen months, the oldest, four years. The number of trusteeships established by this organization was unusual and was the result of a dual movement in many of the locals which had been outraged by the disclosures by the McClellan Committee of the behavior of the President and several officers. The Operating Engineers terminated six trusteeships, all of which were in existence for more than eighteen months, the oldest for almost twenty years. However, one-fourth of all national unions subject to the Act "have not reported any trusteeships," and out of the seventy organizations that have, twenty-three had only one trusteeship during the period between September 14, 1959, and March 13, 1962. Moreover, an examination "of the financial reports shows that the typical union under trusteeship is small, with assets of about $1,750 and annual receipts slightly in excess of $6,000."[11]

Based upon the only exhaustive investigation that has ever been made and with information upon every existing trusteeship during the operation of the law, many of which had been established before the latter's enactment, the Secretary concluded: (1) that "trusteeships have never been widely established except in a few unions"; (2) that the "Act has been effective in correcting the malpractices disclosed by the McClellan Committee"; (3) that the law has stimulated the amendment of union constitutions to provide greater safeguards against unnecessary suspension of autonomy; and (4) that the law has not interfered with the establishing of trusteeships whenever genuinely necessary to achieve a proper purpose.[12]

The analysis of the first 777 reports on trusteeships showed that 707 of them state substantive reasons for their imposition (Table 8). These were classified, and, in some instances, more than one reason was given.

A number of local unions were placed under trusteeship as a result of the revelations of the McClellan Committee and were

TABLE 8. Reasons for Establishing Trusteeship, September 14, 1959, Through March 23, 1962, for Local Unions and Intermediate Bodies[1]

	Number	Percent
Total trusteeships	777	100
With reasons for establishment	707	
Without reasons for establishment	70	
Total reasons for establishment	764[2]	
Correct for financial malpractice or corruption	57	7
Assure performance of collective bargaining agreements	82	11
Restore democratic procedures	50	7
Otherwise carry out legitimate objects	575	75
Caretaker	259	34
(a) Plant closing	123	16

TABLE 8 (Continued)

(b) Small, scattered or itinerant membership	65	9
(c) Loss of Leadership	39	5
(d) Newly established labor organization	32	4
Mismanagement		
(a) Financial	90	12
(b) Administrative	30	4
Dissension	114	15
Disaffiliation	70	10
Miscellaneous	9	1

[1] *Summary of Operations*, 1963, p. 52.

[2] The reasons for establishment are greater than total trusteeships because of more than one reason given in a number of instances.

still retained under trusteeship when the report to Congress had been made. The International Longshoremen's Association placed one of its locals under trusteeship after the local officers had been convicted of extortion, and the International Union of Operating Engineers placed Local 3, of San Francisco, under trusteeship after its officers had been convicted of diversion of funds and property of the local union. The information had been disclosed by the McClellan Committee. Several officers, including the head of the local union, had sold property to the local at inflated prices. In seventeen of the fifty-seven trusteeships in this group, the internationals had reported that funds or property had been stolen. The Plumbers' Union placed a local under a trusteeship after the Secretary-Treasurer had been indicted for embezzling $24,000.

In this group are trusteeships which were imposed on weak locals which had failed to negotiate adequate agreements, had engaged in unauthorized strikes, or had failed to carry out the collective bargaining agreement which had been negotiated. In several instances, the International assumed authority over a subordinate unit because it had failed to gain an agreement with the employer, or it was unable to compel the employer to carry out the standards embodied in an agreement.[13]

In this group are also the trusteeships imposed by the parent organization because of failure to follow proper election methods, inability to keep order at meetings, coercion of the rank and file members, and denial of democratic rights to the membership. Fifty trusteeships listed by twenty-nine internationals were established for this purpose, the largest number for abuses of election procedures. Among the actions that caused these interventions were the stealing of ballots, marking the ballots by an officer of the election, and allowing unqualified persons to vote. In two instances, the local unions were placed under trusteeship so that elections would be rerun under international supervision. They constituted 11 percent of all trusteeships.

Thirteen trusteeships were established because local union meetings were not held or were marked by violence resulting in the denial of free speech to members. The Hotel, Restaurant Employees assumed trusteeship over a local because it failed to hold regular meetings. Another trusteeship was imposed by this union because local officers permitted agents of the employer who were not members to participate and dominate the meetings and hired armed private police to thwart free speech of bona fide members.[14]

In another case, a trusteeship was established over a federal labor union by the AFL-CIO because the Secretary-Treasurer had run the local autocratically, "and it was necessary to instruct members in their democratic rights and responsibilities."

"All but 12 of the 70 parent labor organizations reported trusteeships under this broad purpose. This category accounts for 74 percent of all reasons given for trusteeships over local unions and all but three of the 39 reasons cited for intermediate bodies."[15] This is a general category for several sub-groups.

Thirty-four percent of the trusteeships were established because the subordinate body could not fulfill its responsibilities. Twenty-seven internationals imposed 259 trusteeships for this reason. About half of the trusteeships in this group, 123, were required by plant shutdowns in which the members were employed. Another sixty-five trusteeships were imposed because the scattered, or itinerant membership could not effectively administer the business of the organization. The balance of the seventy-one trusteeships were established because the newly established local required assistance because of sudden loss of leadership.

Only twelve of the seventy unions imposed trusteeships because of plant closings, and only one of the twelve was not an industrial union. The conditions under which trusteeships will be imposed may, however, vary. The purpose may be to assure the carrying out of the collective bargaining agreement, to close out the affairs of the local union, or to provide assistance to the local and its members during a period of unemployment. In sixty-three of these instances, the locals were dissolved.

Thirteen national unions reported the above reason for imposing trusteeships on sixty-five unions. The local, in these instances, may not be performing its collective bargaining obligations, it may be insolvent, or it may not have officers. It may have a fluctuating membership, or there may be no member sufficiently skilled and willing to perform the housekeeping tasks of the organization.

Sixteen national unions reported that loss of leadership compelled them to establish trusteeships in thirty-nine subordinate units. In a number of these cases, death was the cause of the deficiency of leadership. Usually the members and also other officers will request the trusteeship.

Eleven internationals have placed thirty-two local unions under trusteeship because they required assistance, had inadequate treasuries or inexperienced leadership. In this group, the membership or local officers of some of the locals requested the assistance of the parent organization and, in fact, initiated the trusteeship.

Thirty-six internationals reported that they had established 120 trusteeships because of mismanagement of the subordinate unit's affairs in matters unrelated to collective bargaining. The group was divided into those cases in which finances were involved, and those in which the imposition was because the local had failed to follow the constitution or rules of the organization. Ninety of the trusteeships were established because the locals failed to pay their per capita taxes or did not maintain prescribed financial records. In some instances, the expenditures of the local were imprudent; in others the dues structure was inadequate. In this latter instance, the parent union assumed a trusteeship to help restore a solvent income and expenditure policy.

Failure to follow prescribed procedures may involve inadequate bonding of finance officers, improper auditing, or not following union rules with deposit or withdrawal of funds. Finally, the parent union may impose the trusteeship to protect or conserve the subordinate unit's property.

The trusteeships in this group were established because the subordinate unit failed to adopt the constitution and by-laws, or the administrative procedures required by the international. Seventeen national unions imposed trusteeships upon their subordinate units for these reasons. In this group are the instances in which members who are not qualified to hold office under the union's by-laws have nevertheless been chosen, membership cards were not issued in accordance with the practices of the union, or as the Bricklayers, which imposed a trusteeship over a local which refused to obey the directives on organizing residential construction and the setting of initiation fees. "One local union was denied autonomy for discrimination on union committees and maintaining separate washroom facilities for white and colored members despite warnings from the international union."[16]

Twenty-three international unions gave the existence of dissension among the membership as the reason for establishing 114 trusteeships. Differences among the officers and others who had held office appears to have been a reason for the dissension in other organizations. Factionalism is another reason. "In most instances the national unions expressed concern over the possible effects strife within the subordinate would have on the general welfare of the members, or, more particularly, on the subordinate's ability to function as a bargaining representative . . . The Boilermakers noted that the three top officers of the local resigned because of severe criticism of the members."[17]

Disaffiliation from the parent union, secession, or dual unionism was given as the reason for the establishing of seventy-three trusteeships by thirty-one international unions. In this group, the Bakery and Confectionary Workers, which faced a rebellion and the formation of a rival union after the revelations of the McClellan Committee had shown extensive corruption among the top officers, had established eighteen. Trusteeships which followed attempts to decertify the local union as bargaining agent are also in this group.

> In addition to stopping an attempted disaffiliation or decertification, the reports showed many of the trusteeships were established also to protect funds and property of the local and to assure the performance of the collective bargaining agreement . . . One report filed . . . said that an attempt to

disaffiliate included activity aimed at disrupting collective bargaining and overthrowing the agreement.

In another instance the local which planned to disaffiliate had ignored the collective bargaining agreement.[18]

Miscellaneous is a catch-all group which does not conform to the other categories listed in the study of the Bureau of Labor-Management Reports. Five internationals had established nine trusteeships which fell into this group. In several of the instances, the trusteeship was imposed to facilitate the merger of locals.[19]

Seventy-two percent of subordinate organizations whose trusteeships have been terminated were given full autonomy; 22 percent of the organizations were dissolved; and the remaining 6 percent were merged with other units of the international. "The smallest percentage of trusteed organizations returned to autonomy was among those local unions placed originally because of plant shutdowns."[20] Only twelve to seventy-five organizations in this group were restored to autonomy following the termination of trusteeship, while 84 percent of the locals were reported dissolved or merged. It is obvious that the basis of this experience is the serious weakening and loss of membership inherent in the shutting down of the plant. The local may not be viable as an independent unit, and dissolution or merger may be the only policies that can give protection to those who remain.

A major abuse exposed by the McClellan Committee was the prolonged maintenance of trusteeships by a number of international unions. Of the 487 trusteeships in effect on September 14, 1959, 312 had been in existence more than eighteen months; 128 for more than five years, and 50 for more than ten years. One active trusteeship, the one established over District 14, Kansas, by the United Mine Workers of America, was established in 1930. Of the 187 trusteeships in effect on March 13, 1962, 74 were more than eighteen months old, 32 of which had been in existence for more than five years and 21 over ten years. "The duration of the 590 trusteeships terminated under the Act ranged from one day to almost 20 years."

11

Trusteeships and the Courts

Section 304 (a) gives a member of a labor organization the right to complain to the Secretary of a violation of Title III (except 301 dealing with filing of reports) and to bring suit in a district court of the United States. The first three cases brought by union members under this provision involved the right of members to challenge imposition of a trusteeship without complaining to the Secretary of Labor.[1] In *Flaherty v. McDonald*, the challenged trusteeship had been imposed in 1958, prior to the enactment of the statute. The court refused jurisdiction on the ground that Title III could not be applied retroactively. The complaint was amended so that the charge read that, although the trusteeship was imposed in 1958, it had, since the enactment of the statute, been unlawfully administered within the meaning of Title III. The amended complaint was also dismissed on the ground that the union member had to appeal initially to the Secretary of Labor who is to determine whether a violation has occurred.

The same view was taken by the United States District Court of New Jersey. Two officers and several members of Local 1262, Newark, New Jersey, brought suit against the International seeking to have a trusteeship voided. In their complaint, they alleged that the International Union was "acting arbitrarily and capriciously," and the hearing held was a "sham and an illusory proceeding" so conducted that the accused could not defend themselves. The court found that Section 304 (a) did not provide "two coordinate alternate remedies for the review of the trusteeship of a local labor organization." Instead, "the procedure through the Secretary of Labor affords the primary and principal remedy for the individual member or for the local itself."[2]

A different view was taken in the suit to set aside the trusteeship established by the International Brotherhood of Electrical Workers over Local No. 28, Baltimore, Maryland. The trusteeship had been imposed as a result of a factional division within the local. Charging misuse of funds and denial of democratic rights a group of members sought termination in the courts. In contrast to the above decisions, the court held that Section 304 (a) provides alternative remedies. The view that the Secretary of Labor is "the sole enforcing medium" was rejected. Any member may bring suit, and such a right is not qualified by the condition precedent that such a violation must have been determined by the Secretary of Labor to exist. A member may rely upon the Secretary to sue or may himself sue for relief. The issues were not disposed as the international abrogated the trusteeship before the case had gone to trial.[3]

The same view was supported in the case of a challenge to the trusteeship imposed by the Boilermakers' Union upon Local 614 in New London, Connecticut. Looked at simply, "one would say that there are two separate and independent routes through which a member or a labor organization may seek a remedy."[4]

The Flight Engineers International Association had established a chapter on Continental Airlines. During a dispute between the parent union and its chapter, the latter dissolved with the aim of eventually affiliating with another International. The parent union imposed a trusteeship and sought to maintain an action against Continental Airlines, which had been initiated by its chapter prior to its dissolution. The constitution of the union contained no provision for imposing a trusteeship, and the trusteeship was established after the chapter had been dissolved. On both of these counts the Court of Appeals held the parent organization had no standing to sue. The claim of inherent power was rejected: "Whatever 'inherent' right notwithstanding . . . that right could at most be exerted for the purpose of preventing the subordinate body from violating some relationship with the international."[5]

In addition to holding that a local union need not file a complaint with the Secretary of Labor or exhaust the internal remedies specified by the union constitution, the Circuit Court of Appeals held a trusteeship invalid because "there were no provisions in the union's constitution and bylaws authorizing the imposition of a trusteeship." Trusteeships are, under Section 302, authorized "only in accordance with the constitution and bylaws of the organization which has assumed trusteeship over the subordinate body." The court held that the "statute is mandatory in its terms and has nullified or removed whatever inherent power an international union had prior to its enactment to impose such a trusteeship. Unless the constitution and bylaws make provision, therefore, such organization has no power to establish over a subordinate body."

The Air Line Stewards and Stewardesses were affiliated with the Air Line Pilots for several years, but, because of dissatisfaction with the service, withdrew from the organization. It secured a charter as an independent from the Transport Workers Union, but recognized the latter's constitution while it continued to operate under its own original constitution and by-laws. Two years after the arrangement had been consummated, TWU placed Air Line Stewards and Stewardesses under a trusteeship and removed its President from office.

The latter sued, and the District Court ordered the termination of the trusteeship and the return of funds to the Air Line Stewards and Stewardesses and restoration of the President to office. The Transport Workers Union appealed, and while the appeal was pending terminated the trusteeship. The Appellate

Court held the trusteeship question moot and ruled that the federal courts could not compel the restoration of the President to his office, though he could seek relief in the state courts.[6]

On what grounds can an International Union impose a trusteeship? Is it limited to achieve the objectives enumerated in Section 302 and must the union specify in its constitution and by-laws the reasons and the methods for imposing a trusteeship? The United Brotherhood of Carpenters and Joiners placed Local 201 in trusteeship for the purpose of compelling it to join a district council and increase its dues. When the action of the International Union was challenged, the Appellate Court said that Section 302 of the LMRDA authorizes the establishment of trusteeships only in accordance with the constitution and by-laws of the union, that the Brotherhood's constitution and laws contained no such provision specifically authorizing the establishment of trusteeships, and that the powers granted the Brotherhood's General Executive Board to take the action necessary for the welfare of the organization were insufficient. More than a vague reference to the power of the parent organization is necessary. The least that is required, said the court, is that the union's constitution and by-laws set forth the circumstances under which a trusteeship may be established over its local unions and the procedure to be followed in imposing it. In addition, the Appellate Court agreed that the trusteeship was invalid because it was not established for one of the purposes enumerated in Section 302, but in contravention of the rights granted in Section 101 (a) (3) which specified that the members must be allowed to determine their dues.

The Appellate Court rejected the argument that a trusteeship is valid for eighteen months, by declaring that such a rule only applies to circumstances in which the trusteeship was established in accordance with the constitution and by-laws of the organization. Finally, the Appellate Court held that an appeal to the Secretary of Labor was not necessary before bringing suit. The court held that the trusteeship was also invalid because it was for a purpose not allowed by Section 302. Moreover, the attempt to compel the local to affiliate with the district council and pay the dues increase which had been rejected by Local No. 201's membership constituted a violation of Title I.[7]

Refusing to merge with another local union in the same International, because of the effect on its members' seniority, was the basis of a trusteeship imposed upon Local 208, Tobacco Workers International Union. Local 208 had been chartered as a segregated local of employees of Liggett and Myers Tobacco Company in 1937, and the International sought to compel it to merge with a white local, No. 176, which had more members. Moreover, the members of Local 208, the segregated local, would have had to accept the agreement negotiated with the company which would have placed "all Negro workers behind the white workers with respect to seniority and other rights."[8] When Local 208 filed a complaint with the National Labor Relations Board against the International and Liggett and Myers, it was placed under trusteeship. The court held that under Section 104 the local could not be penalized for bringing suit. It enjoined the trusteeship until the issues in dispute would be determined by the NLRB. Furthermore, the trusteeship would remain suspended until the validity was decided by the convention of the union.

In the absence of an emergency within the meaning of the union's constitution, a parent organization cannot impose a trusteeship upon a subordinate unit.[9] During the counting of the ballots in the election of Local 71, Teamsters, the lights went out, and subsequently the ballots were stolen. The General President placed the local under trusteeship, and the regularly elected officers were removed. The court found the trusteeship had been imposed "without a fair investigation . . . and without having the benefit of the disinterested testimony of the persons who conducted the election and were heard by this court." The trusteeship was set aside because it was not imposed for any reasons enumerated in the statute and in the absence of an emergency which would justify such action.

A temporary trusteeship, imposed because of the existence of an emergency, has been upheld. In this incident, the constitution permitted the General Vice-President in the area to appoint, for specified reasons, a trustee to take charge of the affairs of the local union. Before the appointment of a temporary trustee, the time and place of a hearing to determine whether such trustee was to be permanently appointed had to be announced. Moreover, the Vice-President can only act if he believes that an emergency requires intervention.

In the case involving a California local of the Teamsters' Union, the court found that the constitutional provisions had been followed and that the Vice-President acted in good faith. It also directed that the local union be allowed an accountant to observe the auditing of the local's finances, and that in a pending arbitration the members of the local be permitted to hire an attorney and the local pay for these services up to $2,000.[10]

A trusteeship imposed upon a local union by the International Brotherhood of Telephone Workers was ruled invalid because the union constitution failed in providing a procedure for the imposing of a trusteeship. Congress, said the court,[11] intended that "constitutional provisions allowing the imposition of a trusteeship should be more specific and complete than this one." The provisions in the union constitution failed to meet the requirements of the Act. Therefore, a "trusteeship imposed on the basis of such a defective constitution is invalid and should be dissolved." In addition, the court found that the trusteeship did not meet the requirements of Section 304 (c) for a "fair hearing" before the imposition of a trusteeship as no hearing was held. At a subsequent scheduled ratification hearing, the local was denied the right to cross examine witnesses and the presence of counsel. Under the circumstances, the scheduled hearing would not meet the statutory requirements of a "fair and full" hearing.

The standards of fairness were further elaborated in *Luggage Workers, Local 167* v. *Leather Goods, Plastics and Novelty Workers* as including "written charges and fair notice of a hearing so that the local can prepare its defense. The charges must state the acts upon which the International relies, the manner in which they violate the constitution or otherwise justify the trusteeship, and whenever possible the persons who committed them. Vague references to constitutional violations or misconduct are not adequate."[12] Because the International had failed to meet the above standards, the court suspended the trusteeship, but gave the International an opportunity to institute new proceedings in conformity with the decision. The court observed that while a union tribunal need not provide a hearing on the level of a judicial proceeding, the acts upon which the trusteeship is to be based should be stated.

A trusteeship, even if properly imposed, but whose purpose is not an allowable one, will not be sustained.[13] Martin Rarback was suspended as Secretary-Treasurer and District Council No. 9, International Brotherhood of Painters, Decorators and Paperhangers of America, placed in trusteeship, after Rarback had been indicted for accepting kickbacks from contractors employed on public housing projects. A trustee was appointed, and Rarback was placed on the payroll of the International as an organizer. During the trusteeship, a number of members sought to have the trusteeship dissolved, and an election for Secretary-Treasurer ordered.

The court found that the trusteeship was imposed in conformance with the union constitution, the hearing was fair, did not violate due process requirements and fulfilled the requirements of Section 304 (c) with respect to the conduct of the hearing. However, the court found that the "false testimony . . . the whole pattern and equivocal explanation—all points to the conclusion that there has been bad faith, not good faith, that the trusteeship was imposed to keep the entrenched group in power rather than for one of the allowable purposes." The court concluded that "the appropriate remedy is to postpone the partial election now scheduled, order a supervised election for all offices, including that of Secretary-Treasurer, and then terminate the unlawful trusteeship." The election was ordered under Section 304 (a) which authorizes a court to grant "such relief (including injunctions) as may be appropriate." The election was held under the supervision of the American Arbitration Association, and the reform candidate, Frank Schonfeld, defeated Martin Rarback for the office of Secretary-Treasurer.

A number of trusteeships were established because of financial irregularities or for the refusal to perform required financial functions. Lodge No. 837, International Association of Machinists, was opposed to the policies and the services it received from District No. 9 to which it was affiliated. Meetings became turbulent, and the suggestions of the International disregarded. In addition, a practicing attorney was hired, against the orders of the International, and given membership in the local. On May 24, 1966, the International placed Lodge No. 837 under "direction, control and supervision" of the District Secretary, Eugene Glover. During the "supervision," leaders of the opposition to the International won the local offices. The "supervision" was not severe. Regular meetings were conducted and, as noted, the election held, but expenditures had to be approved by Glover or his deputy.

On March 1, 1967, the International suspended Lodge No. 837 and its officers and directed the trustee to take over the lodge's affairs. The suspended officers staged a sit-in, seized the union seal, advised the bank which held the funds of the local not to honor the checks signed by the trustee, and urged the members to leave the International Association of Machinists for another union. As a result, they were brought up on charges, found guilty and expelled. They challenged the trusteeship in the courts. The court noted that the union constitution does not use the word "trusteeship," "but the circumstances under which both 'supervision' and 'suspension' may be imposed are sufficiently specific to meet the requirements of Title III, LMRDA." It found no violations of procedural due process and found the trusteeship had been imposed for reasons permitted by Section 302. Moreover, the existing circumstances "justified the imposition of supervision to 'restore' democratic procedures, or otherwise carry out the legitimate objectives" of the union. The court found that passage of illegal motions at union business meetings threatened "the organizational unity of the IAM and the improper expenditure of local funds . . . justified the suspension of Local 837 on March 1, 1967."

The expelled officers claimed their expulsion violated their rights under Section 101 (a) (1) and (5), but the court ruled these rights were limited by two exceptions: (1) unions were given power to enforce reasonable rules as to the responsibility of members toward the organization as an institution, and (2) they were allowed to prevent interference with the union's contractual and legal obligations. The court noted:[14]

When local officers encourage local members to break away from the national organization and form an independent union, it clearly undermines the responsibility of members to the national organization, and threatens the enforcement of contractual obligations. Therefore, the advocation of dual unionism is not protected under Title I, LMRDA, or Section 7, NLRAA.

In another trusteeship involving financial matters, District 3, International Union of Electrical, Radio and Machine Workers, charged that the district President, and the Treasurer had diverted $140,000 of union funds. At the request of delegates from the district locals, the International appointed two trustees to manage the district's affairs. The President of the district, Milton Weihrauch, contested the trusteeship in the courts, but he was unsuccessful, although the court refused to dismiss his suit. In denying Weihrauch's plea for an injunction, the court rejected his claim for prospective damage. His pension and hospitalization rights were unaffected. In denying the injunction, the court noted that Weihrauch faced no irreparable injury, and there was little indication that he would prevail at trial.[15]

Recall proceedings were brought against Weihrauch and Joseph Iozzi, the Treasurer, and the members voted to remove them from office. The trusteeship was lifted in February 1968, and new officers were elected. Both men were convicted of embezzlement.

The Laborers' Union placed Local 332 in trusteeship, but failed to give the officers against whom the trusteeship was directed an opportunity to be heard and to rebut the evidence presented. John Plenty, one of the officers removed by the International, and Reginald Lopes, a member of Local 332, sued for an order voiding the trusteeship because it was not established after a fair hearing on the reasons for imposing it.

The District Court held that a trusteeship imposed upon a subordinate unit of a labor organization is invalid unless a fair hearing was given on the charges upon which the imposition of the trusteeship was based. The court noted that a fair hearing had been a requirement under the common law, and that, in enacting Title III, Congress sought to limit further the power of unions to impose and maintain trusteeships, and provided means whereby they could be challenged. The court noted that a trusteeship is presumed valid for eighteen months, under Section 304 (c). This presumption was included in order to encourage unions to adopt a fair hearing procedure in their constitutions and by-laws:

> To read the Act as requiring a fair hearing to authorize or ratify the imposition of a trusteeship not only comports with the legislative history but also with the general purpose of the Act, namely, to require disclosure of the reasons for union actions in matters touching the governance of local union affairs.

The International was enjoined from continuing the trusteeship, but its effectiveness was suspended to give the International an opportunity to hold a fair hearing.[16]

The International scheduled a new hearing from which the accused officers withdrew because their lawyer was not allowed to be present. Nevertheless, the hearing continued and the charges made were substantiated. The court followed the earlier ruling in the Third Circuit, that "there is no guaranteed right to counsel at an internal union hearing."[17] The trusteeship was upheld. The court found the hearings were "full and fair" in all respects. Furthermore, it was "consistent with our order and the International did what it should have done originally, and the reprieve, so to speak, as previously stated was based on equitable principles rather than our expressed legal conclusion in the original opinion."

The right of an international to impose a trusteeship upon one of its locals which had insisted on engaging in an unauthorized strike was unsuccessfully challenged.[18] The dispute involved Local 5-443 and its parent organization, the International Woodworkers of America. The members of the local, located in Laurel, Mississippi, and employed by the Masonite Corporation, went out on an unauthorized strike on April 21, 1967. When informed by the parent body that the strike violated the agreement with the company and the obligations of the union, the strikers refused to return to their jobs. Thereupon the company sued the local and the International for a breach of contract. The International, nevertheless, continued to seek an agreement with the employer, and succeeded, on December 7, 1967, in reaching a settlement which called for the return of the strikers without loss of seniority and for mutual withdrawal of lawsuits. At the same time, the International imposed a trusteeship on the local.

This imposition was challenged by the local in the courts. The union's claim that the trusteeship was illegal was rejected by the United States District Court. It found that "local officers were advised repeatedly through written and oral communications from the international officers that the strike must be ended." To the claim that there "was no literal compliance with the International constitutional procedures for establishing a trusteeship before its imposition," the court held:

> There was more than sufficient compliance with both the constitution and statutes thereafter . . . The court finds on the basis of the facts . . . that there were numerous notices of the charges against the union, opportunities given for compliance, a valid appointment of a trustee which was later approved and ratified by the international executive board . . . all in compliance with the union's constitution and bylaws. The court further finds that in compliance with the federal statutes, the trusteeship was established for a valid

purpose, that of assuring the performance of collective bargaining and in order to restore democratic procedures, and, further that such trusteeship became valid after a fair hearing and when it was ratified by the international executive board.[19]

On the validity of the agreement made by the International and not ratified by the local, the court ruled that it was valid even though the local officers did not participate in the negotiations. The court found nothing in the union constitution and by-laws which denies such authority to the International.

The local appealed, and the Fifth Circuit Court affirmed the decision of the trial court. It noted that Section 302 allows a trusteeship to be imposed to end an unauthorized strike. On the failure of the union to follow the procedures outlined in the union constitution for establishing a trusteeship, the Appellate Court found the variations were not significant and that precise compliance with a labor organization's constitutional procedure is not necessary as long as there is substantial compliance with the provisions of LMRDA. The Appellate Court found the union's negotiation of the contract proper and justified as an attempt to mitigate the ill effects arising from the unlawful strike which had been ended by the trusteeship.

Electrical Workers Local 1186 (BEW) v. Eli[20] also involved the imposition of a trusteeship before a fair hearing. Local 1186 had been suspended and the business manager, Akito Fujikawa, removed from office for engaging in unauthorized strikes. The local sued on the ground that the trusteeship was invalid, since it had not been preceded by a hearing of the charges. The court disagreed and ruled that Title III provides a permissible trusteeship which can be ratified by a fair hearing after the fact. The argument of the local that the absence of a detailed trusteeship in the union constitution acts as a bar to the right of the International to impose a trusteeship upon its locals was also rejected by the court.

The court held that the lack of constitutional procedures does not prevent intervention by the International Union; as long as the method is a "just and reasonable one and preserves the local's right to due process, it is valid." Under the IBEW constitution the President is authorized to take charge of local affairs whenever deemed necessary and the statement on International Charge of Local Affairs complies with the requirements of due process. To the argument that the trusteeship was not imposed for an allowable purpose specified in Section 302, the International Union claimed it was imposed to end the unauthorized work stoppages which the court held to be a proper cause.

Two locals of the American Federation of Musicians were active in Chicago, and the International sought to have them merge. Local 10 had about 12,000 predominantly white members, and Local 208 had only about 1,200 members, mostly black. The International presented a merger plan whereby each local would elect officers during a transitional period ending in 1972. Local 10 was dissatisfied with the plan, but its appeal to the International's convention was rejected. The members of Local 10 overwhelmingly declined to approve the merger plan. Thereupon the International imposed a trusteeship upon the local in order to enforce it.

The proposed plan was attacked on the ground that it violated the equal rights provision of Section 101 (a) (1) because the plan deprived non-black members of the merged union from voting for all officers of the local. The court held that this provision was temporary and that "the 'subject to reasonable' exception," in Section 101 (a) (1) "becomes controlling." Reasonable must be determined on practical grounds "in order to effectuate the merger. The attack of dissident Local 10 upon the validity of the trusteeship was also rejected by the court. As the union constitution allowed a trusteeship upon a subordinate unit for disobeying a lawful order of the executive board, and as Local 10 had disobeyed the order to merge, the court held it was in "consonance with the authority under the constitution and by-laws of the union. As merger was legitimate objective of a labor union, the trusteeship was imposed for a purpose permitted by Section 302."[21]

When Branch 36, National Association of Letter Carriers

(NALC), urged its members to join a strike conducted by a rival union, a trusteeship was imposed upon the offending local after an investigation had confirmed the accuracy of the charge. However, Branch 36 refused to recognize the trusteeship. Thereupon NALC sought a preliminary injunction to compel the local to comply. The District Court refused to issue the order, holding that no showing had been made that the national organization would suffer irreparable harm if it did not receive the requested relief.

On appeal the circuit court reversed the decision of the trial court and held that Section 304 (c) LMRDA decrees that a trusteeship established in accordance with the constitution and by-laws of the parent union and authorized or ratified after a fair hearing is presumed valid for eighteen months, unless it is shown by "clear and convincing proof" that the trusteeship was not established or maintained in good faith for a purpose allowable under Section 302. To permit the local union to ignore the trusteeship would reverse the statutory burden.[22]

In 1968, the Laborers' International Union established at the request of seven of the locals in Oklahoma a Laborers' District Council. The convention directed that the council be the bargaining representative of the locals in the state, and that the contract negotiate contain provisions for a health and welfare program and for training. Local 612 refused to negotiate its agreements through the council and made its own contract with the contractors association, which did not contain the provisions mandated by the 1969 convention of the union.

The International notified Local 612 that an investigation would be held to determine whether a trusteeship should be established and its autonomy suspended. Grounds for the investigation were specified in the notice. The investigation commission recommended the imposition of a trusteeship which the International carried out.[23]

Title III, judging by the results attained, could be described as virtually a perfect example of efficient law-making. Without diminishing the ability of unions to place their locals and other units of their organizations under a trusteeship, the evils that grew up as a result of the abuses by less than a dozen unions have been eliminated.

As soon as the LMRDA was passed, unions like the Operating Engineers, the Teamsters, and Meat Cutters had to divest themselves of trusteeships that had been held for longer than the statutory period. As a result, locals that had been held in subjection for a number of years were given their autonomy, and some have carried on effectively and democratically. Operating Engineers Local No. 150, in Chicago, for example, has run democratic elections for union office, and it appears to have been as effective since the departure of the trustee as it had been before. No one has claimed that the other trustee locals, either in the Operating Engineers, the Teamsters, or any other union had not been able to manage their affairs effectively since regaining their autonomy.

While the statute allows a trusteeship for eighteen months without challenge, the Labor Department has prolonged the term upon a showing of need for an extension. The funds of the local are inviolate against "seizure" by the parent union or diversion by the trustee. There are notorious examples of these abuses that were challenged in the state courts and exposed by the McClellan Committee. Prior to the reform legislation, the preventing of looting or dissipating of the trusteed local's funds could have required a long law suit with the outcome uncertain. Complaints of improper behavior of a trustee can now be made to the Secretary of Labor or challenged in the federal courts. More important, the trustee must conform to the statutory standards.

The requirements that trusteeships can only be imposed for specified purposes also acts as a constraint upon officers who might wish to curb opposition. Challenge to a trusteeship is not difficult on jurisdictional grounds, for it is authorized in the statute. Under the common law, the courts were generally satisfied if the union gave notice and a hearing. Under Title III, the substantive purpose is examined, and, in one instance, the absence of good faith was held to be a basis for setting a trusteeship aside by the court. There appears to have been no complaints on the operation of the trusteeships from the union side. As noted in the above discussion, several unions have imposed many trustee-ships without challenge from the Secretary of Labor or the members. The changes sought by Congress seem to have been achieved. The abuses have been eliminated, but the ability to impose a trusteeship by a parent body under the proper procedure and for a legitimate purpose has not been impaired.

12

Regulating Union Elections

In theory at least, unions were always democratic. Virtually all labor organizations, prior to the enactment of the LMRDA, required that elections for office be held at specified periods of time and that members be notified in advance of nomination and voting. Only those in good standing were eligible to vote or to be candidates for office. Good standing was defined as being currently paid up in dues and assessments levied by the organization. Additional qualifications were imposed upon those who sought to be candidates, and the severity of the qualifications was related to the importance of the office sought. A requirement that candidates for local office had to attend a stipulated number or percentage of union meetings in a given period of time was also found in the eligibility standards of a number of unions.

Generally absent from the election provisions were clauses giving all candidates access to union publications or the use of other union resources in electoral campaigns. While a secret ballot might be required, the parent union could not always determine if this were really followed when the results were challenged. Members, if dissatisfied with the conduct of the election, had the right to appeal to the central organization, and gross violations might be grounds for setting the election aside and the ordering of a rerun with or without the supervision of the parent union.

The McClellan Committee found abuses which showed that some labor organizations would scarcely qualify as perfect democracies. In the International Union of Operating Engineers, for example, "only 131,000—some 46 percent" of the members were allowed to vote. Only senior members were qualified.[1] In addition, testimony was given that Victor S. Swanson, manager of its Local 3 San Francisco, was guilty of rigging the election by stuffing of ballot boxes. "His justification that he was only doing what everybody else in the International was doing" was "only further proof," in the committee's opinion, "of the lack of democracy within this union."[2] The comments on the Teamsters' Union's concept of "democracy" were equally scathing. The McClellan Committee reported: "Teamster officials have crushed democracy within the union's ranks. They have rigged elections, hoodwinked and abused their own membership, and lied to them about the conduct of their affairs. They have advanced the cause of union dictatorship and have perverted or ignored their own constitution and bylaws."[3] In order to gain control of the New York joint council through a candidate favored by James Hoffa, a large number of "phony" locals were chartered with the aid of an extortioner who had been convicted before and since of an assorted number of crimes.[4]

While the number of unions in which abuses as serious as those which permeated the above and a number of other organizations was not large, there appeared to be lack of interest to run for office in a number of organizations, an interest which emerged after the enactment of the reform legislation. The rank and file, especially in unions which operated a hiring hall, seemed apathetic as far as elections were concerned. It was difficult to challenge violations of the electoral process. In some organizations, members could not organize to oppose incumbents or to circulate electioneering materials on behalf of candidates of their choice.

In introducing the section dealing with the election of officers, Senator John F. Kennedy said:

This is a critical area, and I am very pleased to say that on the basis of information available to me, most trade unions, both local and international, conduct their elections in an exemplary fashion. However, there has been evidence that some few unions have not conducted their affairs in a democratic manner, and since free secret elections are the cornerstone of the democratic union movement, it appears appropriate the public safeguards be established.[5]

Senator McNamara, of Michigan, believed that the "section represented an unwarranted . . . extremely dangerous, Federal intrusion into the internal affairs of a nonprofit organization."[6] Furthermore, Senator McNamara, who had served as a union official, could "recall little or no evidence of local union election abuse before the Committee on Improper Activities in the Labor or Management Field that would in any way necessitate this extreme step by Congress."[7]

However, the desire to legislate restrictions upon union-held elections had wide support in Congress, with several senators of the more conservative persuasion favoring added provisions allowing for the recall of union officers. These proposals were rejected and a comprehensive law designed to protect the right to vote, support and nominate candidates, and prevent use of union funds and facilities on behalf of candidates was enacted.

Rules for Elections

Section 401 provides that officers of national and international organizations[8] "shall elect its officers not less often than once every five years either by secret ballot among the members in good standing or at a convention of delegates chosen by secret ballot." Officers of intermediate bodies, such as general committees, system boards, joint boards, or joint councils "shall be elected not less often than once every four years by secret ballot among the members in good standing or by labor organization officers representative of such members who have been elected by secret

ballot." Local labor organizations are required to "elect . . . officers not less often than once every three years by secret ballot
among the members in good standing."

Section 401 (c) requires labor organizations

> to comply with all reasonable requests of any candidate to
> distribute by mail or otherwise at the candidate's expense
> campaign literature in aid of such person's candidacy to all
> members in good standing of such labor organization and to
> refrain from discrimination in favor or against any candidate
> with respect to the use of lists of members, and whenever
> such labor organizations or its officers authorize the distribu-
> tion by mail or otherwise of campaign literature on behalf of
> any candidate or of the labor organization itself with refer-
> ence to such election, similar distribution at the request of
> any other bona fide candidate shall be made by such labor
> organization and its officers, with equal treatment as to the
> expense of such distribution. Every bona fide candidate shall
> have the right, once within 30 days prior to an election of a
> labor organization in which he is a candidate, to inspect a list
> containing the names and last known addresses of all mem-
> bers of the labor organization who are subject to a collective
> bargaining agreement requiring membership therein as a
> condition of employment, which list shall be maintained and
> kept at the principal office of such labor organization by a
> designated official thereof. Adequate safeguards to insure a
> fair election shall be provided, including the right of any
> candidate to have an observer at the polls and at the counting
> of ballots.

The above section concerns itself with conditions surrounding
the election, and it seeks to equalize the advantages of candidates
insofar as these objectives can be attained. Section 401 (e)
specifies:

> In any election required by this section which is to be held by

secret ballot a reasonable opportunity shall be given for the nomination of candidates and every member in good standing shall be eligible to be a candidate and to hold office (subject to Section 504 and to reasonable qualifications uniformly imposed) and shall have the right to vote for or otherwise support the candidate or candidates of his choice, without being subject to penalty, discipline, or improper interference or reprisal of any kind by such organization or any member thereof. Not less than fifteen days prior to the election notice thereof shall be mailed to each member at his last known home address. Each member in good standing shall be entitled to one vote. No member whose dues have been withheld by his employer for payment to such organization pursuant to his voluntary authorization provided for in a collective bargaining agreement shall be declared ineligible to vote or be a candidate for office in such organization by reason of alleged delay or default of dues. The votes cast by members of each local labor organization shall be counted, and the results published, separately. The election officials designated in the constitution and bylaws or the secretary, if no other official is designated, shall preserve for one year the ballots and all records pertaining to the election. The election shall be conducted in accordance with the constitution and bylaws of such organization insofar as they are not inconsistent with the provisions of this title.

Section 401 (g) declares:

No money received by any labor by way of dues, assessment, or similar levy, and no moneys of an employer shall be contributed or applied to promote the candidacy of any person in an election subject to the provisions of this title. Such money of a labor organization may be utilized for notices, factual statements of issues not involving candidates, and other expenses necessary for the holding of an election.

Enforcement

The enforcement of this title is lodged in the Department of Labor on condition that the complaining member meets the requirements of Section 402 (a), that is, he

> has exhausted the remedies available under the constitution and bylaws of such organization and of any parent body, or (2) who has invoked such available remedies without obtaining a final decision within three calendar months after their invocation, may file a complaint with the secretary within one calendar month thereafter alleging the violation of any provision of Section 401 (including the violation of the constitution and bylaws of the labor organization pertaining to the election . . . of officers). The challenged election shall be presumed valid pending a final decision thereon (as hereinafter provided) and in the interim the affairs of the organization shall be conducted by the officers elected or in such other manner as its constitution and bylaws may provide.
>
> (b) The secretary shall investigate such complaint and, if he finds probable cause to believe that such a violation of this title has occurred and has not been remedied, he shall, within sixty days after the filing of such complaint, bring a civil action against the labor organization as an entity in the district court of the United States in which such labor organization maintains its principal office to set aside the invalid election, if any, . . . under the supervision of the secretary and in accordance with the provisions of this title and such rules and regulations as the secretary may prescribe. . . .
>
> (c) If, upon a preponderance of the evidence after a trial upon the merits, the court finds
>
> > (1) that an election has not been held within the time prescribed by Section 401, or
> >
> > (2) that the violation of Section 401 may have affected the outcome of an election,

the court shall declare the election, if any, to be void and direct the conduct of new election under supervision of the secretary and, so far as lawful and practicable, in conformity with the constitution and bylaws of the labor organization. The secretary shall promptly certify to the court the names of the people elected, and the court shall thereupon enter a decree declaring such persons to be the officers of the labor organization.

The order of the district court to dismiss the complaint, or designate elected officers of a labor organization is appealable "in the same manner as the final judgment in a civil action, but an order directing an election cannot be stayed pending an appeal."

This type of legislation had not been enacted by any state or in other countries in which democratic labor movements function. The first task facing labor organizations was to bring their constitution and by-laws into conformity with the LMRDA. Constitutional officers, governing bodies or regular or special conventions were aware of the Secretary's power to sue or not to sue. Decisions not to sue are seldom popular with the complainant and his supporters within or outside of the union. However, the courts have upheld the Secretary of Labor's right to determine the disposition of a complaint under Section 401.

The attempt to compel the secretary to institute a civil action to set aside an election failed.[9] In rejecting the appeal of a member of Teamsters Local 377 that the Secretary bring suit to set the election aside, the District Court held that the directive to file suit requires the Secretary to act only under certain circumstances. In a challenge to the Secretary's authority to investigate the conditions surrounding an election by Connecticut Teamsters' local, the Appellate Court of the Second Circuit said that the Secretary had the legal authority to investigate possible violations of election standards regardless of whether the complainant had exhausted his internal remedies.[10] In upholding the right to election records, the court said the Secretary had authority under

Section 601, regardless of whether the complaining member had met the requirements of Section 402, or even whether any complaint had been filed.

A percentage of complaints received are found without merit. The remainder may be settled by voluntary compliance which may consist of an agreement between the union and the LMWP to introduce remedial procedures at the next election, or to rerun the election under the supervision of the LMWP or without such supervision. In some instances, the union will refuse to agree to any of the LMWP's suggestions initially, but will accept the arrangement with the filing of civil suit. In other instances, a suit will be challenged by the union involved.

In the ten years between July 1, 1963, and June 30, 1973, 1,289 union elections have been investigated by the Department of Labor. (Table 9). Comparable statistics are not available before 1963 because of changes in computing from an "alleged violation to a case basis." In this period, 29 percent of the cases were closed because the Department of Labor concluded that the evidence was insufficient, the complaint untimely, or that union remedies had not been exhausted. In 27 percent of the cases the evidence did not show that the violations had affected the outcome of the election and the complaints were dismissed, and in 18 percent the union voluntarily agreed to hold another election. In 13 percent of the latter, the election was held under the supervision of the Department, and in the remainder without such provision. Other corrective action includes an agreement to eliminate provisions in the union constitution and by-laws and practices held to impede the holding of a fair election. Because of the many questions raised by union officers desiring to carry out the requirements of the election regulations, the Secretary of Labor "found it necessary to issue on December 12, 1959, an *Interpretative Bulletin* concerning the election provisions."[11]

The BLMR sought to stimulate self-improvement of the election machinery and it believed "there are areas in which unions can, with little additional effort, improve the handling of their own election contests."[12] Despite the educational efforts, there were 414 investigations into alleged violations of the election provisions in fiscal 1961. Some 283 were closed when no basis for the charges was disclosed. The remainder, except 14 taken to court, were still pending on June 30, 1961. In February 1961, the first court-directed election, by the Independent Workers Union of Florida, was conducted under the supervision of the Secretary of Labor. The union had failed to give the statutory notice of the election and did not provide adequate safeguards. Its election was voided by the United District Court.

The Secretary is authorized to investigate complaints by members and on the basis of the evidence he decides whether to file suit for relief under Section 402 (b). The affiliation of 257 local unions in this group is known publicly. Forty-two of the complaints have been against independent unions; the other 213 locals belonged to national and international organizations of the AFL-CIO, the Teamsters', Mine Workers', and Automobile Workers' Unions. The Secretary has filed ten or more complaints against affiliates of seven national and international unions. The Steelworkers with twenty complaints headed the list, and were followed by the Carpenters and the Operating Engineers, each with sixteen; the Laborers, fourteen; Teamsters, thirteen; International Longshoremen's Association (ILA), and the International Brotherhood of Electrical Workers (IBEW), each with ten. Ninety-nine of the 255 suits were filed against affiliates of the above seven organizations.

In the case of the Steelworkers, the Secretary attacked the attendance requirements of a number of its locals, but was not uniformly successful in demonstrating that they were unreasonable. The suits against the International Union of Operating Engineers were directed to the lengthy time period between the requirement for candidacy and the local elections and at the denial of the right to hold office by members of branches, and the continuous good standing requirement. These requirements have since been abolished. The Glass Bottle Blowers Association, a relatively small organization, has had nine suits filed against its elections because of its stringent attendance requirements, since modified. The Machinists' Union with eight suits, and the Automobile Workers' and the Printing Pressmen each with five suits

TABLE 9. Election Complaints and Their

	1961	1962	1963	1964	1965
Complaints Received			179	139	99
Election cases closed			134	113	94
No violations found, complaint untimely or closed for other reasons			9	15	41
Insufficient evidence on influence of election			60	63	25
Voluntary compliance			30	26	16
Election supervised by LMWP Management Reports			14	26	10
No supervision of election by LMWP			16		4
Other corrective action taken					2
Civil actions filed by Department of Labor	14	9	15	25	12
Election supervised under court order			11	9	8

[1] Data for 1960-1962 are not comparable.

Compilations are from Compliance and Enforcement of Office of Labor-Management and Welfare-Pension Reports.

Disposition in Fiscal Years 1963-1972[1]

1966	1967	1968	1969	1970	1971	1972	Total, 1963-1972
149	92	118	110	134	132	137	1289
151	90	106	128	127	126	134	1203
25	27	42	58	48	49	47	371
56	27	24	20	24	22	35	356
35	21	17	21	21	20	29	236
26	14	11	19	10	13	18	161
9	4	3	2	7	6	7	58
	3	3		4	1	4	17
35	15	23	29	34	35	23	269
10	7		11	17	35	27	135

are the next highest on the list of organizations. Twenty-five international unions have each had only one suit filed against its affiliates.

The complaints that are made to the LMWP are basically of two kinds. (1) Charges that the elections were not conducted in accordance with the requirements of the union's constitution and by-laws or the LMRDA. These charges may be failure to circulate campaign literature, give notice, or permission for an observer. Miscounting and ballot-tampering fall into this group. (2) Complaints and suits are also based on the claim that the eligibility standards for union office are unfair and discriminatory against some members or groups of members. The LMWP has interpreted its duty under the statute to eliminate or rectify both deficiencies in the election procedures.

Unions are likely to be more willing and ready to adjust shortcomings which arise as a result of human failure or a desire to deceive or to gain an unfair advantage than to change a practice based upon its constitutional procedures. An example is the reaction of the Steelworkers to the LWMWP's challenge to the election of the director of District 28 in the 1965 election. The opponent to the incumbent was unable to obtain from the district a list and location of the local unions' offices and the time of meetings so that the opposing candidate might meet the members and circulate his campaign literature. After his defeat, the opponent of the incumbent protested the conduct of the election to the International Union. The executive board sustained the results of the election. Thereupon, the defeated candidate took his complaint to the LMWP. In the end, the Steelworkers accepted a stipulation that in the next election for director in District 28 candidates would receive, upon their request, the name and address of the recording secretaries of all the district's locals and that campaign literature would be promptly distributed by the International Secretary-Treasurer at the candidates' expense. Approved by the District Court of Western Pennsylvania, the terms were incorporated into the International constitution. The stipulation also included an agreement that the 1968 election in District 28 would be under the Secretary's supervision.

On the other hand, the Steelworkers believed that the requirement that candidates for local office attend at least 50 percent of the business meetings of their local union in the preceding thirty-six months of the election was fair. It also allowed credit for attendance whenever the candidate was employed on a shift which coincided with the meeting. As a result, the LMWP brought suit against a number of local unions, but the results were not uniformly favorable to it. A number of district courts held the Steelworkers' attendance provisions reasonable. The Glass Bottle Blowers Association whose attendance requirements were more severe and which virtually allowed no exemption were also attacked in a series of suits, and the LMWP was uniformly successful in compelling an amendment of these qualifications.

Another example of an attack of discriminatory qualifications was the series of suits against a number of local unions of the International Union of Operating Engineers. Some locals were composed of a parent body and three branches. The parent body contained members who were the most skilled and the branches those of lesser skill. The initiation fees differed, but the branch members had all the rights that were enjoyed by those belonging to the parent body except the right to hold office. In addition, the LMWP regarded the need to file a declaration of candidacy five months before the election and continuous good standing for five years before an election, with monthly or quarterly payment of dues in advance without variation, as unreasonable, in that it denied a fair opportunity for members to be nominated for office.

Several District and Appellate Courts regarded these restrictions as violations of 401 (e) which requires that "a reasonable opportunity shall be given for the nomination of candidates and every member shall be eligible to be a candidate and to hold office (subject to . . . reasonable qualifications uniformly imposed)."[13] The Operating Engineers, to avoid further litigation, amended the constitution so as to eliminate the need for a declaration of candidacy, to provide a thirty-day grace period for the payment of dues and to reduce the continuous good-standing rule to three years for business manager and one year for candidates for other local offices. The amendments also required locals to hold elections in August, with nominations to be made not earlier than the preceding May.

The LMWP continued its attack upon the limiting of the right to hold office to members of the parent body. The District Court of Northern Ohio held that it was an unreasonable requirement because the union's rule permanently deprives members of Local 18 "who neither choose nor have the ability to operate machinery of the right to become officers of the union." Moreover, the court held that "officership should not be qualified by a requirement that one be qualified to operate certain machinery with enough skill to earn a living thereby in a local union, the structure of which is comprised of men organized across craft lines, some of whom are skilled, others unskilled, some employed in the construction area, others operating in a factory environment."[14]

The union appealed. The Sixth Circuit Court of Appeals upheld the lower court and noted that the membership requirement being challenged had no relation to the branch members' fitness to hold union office. Moreover, the disqualification of 60 percent of the local's members from running for office violated the intent of congress to make labor organizations more democratic. As far as the ability of members of the branches becoming affiliated with the parent organization by the payment of an additional initiation fee, the court held that requiring a member who had met his financial obligations over the years to pay a fee in order to run for office was unreasonable and void.[15]

After the Supreme Court denied *certiorari* in October 1971, the Operating Engineers convention eliminated the requirement from the International constitution. The campaign against this clause was conducted for virtually the entire period in which the LMRDA was in effect. It is this persistent and unnoticed activity of the LMWP which is making the mandate of the LMRDA's "a member shall be eligible to be a candidate subject to reasonable qualifications uniformly imposed," a reality.

The LMRDA had an effect upon the willingness of members to challenge the leadership in several unions. It is likely, although not provable, that without the participation of the LMWP, the incumbent James Carey would have remained the head of the International Union of Electrical, Radio and Machine Workers despite the fact that more than 22,000 members voted for his opponent than for him in the union's 1965 election. The election committee had diverted a sufficient number of votes to have him declared elected. No relief could be obtained through the courts until the director of the LMWP, acting under Section 601 (a), took possession of the ballots, the counting of which showed the true course of the election.

Would there have been a challenge to the head of the Steel-workers Union, or would the opposition within the Retail Clerks International Association have been willing to mount a campaign against the administration-supported ticket? The long campaign in the United Mine Workers of America might not have suc-ceeded without the efforts of the LMWP, supported by the con-siderable resources of the government. Although there have been no revolutionary changes in the official staffs of the organi-zations of labor, it cannot be successfully maintained that the absence of opposition is the result of fear of reprisals. It is difficult to organize a slate of opposition candidates in many unions be-cause few persons have developed a large enough constituency. It is noticeable that, in virtually every union in which opposition to one or more general officers appeared, the opposition candidate had come from the ranks of long-term office holders. In the International Association of Machinists, a long-term Vice-President ran against the incumbent Secretary-Treasurer and was defeated. I. W. Abel, who successfully headed an opposition slate in the Steelworkers' Union, against the incumbent Interna-tional President, had served the union almost from the beginning of its existence. The opposition in the Retail Clerks International Association was headed by a serving International Vice-President, and the task of challenging the incumbents was made easier by the retirement of James Suffridge, the President at the time of the challenge. Joseph Yablonski was also a well-known officer of the United Mine Workers of America, who had headed the union's Labor's Non-Partisan League. However, after the death of Yablonski, Miners for Democracy nominated an opposition ticket which was headed by three candidates who had not held an important office in the union.

The effect on local elections may have been greater. Two examples will suffice. Local 825, Operating Engineers, Jersey City, New Jersey, had been headed by Peter W. Weber, an International Vice-President and one of the more powerful individuals in the construction industry within his jurisdiction. In the ten years that Weber had been President and business manager, he had not faced an opponent. In 1962, an opposition candidate appeared. Though a new experience for Weber, the challenge was easily repelled. A significant development followed in that the opposition to Weber continued to function. Weber, in the meantime, was exposed as one of the directors of a large-scale shakedown of contractors building the Texas-New Jersey pipeline. He was indicted and convicted for extortion and for violating Section 302 of the National Labor Relations Act. Sentenced to prison, his office was inherited by his brother and the faction that had dominated the local continued to rule.

However, the opposition did not fade away. It was formally protected by the prohibition upon reprisals of Section 401 (e). It continued its existence, and in the 1971 local elections an opposition candidate for business manager and President appeared to have won the election. There was a dispute over the counting of challenged ballots. The opposition candidate was declared elected by the Election Committee and under Section 402 (a) (2), was entitled to take office. The incumbent was not ready to surrender without a contest, and wanted the challenged ballots rejected and himself declared the victor. Fearful of this eventuality, the opposition appealed to the District Court under Section 101 (a) (1) which guarantees equal rights to members of unions to nominate and vote.

On the basis that, as the election had not been certified, there was no ground to appeal to the Secretary of Labor, the court ordered the retention of the ballots until a supervised recount could be made. The incumbent officer appealed, and the Circuit

Court reversed the lower court. It held that an election for union officers is "completed upon the termination of the balloting, rather than upon the certification of the results." Moreover, the District Court lacked jurisdiction to hear an individual member's precertification suit to enjoin a recount under the Bill of Rights provisions of the Act. As the opposition candidate was declared elected, the incumbent whose group had controlled the union for at least two generations would have to proceed by a Title IV protest.[16]

Obviously the opposition did not win an overwhelming victory, but its ability to maintain itself and field candidates against the incumbents and their supporters is an achievement of importance. It may also show that the rank and file may not be as tolerant of corruption as has been generally assumed, and if given an opportunity will take action to oust those who betray their trust.

The challenge to the administration in Local 560, Teamsters in Jersey City also reflected the presence of the LMWP. Dominated by Anthony Provenzano, an International Vice-President, two opposition slates appeared to contest the election of 1962. Operating in Bergen, Hudson, and Passaic Counties, New Jersey, and Monroe County, New York, the local was one of the larger and more powerful in the Teamsters' Union. Slightly more than 50 percent of the approximately 12,000 members voted, and the margin of victory for the incumbents was about 550 votes. Complaints of inadequate safeguards of the ballots, and voting by ineligible members led to a stipulation that the 1965 election would be held under the supervision of the Department of Labor. Despite the indictment and conviction of Provenzano for extortion, he managed to increase his margin of victory substantially.[17] Complaints against both elections were made to the LMWP, but the Office of Labor-Management and Welfare-Pension Reports found violations in the Teamsters' Local 753 of no significance and dismissed the charges.

There are simple violations of Title IV such as when the members have not received adequate notice of the election, safeguards for the election have not been provided, or the ballot has been mishandled. If it can be established that such violations may have affected the outcome of the election, the courts will set the results aside and order that another election be held under the supervision of the Secretary of Labor.

13

Title IV
and the Courts

Some of the court cases concerned charges of false counting, improper manipulation of the voting lists, failure to allow an opposition to the incumbents to circulate campaign material. In addition, the courts were called to rule on a series of challenges to the standards established for voting and holding office. As neither federal, state nor municipal governments had legislated on such issues, the courts were called upon to decide *de novo* these questions for which no direct precedents existed.

Unions have assumed that their election procedures were fair and reasonable, and made minor if any changes in these provisions after the enactment of LMRDA. If the changes were insufficient the union election rules could be challenged. For example, the Department of Labor, in response to complaints of members, sought to have the International Union of Operating Engineers eliminate the restrictions on office holding by members of its branches. The union declined, and the cases were taken to the federal courts. The Steelworkers believed that its attendance requirements for candidacy were reasonable, and other unions shared that opinion with regard to their own election procedures.

Neither Local No. 6 of the Hotel and Restaurant Employees Union nor the National Maritime Union considered the requirement of prior office holding for candidacy for the top offices as a violation of LMRDA. Interpretation of other election clauses or the name or location of polling places might come under attack.

The Department of Labor also compelled several unions to hold elections for officers. These were independents or unions that were not affiliated with the AFL-CIO, or one of the International unions outside the federation. One of those was Teamsters, Warehousemen and Production Workers, Local 424, not affiliated with the Teamsters' International.

It operated in Eastern Long Island, where it had recruited about 350 workers, mostly engaged in potato-picking. It had agreed to hold a supervised election, but its Secretary-Treasurer sent out inaccurate information on the time and place where it would be held. The Department of Labor secured its first restraining order to prevent interference with the balloting. In the election, held in two different communities, only thirty-two votes were cast. The President and the Secretary-Treasurer of the local were ousted from their offices.[1]

Amalgamated Local Union No. 355 was also an independent organization. It recruited workers in the New York-New Jersey area. It had failed to hold an election in accordance with its constitution and it also violated the provisions of LMRDA which require local unions to conduct elections "not less often than once every three years." It agreed to amend its constitution to make a number of positions elective and to hold tri-annual elections.[2]

The election was held in March 1963, and polling places were set up in five different communities in which members of the union were located. Only fifty-six votes were cast by a membership of approximately 1,700. The members appeared disinterested, and the candidacy of the incumbents was not contested.

Another independent, the Independent Service Employees Union, followed a similar pattern. It also refused to make contracts available to its members on request, required by Section 104, and dissidents who protested the election were brought up on charges. The officers then held an election in which they were unopposed. At the request of the LMWP, the election was voided by the U.S. District Court for Eastern New York, and a new election stipulated by the agreement of the union office. An attempt by the officers to evade the stipulation led the LMWP to institute contempt proceedings.[3] In the end those who had been expelled were reinstated with full rights to vote.

A full slate was nominated against the incumbents, but the latter were able to win by a vote better than two to one for the two principal officers and by a slightly lesser margin for the two others.

The reelection of the officers under these circumstances may be puzzling to the reader. One factor may have been the support given to the incumbents by the employers with whom the organization bargained. They cooperated in discharging one of the dissidents who was then ordered reinstated by the court. The union, charged with failing to hold regular elections, was made up of workers who were members of minority groups and had low skills. The employers were engaged in labor-intensive activities and were anxious to keep a more aggressive union from gaining bargaining rights. Turnover of labor was high, and the workers were disinterested in the organization. Thus labor reform was difficult to gain despite the support from government.

The attempt to penalize a candidate by inducing employers to deny him employment as a longshoreman was discontinued when the LMWP secured an injunction restraining Longshoremen's Local 1752 and its officers from compelling employers to discriminate in hiring of the opposition candidate.[4]

Failure to notify a large number of members of an impending election was a violation of Section 401 (e) and a basis for setting the election aside in Local No. 1622, Carpenters.[5] The charge had originally been made by a candidate for office that the ballots had been miscounted, but the suit by the Secretary of Labor had also included the charge of inadequate notice. Basing its decision on the Supreme Court's ruling in Laborer's Local 125,[6] the District Court of Northern California held these matters could be included in the Secretary's complaint because "notice of election is too fundamental requirement to be made dependent on a private complaint, to put it in issue when the election is being contested." The court also refused to accept the union's contention that the holding of an uncontested election in 1967 rendered the disputed 1965 election moot. The court ordered another election, finding that the union had failed to give adequate notice, a reasonable opportunity for nomination of candidates, and failed to safeguard the accuracy of the ballots.

Section 401 (b) requires that local elections be held by secret ballot. The Department of Labor unsuccessfully challenged the 1960 election of Laborers' Local No. 11 on the ground that there had been a violation of the secrecy provision because the "ballots issued to the voters in numerical order, and all of the cast ballots tallied after the election bore serial numbers." It was the view of the Department that the voters could be identified.

A secret ballot, as defined in 3(k), "means the expression by ballot, voting machine, or otherwise, but in no event by proxy, of a choice with respect to any election or vote taken upon any matter, which is cast in such a manner that the person expressing such choice cannot be identified with the choice expressed." Judge H.C. Sorg, of the United States District Court for Western Pennsylvania, found a number of irregularities but he held they did not affect the election. Voters were required to identify themselves in the presence of watchers, the financial secretary, and judges of the election. The secretary stipulated that no voter cast more than one ballot. Even though the record of eligible voters and the list of voters were made available to the secretary, there is no evidence that any unauthorized person voted in the election.[7] The court noted that there had been some deviation from literal compliance with the terms of the act, and urged that steps be taken "for safeguarding the secrecy of the ballot," but the "preponderance of evidence did not show any violation which may have affected the outcome of the election."

Following the June 1963 election of Hod Carriers' Local 169, Reno, Nevada, two members complained that they had been denied the right to vote, that the membership lists were inadequate, and that the local had failed to send notices of election to each member. In addition, the Secretary of Labor raised the issue of the adequacy of one polling place in view of the fact that some members lived more than 60 miles from where the polling place was located. The court found that the failure to allow some members to vote may have affected the outcome of the election.[8] The court directed the next election be held under the supervision of the Secretary. However, the court rejected the claim that additional polling places or a mailed ballot should have been utilized. The court found "that it was not wholly impractical for a member of Local Union 169 to travel from any place within its jurisdiction to Reno, Nevada, to vote once every three years for union officers." It noted that a worker in Elko, Nevada, for example, who joins the union, does so freely and not under the same economic compulsion as if the collective agreements did require union membership and does so with the knowledge that the seat of the union is in Reno where union elections have historically been held. The court did not believe that members were deprived of the right to vote as a result of the single polling place, although it might be reasonable to establish polling places more convenient to members living a distance from Reno.

The refusal of the officers of the American Guild of Variety Artists to circulate the campaign literature of an opposition slate was held to be sufficient ground for setting the election aside and directing the holding of another in its place.[9] "A fair election here depended on the provision of adequate safeguards with respect to candidates' campaign literature distribution by the union's access to the use of a single membership list."

In a private suit, the District Court of Western Pennsylvania held that a candidate for district office must be permitted to use the union's addressograph machinery containing names and addresses of union members. The opposition candidate was limited to one mailing.[10] However, in a similar case, it was held that a member did not have the right to copy the membership list for purposes of using it for circulating campaign literature.[11]

When proof of the use of funds on behalf of an incumbent officer was presented, the District Court ordered the funds returned to the union and permanently enjoined the use of union funds on behalf of candidates in a court-ordered election.[12]

The District Court of Eastern Pennsylvania found the rule allocating certain offices in Local 1291, International Longshoremen's Association, to members of the "white" race and others to members of the "colored" race unreasonable, in that the rule had no objective relationship to the duties to be performed, and that the rule would permanently exclude certain individuals from holding office who fall into neither racial category. A stipulation was reached which would allow the Secretary to conduct a supervised election without the objectionable racial clause governing nominations or election.[13]

On the grounds that a union could not limit certain offices to a particular group of members the District Court of Western Pennsylvania set aside the election in Local 610, United Electrical, Radio, and Machine Workers, in Wilmerding, Pennsylvania. The court held it was unreasonable to specify in the constitution that only members of the Air Brake Division could be candidates for certain offices and only members of the Switch and Signal Division could be candidates for the remaining offices.[14]

One of the first cases in which the court was called upon to interpret the meaning of sections of 401 (e) involved a group of members of Amarillo Drivers, Local 577, Teamsters, who, after exhausting their internal remedies, complained to the Secretary that they had been denied an opportunity to run for local office.

The Teamsters' International constitution provided that continuous good standing for the 24-month period preceding the election was a requisite for candidacy for office. The Secretary charged that the requirement was unreasonable and violated Title IV.

Another basis claimed by the Secretary for invalidating the election was the disqualification of members whose dues were being paid to the union through a voluntary check-off. Under Section 401 (3), "No member whose dues have been withheld by his employer for payment to such organization pursuant to his voluntary authorization provided for in a collective bargaining agreement shall be declared ineligible to vote or be a candidate for office in such organization by reason of alleged delay or default in the payment of dues." The Secretary contended that where the member is employed under a check-off system, he is relieved by the statute of the responsibility of seeing to it that the dues deductions are actually made in order to protect his eligibility for office.

In the opinion, in January 1963,[15] the District Court upheld the government's argument that the check-off was a system for the benefit of the labor organization. The court noted that the employer had followed an irregular pattern in making its dues deductions from the wages due the employees, but that the union did not protest the irregularity. Moreover, the union suffered no financial loss because the dues arrearage had been wiped out by subsequent contributions, and the complaining members had paid up all of their back dues at the time of the nomination. Delay or default in making the deductions, the court held, was due to the laxity of the employer or the union in administering the check-off program. Whatever caused the failure to make timely dues deductions, it could not serve as a basis for prejudicing the right of the individual union member.

The court also found the absence of any grace period for payment of dues unreasonable. At the next convention of the Teamsters' Union, held after the suit against Local 557 had been filed, the union changed its rule for paying dues so that members "paying dues to local unions must pay them on or before the last day of the current month."

A check-off case also arose in Local 191, Teamsters, Bridgeport, Connecticut. As in *Goldberg* v. *Amarillo General Drivers Local 577*, the dispute seems to have arisen as a result of deficient record keeping by the employer. In fact, the District Court of Connecticut found the employer's compliance with the check-off provisions "whimsical," and the union's records "confused." However, said the court:

Where the check-off system is used and specific authority is given by the employees for its exercise at particular times with payment of the dues directly to the union the burden of record keeping rests upon the employer and the union. It is not up to the individual employee to take issue with the employer where the employer departs from the terms of the check-off system instituted under the terms of the collective bargaining agreement. It is only where the employee has not been employed and is not on the payroll for the payday on which the check-off is authorized to be made that he must see to it that he pays his dues himself in advance.[16]

The member did not know he was delinquent in his dues payments until the union notified him. He brought his payments up-to-date before election, but he was ineligible because he had lost his continuous good standing for the 24-month period which the constitution of the union required.

The court held that the union and the employer were responsible for the failure of the member to keep current.

If the employer and the union had adhered to the provisions of the written authorization, which was the only source of authority they had to check-off and receive dues out of [the member's] wages, [his] ... dues would have been paid.... To say, therefore, that a union member loses the protection of . . Section 401 (e) . . . because the employer, with the tacit consent of the union, makes the check-off in any week which suits its fancy other than the one in which it is authorized to do so, and thereby loses so valuable a right as his eligibility to run for union office, would be a mockery of just and fair procedure.

There is one difference between the two decisions on the member's responsibility. The decision in *Amarillo* does not deal with the problem of the member's responsibility for payment of dues when he does not have any money on deposit with the employer because he has been on temporary layoff, vacation or illness. On the other hand, the decision in Local 191 recognizes the member's responsibility where he "has not been employed and is not on the payroll for the payday on which the check-off is authorized to be made . . . he must see to it that he pays his dues himself in advance." This requirement is not only a reasonable one, but is in harmony with the Congressional desire to promote democratic unions.

A member who aspires to office within a union, it seems, should be sufficiently interested in the organization to realize that he must pay his dues in order to retain his good standing when he is not working because of his own decision or layoff. An employer only functions as a transmitting agent and has no duty to keep his employee's dues paid up unless the latter has sufficient funds to cover the amount going to the union. The rights of a member should not be "destroyed through connivance or chicanery," but the member, certainly one who aspires for office, should be sufficiently concerned with the union's rules and its welfare to be aware of the need to pay his dues directly. This is not a great burden, and by no means unreasonable. Responsible unions require that members show an interest in the organization, and interest begins by a member meeting his financial obligations.

Are workers for whom the union performs the normal membership functions to be regarded as members, or are members only those who have been formally admitted after paying a required initiation fee and taken the oath of membership? This question was raised in *Goldberg* v. *Marine Cooks and Stewards* in which only those with A ratings who sailed regularly as employees in the stewards and galley department on the vessels under agreement with the union were regarded as members. Other employees, in Class B, and C ratings, were not regarded as full book members and were denied the right to vote in union elections. This was the principal charge, but another was that the candidate opposing the Secretary-Treasurer was denied an opportunity to circulate his campaign material at his own expense. The union was willing to rerun the election for Secretary-Treasurer, but refused to concede that Class B and C employees were members of the union.

The District Court directed a rerun of the election for Secretary-Treasurer, but accepted the union view on B and C members. They had not paid the required initiation fee, nor had they taken the oath of members. The charges which they paid to the union were reimbursement for costs of the registration facilities, hiring halls, bargaining with employers, handling of grievances and the general administration of the union contract.[17] The Secretary, in fact, had attacked the union's admission policies, not the right to vote.

Justification of the class divisions was based upon the time spent in the industry. The union's position, which the court accepted, was that only those who have committed themselves to going to sea as a permanent occupation should be considered full book members and thus entitled to vote on union policy and officers. The union also claimed that many are attracted to the sea temporarily, but do not remain in seafaring occupations. They are not permanently attached to the industry, and therefore, should not help decide union policy. They are, however, required to pay a service charge.

The Secretary sought to invalidate an election in Local 9, International Union of Operating Engineers, because a member was disqualified for not maintaining the continuous good standing required by the union constitution and by-laws. The court, in this first case in which continuous good standing was an issue, ruled the provision was not a "reasonable qualification" under Section 401 (e) of the LMRDA. The court held that "while a requirement that a member be fully paid up or that he keep his dues paid on a regular basis, would be perfectly reasonable, provided he has some grace period, defendant's requirement is so strict as to be arbitrary and unreasonable."[18] The court found the disqualification of the candidate was a violation of Section 401 (e) and might have affected the election for Secretary-Treasurer.

Before the settlement agreement between the Secretary and the International Union of Operating Engineers, a number of courts had rendered decisions that one or more of the union's requirements for candidacy for office were in violation of Title IV. The Secretary appealed the refusal of the member's complaint. The union cross-appealed on the ground its qualifications were reasonable. The Court of Appeals affirmed the decision, and the Secretary was granted *certiorari* on the scope of the government's complaint. While the decision was pending, an agreement was reached that the next election would be supervised by the Secretary.

The Department of Labor as well as the courts faced a problem because under certain circumstances unions could avoid the holding of a court-ordered supervised election. As noted above, one of the remedies provided under the LMRDA was that a court could order that a union hold the next election under the supervision of the Secretary. In order not to interfere with the operations of the union, Section 402 (a) (2) provides: "The challenged election shall be presumed valid pending a final decision thereon . . . and in the interim the affairs of the organization shall be conducted by the officers elected or in such other manner as its constitution and bylaws may provide."

In a number of instances, the unions affected appealed the decisions of the trial courts. While the case was being considered on appeal, the term of the officers elected in the contested election expired, and a regular election for officers was then held. In the cases of several locals of the Operating Engineers and of the Glass Bottle Blowers Association, no complaint of the conduct of the second election was made to the Department of Labor. However, when the appeal against the contested election was considered by the Appellate Courts, they found that in the interim between the decision of the trial court and the time of the case under consideration, a regular and uncontested election had been held which rendered the challenge of the complainants to the earlier case moot.[19] The result was that the directives of the courts that an election be held under the supervision of the Secretary of Labor was effectively evaded.

The Second Circuit Court of Appeals noted that it had no power to grant Secretary relief as the cases were moot. The court noted that the IUOE candidacy requirements had been under repeated attack in the courts, but because of interminable delays the issue has not been decided. In addition to suggesting more expeditious handling of the suits, the court noted that "temporary relief may be appropriate to prevent an election from mooting a pending Title IV suit by the secretary."

The Second Circuit overruled the refusal of the District Court of Northern New York to enjoin the 1966 election of Locals 545, etc., International Union of Operating Engineers. "We think," said the Appellate Court,

> the district court has the power to enjoin a union from holding an election, or from giving effect to one already in process, where it is apparent that the secretary is likely to succeed in his claim, that the election under which the union's officers are currently serving was conducted in violation of the requirements of the Labor-Management Reporting and Disclosure Act of 1959 . . . where the impending balloting is apparently being conducted under substantially similar conditions, where it also appears that such injunction will not cause serious injury to the unions concerned, and where the secretary is likely to suffer a very real detriment in his attempt to enforce the law if such restraining order is not granted.[20]

The issue of mootness was decided by the Supreme Court in *Wirtz* v. *Local 153, Glass Bottle Blowers Association*. The Association's election was challenged because of its rule that eligibility for candidacy to office was conditioned on a candidate's attendance of 75 percent of the union meetings held in the two-year period preceding the last election.

Justification for such constitutional clauses have been that regular attendance at meetings is a sign of interest in union affairs, that it promotes democracy by making meetings more representative, and allows the aspiring candidate to become acquainted with the problems of the organization. Opponents have seen it as a device for disqualifying potential challengers to incumbents, for high attendance requirements may not be easily met. Thus it favors the incumbents who are compelled to be present at meetings in the normal fulfillment of their duties.

On the complaint of a member, the Department challenged the 1963 election of Local 153, Glass Bottle Blowers Association, on the ground that its requirement of attendance at 75 percent of the regular meetings in the two-year period since the last election was unreasonable. The District Court agreed, but refused to order a new election because the Secretary had failed to establish that the violation may have affected the outcome of the election.[21]

While the case was pending on appeal, the union held its 1965 election under the same restrictive rules which had been held unreasonable and in violation of Section 401 (e), LMRDA. As no complaint had been made by a member on the 1965 election, the District Court held, when it was challenged by the Secretary, that it had not been shown that the rule requiring a candidate to attend 75 percent of the meetings to qualify for office had affected the outcome of the election since no candidate had been "deterred or disqualified from being candidates by reason of application of said regulations." The decisions of the District Court in both 1963 and 1965 elections were appealed by the Secretary of Labor.

In December 1966, the Third Circuit held that the conduct of a regular election while a Title IV suit is pending renders the latter moot. It vacated the District Court's judgment on its merit, and also its 1966 order denying post-judgment relief for lack of a prerequisite complaint by a union member. The District Court dismissed the complaint as moot and any motion for post-judgment relief. To this decision, the Supreme Court granted *certiorari*.[22]

The issues before the Supreme Court were whether the suit by the Secretary had been mooted by the holding of a regular subsequent election by the union, and whether an unreasonable qualification for office might have affected the election, when 97 percent of the members of the local union were ineligible for candidacy, including one who had been nominated. In January 1968, the Supreme Court in a unanimous decision declared that a suit to set aside an election cannot be rendered moot

> by the happenstance intervention of an unsupervised election. The notion that the unlawfulness infecting the challenged election should be considered as washed away the following election disregards Congress' evident conclusion

that only a supervised election could offer assurance that the officers who achieved office as beneficiaries of violations of the Act would not by some means perpetuate their unlawful control in the succeeding election . . . Congress chose the alternative of a supervised election as the remedy for a Section 401 violation in the belief that the protective presence of a neutral Secretary of Labor would best prevent the unfairness in the first election from infecting directly or indirectly, the remedial election.[23]

The Supreme Court also believed that union members who were aware of the unlawful practices could not adequately protect their interests in an unsupervised election. It said that "the intervention of an election in which the outcome might be as much a product of unlawful circumstances as the challenged election cannot bring the secretary's action to a halt. Aborting the exclusive statutory remedy would immunize a proved violation from further attack and leave unvindicated the interests protected by 401. Title IV was not intended to be so readily frustrated."

Finally the court said: "The only assurance that the new officers do in fact hold office by reason of a truly fair and democratic vote is to do what the Act requires, rerun the election under the secretary's supervision."

The decision has held that whenever the Secretary shows that a section of 401 has been violated that may have affected the outcome of a challenged election, the fact that a union has conducted another unsupervised election does not deprive the Secretary of his right for an order voiding that election and directing another under his supervision. The case was remanded to the Appellate Court with instructions to rule on the merits of the Secretary's appeal. In December 1968, the Third Circuit affirmed the District Court's view that the attendance requirements were unreasonable, but reversed the trial court's decision that the imposition of an unreasonable qualification for office did not affect the outcome of the election. In June 1969, the District Court ordered the union to hold its 1969 vote under the

Secretary's supervision, and explicitly directed that attendance requirements should not be a qualification for eligibility in the supervised election.

The Supreme Court also dealt with another issue, whether the Secretary is able to expand his complaint beyond the charges raised by the member, if, upon investigation, he finds other violations which had not been listed in the member's complaint. Local 125, Laborers, Youngstown, Ohio, had held an election for local officers, in which the candidates for one of the offices were tied. A runoff election was held, and a member complained that members who were not in good standing were allowed to cast ballots. During the investigation, it was found that the same violation had occurred in the initial election.

Both of the elections were challenged by the Secretary and the scope of complaint issue arose, as it did in several other challenged elections. In the case of Local 125, the District Court dismissed the parts of the complaint challenging the general or first election on the ground that the Secretary's right to sue is predicated upon a complaint by a member who had exhausted his internal remedies.[24]

In the election held by Laborers' Local Union No. 125, the Department claimed, the constitution was violated when members in arrears in their dues and not in good standing were allowed to vote in two elections. The second election was the result of a tie vote for business agent which necessitated a runoff. While investigating a complaint against the runoff election, the Department discovered a number of violations in the original election.

It presented the evidence of violations in both the original and runoff elections and asked the United States District Court to void both elections because members not in continuous good standing had been allowed to vote. On June 14, the court dismissed the portions of the suit challenging the original election on the ground that the complaining member had contested only the runoff election and that Secretary's right to sue must be predicated upon a complaint from a member who had exhausted his internal remedies.[25] However, the court granted, on April 1,

1966, summary judgment to the Secretary and ruled that fifty-eight ineligible votes had been cast in the 1963 election and it was therefore void, as that number of votes could have affected the outcome of the election. A new election was ordered.

In accordance with the direction of the court, Local 125 held an election in June 1966. On December 15, 1966, the Sixth Circuit Court of Appeals held that the union's regularly held election in 1966 rendered the lawsuit moot. In order to prevent the District Court's decision, dismissing the Secretary's complaint dealing with the union's general election serving as a precedent, the court directed that this portion of the complaint be dismissed.[26] The Department sought review by the Supreme Court, and *certiorari* was granted to consider whether the Secretary's suit is mooted, if during its pendency the union holds another election, and whether the Secretary is limited in a Title IV action to the particular complaint made by the member and the particular contest challenged.

In a unanimous opinion, the Supreme Court upheld the views of the Secretary that a union may not moot a pending Title IV action by conducting an unsupervised election of officers.[27] The court also rejected

> the narrow construction adopted by the District Court . . . limiting the secretary's complaint solely to the allegations made in the union member's initial complaint. Such severe restriction upon the secretary's powers should not be read into the statute without a clear mandate from or congressional intent to that effect. Neither the language of the statute nor its legislative history provide such an indication; indeed, the indications are quite clearly to the contrary.
>
> First, it is most improbable that Congress deliberately settled exclusive enforcement jurisdiction on the secretary and granted him broad investigative power to discharge his responsibilities, yet intended the shape of the enforcement action to be immutably fixed by the artfulness of a layman's complaint which often must be based on incomplete information. The expertise and resources of the Labor Depart-

ment were surely meant to have a broader play. Second, to constrict the secretary would be inconsistent with his vital role, which we emphasize today in *Wirtz* v. *Local 125, etc.*, ante, in protecting the public interest bound up in Title IV. The Act was not designed merely to protect the right of a union member to run for office in a particular election. Title IV's special function in furthering several goals of the LMRDA is to insure free and democratic union elections, the regulation of the union electoral process enacted in the Title having been regarded as necessary protections of the public interest as well as of the rights and interests of union members. We can only conclude, therefore, that it would be anomalous to limit the reach of the secretary's cause of action by the specifics of the union member's complaint.

While not ruling on whether a member could appeal to the Secretary without exhausting his internal remedies, the court held that "on the facts of this case we think the secretary is entitled to maintain his action challenging the June 8 election, because respondent union had fair notice from the violation charged . . . in the runoff election that the same unlawful conduct also occurred at the earlier election." The court believed the union was under obligation to expand its inquiry beyond the specific challenge made by the complaining member. As the union had failed in its responsibility, the Secretary was entitled to direct relief with respect to the initial election.

The case was remanded to the Appellate Court with instructions to reverse the District Court's judgment of dismissal and directing further proceedings consistent with the Supreme Court's opinion. The action was settled by agreement that the union would conduct its 1969 election under the Secretary's supervision.

The Secretary's power to bring a member's complaint is, however, not unlimited. In the election in Local 6799, United Steelworkers of America, The District Court, Middle District, California, recognized the right of the Secretary to include in his complaint violations "disclosed by his investigation, even though said violations were not raised by the union member in his protest to the union, provided the Secretary gives the defendant a reasonable opportunity to correct the violations, prior to filing suit." On the main issue, the court found the three-year rule on attendance reasonable candidacy qualification under 401 (e) of LMRDA.[28] Furthermore, the court held that any member who wanted to comply with the rule could have done so by attending the necessary meetings, or through the liberal work excuse provision. Use of union facilities for the duplication of campaign material for the incumbent President and denying the service to other candidates was held *prima facie* violation of 401 (g) which could be cured only by rerunning the election for this office.

The Ninth Circuit affirmed the rerunning of the election, but denied the Secretary's right to litigate a violation that had not been included in the member's complaint.[29]

The Supreme Court granted review, and the decision by Mr. Justice Marshall found that the words "a violation" in Section 402 was "susceptible" to more than one meaning. It "might mean 'any violation whatever revealed by the investigation. . . .' In particular, they can be fairly read to mean, 'any of the violations raised by the union member during his internal union election protest.' "[30] Recognizing the Congressional desire "to remedy abuses in union elections without departing needlessly from the longstanding Congressional policy against unnecessary governmental interference," the decision held the requirement that a union member first seek redress for his election complaints within the union before appealing to the Secretary was designed "to avoid unnecessary governmental intervention."

The Supreme Court rejected the Secretary's view because it would reduce the exhaustion requirement to a nullity, for under the Secretary's view " 'exhaustion' would be accomplished given any sort of protest within the union, no matter how remote the complaint made there from the alleged violation later litigated. The obvious purpose of an exhaustion requirement is not met when the union, during 'exhaustion,' is given no notice of the defects to be cured . . .[31] To accept the petitioner's contention that a union member, who is aware of the facts underlying an alleged violation, need not first protest this violation to his union before complaining to the secretary would be needlessly to weaken union self-government. Plainly petitioner's approach slights the interest in protecting union self-government and is out of harmony with the Congressional purpose reflected in Section 402 (a)."[32]

The court was mindful of the possibility that complaints by union members will often be imprecise and based upon inadequate information. Such "deficiencies" should not "foreclose relief from election violations." Courts were urged to impose "a heavy burden on the union to show that it could not in any way discern that a member was complaining of the violation in question." However, "when a member is aware of the facts supporting an alleged violation, the member must, in some discernible fashion, indicate to his union his dissatisfaction with those facts if he is to meet the exhaustion requirement."[33]

The Secretary's right to raise issues not included in a member's complaint has not been impaired, but has been limited to violations which are not likely to be visible to members. In a suit by the Secretary against alleged violations by Local 734, Teamsters, the District Court of Northern Illinois held that "if the members presented an inartfully drawn protest to the union which can be said to cover several violations, the secretary may litigate other claims arguably covered by the protest when the union can be charged with knowledge thereof."[34]

As a result of the decision in the Steelworkers Local 6799 suit, the Secretary agreed to the dismissal of seven suits involving attendance as a qualification for office and the partial dismissal of three others.[35] It appears that the Secretary was seeking to reform union election procedure in accordance with his staff's views, rather than handle only those which members found burdensome.

The requirement of prior office holding for prospective candidates for some union offices was attacked by the Secretary in several suits. The theory behind such provisions is that members should have some experience (usually lower and less exacting) in handling union affairs before they are eligible for other offices.

In the Independent Office Employees Association, only the heads of the eight divisions, into which the union was organized, were eligible to the office of Treasurer. Only six of the heads of divisions (directors) could be elected to the offices of President, Vice-President, or Secretary. After a complaint had been filed by two members, the Secretary challenged the 1965 election on the ground that every member had not been given an opportunity to nominate, be a candidate, or vote for a candidate of his choice. The union agreed to the facts and entered no defense. The court found the rules unduly restrictive and directed a new election under nonrestrictive rules.[36] Prior to the holding of the next election, the organization amended its constitution, providing for the election of the officers by direct vote of the members.

A different result was reached in the challenge to the American Federation of Musicians, Local 174, New Orleans. The 1965 election was challenged, after a proper complaint, on the ground of the unreasonable eligibility requirement for President and Vice-President, the requirement being at least one year's service in an elective capacity during the immediate past five years of membership. The Secretary's calculations showed that only 5.7 percent of 839 members could qualify for the above offices.

The qualification was attacked as undemocratic, purposeless, and arbitrary. The union claimed that it had within its ranks a large variety of members and one who aspires to the top offices should have sufficient recent experience in another union post so as to be acquainted with the needs and problems of all members. The District Court rejected the Secretary's argument.[37] In the decision, the court said: "the requirement of prior office holding during the immediately past five years for the office of President and Vice-President is not an unreasonable qualification and is, therefore, not in violation of Section 401 (e) of the Act." While only twenty-seven members were eligible to run for the offices of President and Vice-President, all members in good standing, the court noted, could be candidates for the 17 other elective offices. The testimony on the requirements in other unions, although found relevant, did not, the court ruled, establish the unreasonableness of the qualifications in question. After the Supreme

Court's ruling in Hotel, Motel and Club Employees' case, an agreement between the Secretary and the local was reached that the prior office holding rule would not be enforced in future elections, and that the next regular election would be held under the Secretary's supervision.

The Secretary was successful in having the national election of the National Maritime Union (NMU) (the union holds no local elections) voided by the District Court, Southern New York, on the ground that the prior office holding requirement of four years as a national officer, branch agent, field patrolman, patrolman, was, as a condition of candidacy for the eight national offices, an unreasonable restriction on the right of members in good standing to become candidates for national office. Moreover, the court concluded that "prior office holding as a qualification for candidacy unduly lengthens the number of years which must elapse before a seaman can qualify for office."[38]

As for the other charges, the court held the rule that candidates must be self-nominated was restrictive. The other charges by the Secretary were rejected by the court as not being unreasonable. Limiting nominations to the month of February, requiring candidates to secure 100 endorsements by members, that endorsements be on official union form, that candidates appear in person before a port verification committee were ruled to be proper rules and not in violation of Section 401. The union rule that candidates for national office must be members for five years and have attained Group 1 shipping status (be employed as qualified seaman on NMU contract vessels for at least 200 days during each of the five years preceding nomination) was upheld as a reasonable one.

The Appellate Court in affirming the decision held that "if there were any doubt in the past as the unreasonableness of a qualification primarily responsible for rendering over 99 percent of a union's membership ineligible to hold voice, that doubt surely has been put to rest by the Supreme Court's opinion." The Appellate Court noted:

While we would hesitate to say that experience gained in one of the lower offices bears no relation to a candidate's ability to perform as a national officer, the Supreme Court quite clearly has pointed out that it is for the rank-and-file union member to distinguish qualified from unqualified candidates.

Having held that prior office holding and self-nomination were unreasonable and restrictive, the election was voided and a new one ordered under the Secretary's supervision. The election was held and the administration slate for eight national offices, fourteen port agents and fifty-nine patrolmen was chosen.

The reasonableness of prior office holding as a qualification for candidacy in a union election came before the Supreme Court in a suit involving Hotel, Motel and Club Employees Union Local No. 6. The disputed election was held in 1965, and after a complaint the Secretary brought suit to have the election invalidated. This local of about 27,000 members functioned in New York City, and it was organized on the basis of departments based on crafts or broad category of work, and districts based on geographic areas. The only exception was the club district in which all members employed in clubs were obliged to join.

The highest body was the assembly, elected from the districts—one delegate to each seventy-five members. Each district also elected a Vice-President as well as its complement of business agents. In the district elections, efforts are made to have various departments represented. The executive board is made up of the general officers and delegates of the assembly elected to this body. An administrative board made up of the general officers and the delegates to the New York Hotel and Motel Trades Council completes the official bodies. A member was eligible for candidacy in the assembly if he had one year of continuous good standing in the local immediately preceding nomination. Members who wished to be candidates for general office, Vice-President or business agent must have been a member of the assembly or executive board, served at least one term of prior service on the executive board, or belonged to the old shop Delegate Council.

The Secretary attacked the qualifications for general office and business agents as unreasonable and adduced evidence that such requirements were not common among other labor organizations. In a decision District Court Judge Inzer B. Wyatt held that any requirement of prior office holding to be eligible for union office would be unreasonable.[39] Citing the aim of Congress "to secure free and democratic union elections," the court noted that Congress provided "specifically and affirmatively that 'every member in good standing shall be eligible to be a candidate' and the only relevant exception was for 'reasonable qualifications.' "

The local's main argument—that the complexity of the problems required minimum experience in union affairs and that prior office holding was, therefore, a reasonable qualification —was rejected. Such a view was based on "the premise that the membership at large cannot be trusted properly to evaluate union experience in casting election ballots. The philosophy of a free democratic society, expressed in the Act, does not tolerate such a premise . . . The members of a union must have a free choice to give weight to experience, inexperience, or to other factors as they see fit." The judge refused to set the election aside, but enjoined the local from enforcing any prior office holding requirement in future elections. The judgment was appealed.

The Court of Appeals for the Second Circuit reversed the decision of the trial court and held that the prior office holding requirement was reasonable. The court stated that unions have been allowed to govern their own affairs, and that the LMRDA "prescribes only certain basic minima and leaves the area not covered by these minimum prescriptions to the decisions of the unions themselves." Furthermore, the Appellate Court did not think "that basic minimum principles of union democracy require that every union entrust the administration of its affairs to untrained and inexperienced rank and file members." Moreover, the one-year membership in the assembly was not unreasonable, as any member with one year's continuous good standing can qualify as a candidate.

The decision of the trial court, and later the Supreme Court decision, noted that it was difficult for a dissident member to be elected to the assembly. However, such difficulty was not because the qualification of one-year continuous good standing was onerous or unreasonable, but because of a lack of organized support. The judgment of the trial court was overruled and the injunction against holding the next election without prior office holding rule was set aside. The Secretary petitioned for *certiorari*, which was granted.

The questions raised in the appeal were: (1) Can the Secretary allege violations which have been disclosed in his investigation, but were not made in the member's complaint? (2) Is a union rule which severely restricts candidacy for office 'reasonable qualification' under the LMRDA? (3) May a qualification for office for candidacy "have affected the outcome of an election when it resulted in the disqualification of a number of nominees and rendered approximately 93 percent of the members ineligible to run for office?"

In a unanimous decision, with Mr. Justice Marshall taking no part, the Supreme Court reversed the Appellate Court and held that "Congress plainly did not intend that the authorization in 401 (e) of 'reasonable qualifications uniformly imposed' should be given a broad reach. Moreover, unduly restrictive candidacy qualifications can result in the abuses of entrenched leadership that the LMRDA was expressly enacted to curb. The check of democratic elections as a preventive measure is seriously impaired by candidacy qualifications which substantially deplete the ranks of those who might run in opposition to incumbents."

According to the court, a rule that disqualifies 93 percent of the members from running for office cannot be a reasonable one. The union defense that it was necessary to test the ability of rank and file members for office was rejected because the Congressional

model of democratic elections was political elections in this country, and these are not based on any such assumption. Rather, in those elections the assumption is that voters will exercise common sense and judgment in casting their ballots. Local 6 made no showing that citizens assumed to make discriminating judgments in public elections cannot be relied on to make such judgments when voting as union members.

On the question of the effect on the outcome of the election, the Supreme Court said:

> Nothing in them necessarily contradicts the logical inference that some or all of the disqualified candidates might have been elected had they been permitted to run. The defeat suffered by the few candidates allowed to run proves nothing about the performance by those who did not. . . . But since 93 percent of the membership was ineligible under the invalid bylaw, it is impossible to know that the election would not have attracted many more candidates but for the bylaw. In short, the considerations relied on by the court are pure conjecture, not evidence. We, therefore, conclude that the prima facie case established by the violation was not met by evidence which supports the District Court's finding that the violation did not affect the result.

The Supreme Court did not pass on the question of whether the Secretary may allege violations not stated in the member's complaint. The case was remanded, and the judgment of the Appellate Court reversed. On September 5, 1968, the District Court ordered a new election under the Secretary's supervision and ordered that those elected should serve the remainder of the term they would have served if they had been elected in the election of May 16, 1968. The orders were carried out.

On the basis of the decision in Local 6, the District Court of Northern District of Ohio, Eastern division, ruled that limitation of office holding to members of the parent body of Local 18, Operating Engineers, was unduly restrictive within the meaning of Section 401 (e).[40] Similar to a number of other local unions of the International Union of Operating Engineers, Local 18 was made up of a parent body and several branches. Members of the parent body received no wage benefits greater than members of the branches. Wages were determined by the equipment operated or function performed. Members of the parent body had to be able to operate one or more types of equipment within the jurisdiction of Local 18 and pay a higher initiation fee than required of members of branches. However, the members of the branches were full members of the union, with the exception that they cannot be officers. They were nevertheless permanent members of the union.

Relying upon the decision in *Local 6*, the court said:

> case has severely circumscribed a union's power to use this kind of rule as a qualification for candidacy. Without regard to whether a given leadership is malevolent or benevolent, the court has suggested that qualifications which assume that rank and file members are unable to distinguish qualified from unqualified candidates are unreasonable. The Supreme Court emphasized that the proper model for union officer elections is Congressional elections in which the assumption is that the voters will exercise common sense in judgment in casting their ballots. Of course, the facts in the Local 6 case are arguably distinguishable. Local 6 dealt with a "prior office" requirement; and the union in that case had inconsistently administered its own rule. But the broad language and implication of the High Court would indicate the same result here, where the union's rule admittedly is not directly related to the candidate's ability to serve as an officer, but rather relates to motivation.

The Sixth Circuit affirmed the decision that restricting office-holding to the members of the parent local was "manifestly unreasonable."[41] The court found the union's argument "misplaced."

> The determinative question is not whether the parent local's package of benefits is reasonably priced, but whether the right to run for union office may be packaged and sold. . . . We hold that it is unreasonable to require that all candidates for union office purchase union sponsored life insurance

and the right to a paid-up union membership as a prerequisite to eligibility to hold office.

The 1965 election, which had been challenged, was set aside, and the parties were directed to confer on planning future elections in accord with the opinion of the court. After the Supreme Court denied *certiorari*, the International Union of Operating Engineers, in October 1971, eliminated the restrictions upon office holding and made members of branches eligible to serve as officers.

The LMWP also intervened in similar cases, at the request of members who had been denied the opportunity to run for office as a result of improper expulsion from the union.

In Local No. 34, located in Peoria, Illinois, with a membership of about 365, four dissidents issued a leaflet announcing their intention to run for office. Charges were preferred against them and after being tried and found guilty of slander, they were barred from attending meetings of the union for three years and running for office. Their penalties were reduced to two years by the district Vice-President, and the decision was subsequently upheld by the International Executive Council.

The expelled continued their membership by paying their regular dues, and when they were denied the right to participate in the elections, they appealed to the Department of Labor. The Bureau challenged the election on the ground that four members in good standing had been denied the right to nominate and to vote for candidates of their choice. An agreement was reached that the four would be allowed to take part in the 1967 election for officers. The incumbents won twelve out of the thirteen offices.[42]

Under similar circumstances, the LMWP challenged the election in Local 611, IBEW, Albuquerque, New Mexico. In 1962, Charles J. Stein, a candidate for business-manager/financial-secretary, distributed leaflets critical of the union officers. He was charged with defaming their character, found guilty and expelled. His expulsion was reduced to a suspension from the union for five years, but, when he sought to attend union meetings, he was again expelled. He tried to challenge the union election, but, as an expelled member, he had no standing. He filed a Title I suit, and the United States District Court for New Mexico voided the expulsion on the ground that the issuance of leaflets by a union member on union business was protected. The court also restored his membership to the time of expulsion.

Stein now invoked his appeal against the election of 1964 within the union, and when it was rejected he carried his petition to the LMWP. His complaint was accepted on the ground that the union had been put on notice that he would challenge the election, once he regained membership. As long as his expulsion was effective, Stein was unable to get relief through the LMWP. However, once reinstated, his complaint was valid and actionable. An agreement was reached with the union that Stein would be allowed on the ballot in the election of 1966. His effort to intervene in the suit was rejected by Tenth Circuit Court of Appeals.[43] In the supervised election, Stein was a candidate for business manager. He was defeated by a vote of 557 to 178.

By such activity, the Department adds another protection for dissidents penalized for activity within the union. Wrongful suspension or expulsion does not insulate such members from the political life of the union in the sense that they lose their rights to participate because of their improper exclusion. These rights can be asserted once they have been reinstated which means that it is not possible for an incumbent to rid himself of an opponent by utilizing the disciplinary machinery of the organization.

A union could not disqualify a candidate from the ballot on the ground that he could not meet the bonding requirement of the LMRDA.[44] A prospective candidate for financial secretary-business representative in Carpenters' Local 559 was disqualified because he had been expelled from membership in Iron Workers Local 595, in 1953, and removed as Secretary-Treasurer. After his expulsion the candidate sought to control the local and its assets. With the approval of the membership, he transferred $30,000 to Iron Workers Incorporated. He was compelled to return the funds to the International.[45] Then he joined Carpenters' Local 559, where he sought office. He was ruled off the ballot by the First Vice-President of the International because he was presumably unable to secure a bond as required by Section 502 (a) of LMRDA. He appealed to the Secretary on the ground that his disqualification violated Section 401 (e). The union refused to modify its ruling; a suit to overturn the 1963 and 1965 elections, in which Sanders, the prospective candidate, was disqualified, was initiated.

The court found that the disqualification was in violation of Section 401 (e) and might have affected the outcome of the election. A determination that a candidate is not bondable, said the court, is "not a valid ground under Section 401 (e) of the Act for denying the right of such member to be a candidate for office, or for excluding or omitting his name from the ballot when he was duly nominated for office." The judge noted that the requirement that certain officers be bonded is

> not a valid condition precedent to the right of a member in good standing of a labor union to be a candidate for office. In the absence of unusual circumstances, not established in this case, the question of the bondability of a union member cannot be raised upon his nomination as a candidate for office or to question his eligibility as a candidate, but can only arise upon his election to an office requiring bonding under Section 502 of the Act.[46]

The 1963 and 1965 elections were set aside, and a new one ordered under the Secretary's supervision. The election was held, and Sanders was a candidate. He was defeated for office.

The efforts of the Secretary to invalidate the election in Local Union 582, Plumbers, because the local had not provided for absentee ballots failed. The number of absentees from the election was relatively large, but the court was of the opinion, "their numbers *per se* would not make the election procedures actually employed incompatible with democratic procedures."

The local's jurisdiction covers Orange County, California. It has 1,176 members. Two-thirds of the number voted in the election. In rejecting the petition of the Secretary, the District Court noted that absentee voting is not to be determined on the

basis of whether it is more convenient for some people to vote
"but whether the court finds the actual arrangements so lacking
in democratic principles and so unfair, in denying a reasonable
opportunity to vote to a significant number of members, that the
election must be voided. The arrangement employed must be
held to be beyond the permissible discretion of the union. . . . The
plaintiff has not met the burden in the instant case."[47]

This case is an example of the LMWP seeking to impose voting
practices on labor organizations. A union cannot monitor absentee ballots as well as the government, nor can it prosecute for
fraud. The two-thirds of the members voting should be used as a
good example, rather than a bad one. If the members of the
LMWP administering this phase of the law would take notes, they
would find that many local and gubernatorial elections fail to
produce that percentage of voters, and that the voting for Boards
of Education and bond issues seldom attains as high a percentage
of votes.

A suit by Local 1337, International Brotherhood of Electrical
Workers (IBEW), to compel the Secretary of Labor to certify the
results of an election held under the LMWP supervision was
successful, and the Secretary was ordered to certify the results.

The case had its origin in the expulsion of a member of Local
1337, for bringing suit against the union under 501 (b). After his
reinstatement in the local at the orders of the court, he complained that he had been denied the right to be a candidate for
office in the local election. It was agreed that new elections would
be held, under the Secretary's supervision. After the elections,
the Department refused to certify the results because the limited
election facilities resulted in long waiting periods for prospective
voters, many of whom had to remain outside in inclement
weather. Some of the voters were harassed, and the police had to
be summoned to preserve order. The request of the Secretary
was rejected by the court. The charges, in view of the court, were
vague and the evidence inconclusive. Moreover, the court ruled
the statute placed "a mandatory duty on the Secretary to certify
the election which it supervised, and furthermore, such acts of

the secretary in this case were arbitrary and prejudicial to the rights of the union."[48]

The overwhelming majority of the complaints to the Secretary concern local unions. Occasionally, charges have been presented against an intermediate body and against International Unions less frequently. In the charges against the National Maritime Union of America, the United States District Court of Southern New York voided the election and ordered another. In a dispute involving the vote in the 1964 election in the International Union of Electrical, Radio and Machine Workers, the attempt of the supporters of the incumbent President to steal the election was frustrated by the intervention of the Secretary of Labor, acting under Section 601 which empowers him to investigate in order to determine violations of the act. The United States District Court of the District of Columbia had refused to intervene because of lack of jurisdiction,[49] and the Board of Trustees, charged with counting the ballots, had announced that James Carey, the incumbent, had been elected by 2,193 votes. Despite the obstruction by the incumbent officers, the Secretary was able to obtain access to the ballots, which, when counted by members of the Department of Labor, showed that Paul Jennings, the opposition candidate, had been elected by a majority of 23,316 votes. It is doubtful if the rightfully elected candidate could have taken office without the support of the Department of Labor acting through the LMWP.

Intervention in the 1964 election in the International Typographical Union followed a complaint by the defeated candidate for Vice-President, whose challenge to the election had been rejected by the union's Executive Council. Political activity is well established within this organization, and two political parties, the Progressive and the Independent, have functioned for more than fifty years. The political parties function under the union constitution, and each must file financial statements with the union's secretary, showing the amounts received and expended for political purposes in the last two years. None but members may donate for political purposes.[50]

The election was an unusually bitter one, and the returns were contested by the minority. After the appeal had been rejected by the union tribunal, a complaint was made to the Secretary of Labor, charging a number of irregularities. When the union was informed of the investigation by the Department, it instructed its locals to cooperate, but objected when the Department insisted that the records of the Progressive Party be made available.[51] The union demurred, and claimed that the party was not part of the union, but in the end, the union and Progressive Party made their records available to the Department.[52]

In June 1965, the Department informed the head of the union that the organization had failed to provide adequate safeguards for the 1964 election. A number of other violations were noted. The charges were rejected by the union, but the charges may demonstrate the difficulty of running an election in reasonably large unions without avoiding some violations of LMRDA. The Typographical Union has consistently practiced democracy. If there is virtue in opposition tickets, it has achieved it in a larger measure than any other labor organization. Yet flaws were found in its conduct of the balloting.

A less controversial role was played by the Department in the hotly contested national election in the Steelworkers Union in 1964-1965. There were two tickets in the field, the opposition candidate for President being the Secretary-Treasurer I.W. Abel. Headquarters were opened by each slate and candidates campaigned throughout all of the districts in which the union had members. Votes were cast at the local unions and were sent to the tellers after they were tabulated. At the joint request of the parties, the Secretary of Labor appointed two observers for the counting. Of the over 607,000 votes, Abel was elected by more than 10,000. His running mates received greater majorities—the Abel candidate for Vice-President won by more than 21,000, and the candidate for Secretary-Treasurer, by almost 47,000. In this election, the alertness of the Department of Labor and its making observers available were factors in making possible the peaceful transition.

The 1968 election of the Retail Clerks International Association, and the 1969 election in the United Mine Workers of America were also challenged. The contest in the Retail Clerks followed an announcement of President James A. Suffridge that he would not be a candidate for another term. Suffridge had served as President for 25 years, and during his tenure the membership had grown from 60,000 to more than ten times that number.

Suffridge, in the announcement of his retirement, had recommended a full slate of candidates, which was to be challenged by an opposition, the Committee for the Reformation, Revitalization and Reconstruction of the Retail Clerks International Association. The opposition was led by two Vice-Presidents and included a number of local leaders. The opposition also published an eighteen-point program, part of which had to do with internal reform and strengthening of internal democracy. As soon as it was announced that the administration slate had won, the results were challenged by the Committee for a Democratic Election. The union appellate procedures rejected the appeal, and a complaint was made to the Secretary. The investigation by the Department "did not disclose sufficient evidence to establish that two announced candidates . . . were coerced into withdrawing therefrom and supporting the Administration slate, as alleged in the complaint."[53]

The investigation revealed violations by both parties, but, in the opinion of the Department of Labor, the violations had not affected the outcome of the election. Suit to compel the Secretary to institute an action against the Retail Clerks was started by the dissidents in the United States District Court for the District of Columbia. District Judge Gesell questioned the decision of the Secretary that he was "obliged automatically to conclude that the serious irregularities found did not affect the outcome of the election."[54] He held, furthermore, that the complainants had a "judicially enforceable right to demand that the secretary exercise his discretionary authority in a manner consistent with the requirements of the act and not capriciously." The court indicated it would not substitute its judgment for the Secretary's, but held that the Secretary must provide the petitioners "with an adequate written statement for his reasons for non-intervention."

Upon review of the findings, the Department reaffirmed its earlier decision that the evidence was not sufficient to support the allegations that violations disclosed may have affected the outcome of the 1968 election. The court, upon reconsideration, noted that "the secretary has made a determination that he will not proceed and he has made that in the exercise of his discretion, reached after obviously careful investigation. If, as the court concludes, there is a rational and defensible basis for his determination, then that should be an end of this matter, for it is not the function of the court to determine whether or not the case should be brought or what its outcome would be."[55] The court held "as a matter of law that the secretary is not required to sue to set aside the election whenever the proofs before him suggest the suit might not be successful. There remains in him a degree of discretion to select cases and it is his subjective judgment as to the probable outcome of the litigation that must control. Accordingly, it would appear that the appropriate action to take in this case is to grant the secretary's motion to dismiss."

The disputed 1969 election in the United Mine Workers of America attracted the greatest national interest of any union contest and led to severe criticism of the Secretary of Labor and the LMWP for not intervening. For the first time since 1926, the incumbent officers were challenged by opposition candidates. Joseph Yablonski, the head of the union's Labor Non-Partisan League, announced his candidacy for President, and Elmer Brown was on the opposition ticket for Vice-President.

The first complaints were made to the Secretary during the nomination period by the attorney for Yablonski, who charged numerous violations of the LMRDA election requirements and asked for an "immediate investigation." Secretary of Labor George P. Shultz replied that it was "the Department of Labor's long-established policy not to undertake investigations of this kind without having a valid complaint under Section 402 (a) after an election has been completed." He said, further:

the Department of Labor, as a matter of policy, has never initiated or conducted an investigation election prior to the actual conduct of the election. In those very few situations where investigations have been conducted prior to the receipt of a valid complaint under Section 402 (a), the Department acted only after the election had been completed or a request for intervention had been received from the parties involved.[56]

During the campaign, Yablonski accused the Mine Workers, W. A. (Tony) Boyle and the editor of the *United Mine Workers Journal* of discriminating against him in connection with his campaign for union Presidency. The court found that the membership lists were being used against Yablonski in violation of Section 401 (c). The United States Court of Appeals upheld the order against the discrimination.

The District Court found that the journal of the union had been used to promote Boyle's candidacy. It cited the excessive coverage given to Boyle and the absence of Yablonski's name from its pages. However, the court stated:

> The fact is that, in the context of a bitterly contested election, the contents and emphasis of a union periodical such as the *Journal* must be judged in the light of the Landrum-Griffin Act. It should be understood that this court is not attempting to tell the Journal what it can and what it cannot print; this would violate the First Amendment and is beyond our statutory authority. Irrespective of the question of remedy, it is our conclusion that the conduct of defendants is in violation of Section 401 (c) of the LMRDA and that plaintiff has made a showing that he is likely to prevail on the merits.

The court refused to order the journal to give Yablonski sufficient space to present his views so as to offset the excessive presentations previously allowed Boyle. The court believed that such action was beyond the court's statutory authority and would involve serious constitutional questions under the First Amendment.

However, the court ruled that the burden is on the defendants to avoid misuse of the membership list and enjoined the defendants from discriminating in the use of them.[57] Yablonski filed several other suits. In one he sought to have the editor of the *United Mine Workers Journal* held in contempt, but the court ruled "plaintiff has not produced sufficient evidence to show that the November 1, 1969 issue of the *Journal* is ·or was a campaign instrument in favor of defendant Boyle which was distributed to the union membership in violation of this court's order that defendant refrain from discrimination in the use of UMWA membership lists."[58]

Yablonski, who was head of Labor's Non-Partisan League, was removed from his post by Boyle. He then sued for reinstatement, and the court ordered his reinstatement since his removal was in violation of Section 101 (a) (1) and Section 401 (e).[59] There were also suits over the distribution of mail at the candidate's expense, which Yablonski claimed the union had refused to do. The court directed that the union comply with the requests.[60]

Both Yablonski and W. A. (Tony) Boyle received sufficient endorsements to go on the ballot. In the meantime, the LMWP initiated an investigation which showed extensive misuse of the finances of the organization. A federal grand jury in Washington also launched an investigation of the use of funds collected illegally from members to finance the election campaign of Boyle and his associates. The election was conducted on December 9, 1969, and approximately 126,000 members cast their ballots in the election. Boyle defeated Yablonski by a vote of about two to one. Yablonski charged numerous violations including vote stealing, and requested the Department to impound the ballots. The Secretary refused to do so.

In explaining the reasons for the rejection, W. J. Usery, Assistant Secretary of Labor, said that the

impounding of ballots and other records would be an extraordinary action and justified only in the event of convincing evidence that the integrity of the ballots or records were directly threatened. The information you submitted and the argument you presented have been very carefully considered by appropriate officials within the Department and have been reviewed by the secretary. After such consideration, the secretary has determined that there is insufficient evidence for impounding the ballots and records by the Department of Labor at this time.[61]

Yablonski and his wife and daughter were murdered in their home on January 5, 1970. Soon thereafter, the United Mine Workers of America waived the requirement that a member must exhaust his union remedies before filing an appeal with the secretary, and asked for an investigation of the election. It "was the most intensive and widespread . . . ever undertaken by the LMWP, with more than 43,000 man-hours devoted to the case." More than 200 investigators held about 4,400 interviews, 4,200 with UMWA officials and the remaining 200 "with volunteer observers, bank officials, and radio TV stations, newspapers, advertising, and other officials. The investigation covered 882 of the 1,260 locals whose votes were counted and 10 of 28 whose votes were not counted."[62]

On March 5, 1970, the Department of Labor brought suit against the United Mine Workers and also sought to enjoin the union from inadequate record keeping. Numerous violations of Title IV were charged.

During the suit Miners for Democracy sought through its chairman, Michael Trbovich, who had filed the original complaint, to intervene as a party to the law suit. Refused by the district and appellate courts, the United States Supreme Court granted *certiorari*. The court reversed the decisions below and held that a union member who had filed an initial election complaint with the Secretary could intervene in the Secretary's subsequent suit challenging the election. However, such intervention is limited to the claims of illegality presented in the Secretary's complaint but the limitation does not apply to the proposed terms of any new election the District Court may order. Congress intended to prevent "members from pressing claims not thought meritorious by the secretary, and from litigating in forums or at times different from those chosen by the secretary. Only if intervention would frustrate either of these objectives can the statute fairly be read to prohibit intervention as well as initiation of suits by members."[63]

Intervention is permitted to assist the Secretary in the presentation of his case, a limitation in harmony with the Congressional intent to deny union members to institute private suits in union election disputes.

On May 1, 1972, District Judge Bryant found the violations alleged in the Secretary's complaint had been established. Basing himself on the Supreme Court's decision in *Wirtz* v. *Hotel Employees*, 391 U.S. 492 (1968), he concluded that the violations may have affected the outcome of the election. He found the union had failed to elect its officers by secret ballot, failed to provide adequate safeguards, denied candidates an opportunity to circulate their literature, misused the union publication for advancing the candidacy of the incumbents, denied the opposition information on polling places. The court also held that the removal of Yablonski as director of Labor's Non-Partisan League was a clear violation of 401 (e), which forbade reprisals against political opponents.

A new election was ordered under the supervision of the Secretary for officers who would be installed not later than January 15, 1973. In addition, the Secretary was to oversee the union's financial transactions at the international, district, subdistrict and local levels, and the union granted the right to station observers at all the above places.[64] It was the first time the national election of a union was upset, and the drastic restrictions placed upon organization were without precedent, except for the monitors appointed to supervise the Teamsters' Union.

The dissidents waited their time, and by May 30, 1972, the Miners for Democracy had met in Wheeling, West Virginia, and nominated a slate of candidates headed by A. R. Miller, who was nominated for President. The administration renominated

Boyle, and candidates for other national posts. The candidates objected to some of the government rules. The final results were 46,350 for Boyle to 58,732 for Miller. The rest of the ticket of Miners for Democracy was also elected. It was the first time since the defeat of Thomas L. Lewis some sixty years before that the coal miners had ousted an incumbent from national office. The transition to the new administration was uneventful, with Boyle and his staff cooperating fully with the newly elected officers.

The LMWP also succeeded in having the election of District 50, Allied Technical Workers, set aside. Pursuant to a complaint, the agency investigated 850 local unions in thirty-eight regions. The investigation was a response to a complaint by a defeated candidate for President, who had advised merger with the Steelworkers, and a Vice-President who favored joining the International Association of Machinists. District 50 agreed to hold a convention and elect delegates and officers under the Secretary's supervision. The convention met and voted to merge with the Steelworkers.[65]

Title IV has had a significant effect upon the electoral processes of the organizations of labor. It has compelled many of the unions to revise their rules governing elections, and to give more attention to the protests coming from the membership. Even more important is the effect that Title I has had on the rights of union members to organize oppositions, to issue leaflets and other kinds of literature and to circulate it among the members, without the interference of the union and its officers.

Although an incumbent has an inevitable advantage in running for reelection because of his broad acquaintance with the members, he cannot use the publications of the union nor other resources of the organization for the promotion of his candidacy. The requirement of notice and a secret ballot are also helpful to those who are challenging incumbents. As important as these changes are, the elimination of qualification provisions which are difficult for many members to meet is another change which increases the opportunities for members to run for office. The decisions of the Secretary of Labor and the courts have eliminated obstacles to candidacy and have made possible challenges which could not have taken place prior to the enactment of the reform legislation.

Although the challenges to national officers have not been numerous, they have measurably increased. It is not likely that the heads of the Steelworkers, the Mine Workers, the Bricklayers and several others would have been challenged without such a law. The Retail Clerks do not fall into this group because the incumbent had retired, and it is doubtful if he would have been challenged had he run for reelection. What makes it possible to challenge an incumbent is the ability for the opposition to organize and mount a campaign without interference or reprisals.

The role of the Secretary and the Office of Labor-Management and Welfare-Pension Reports has been important in that these agents are charged with protecting the electoral rights of union members. The LMWP, which is the permanent enforcement agency, has performed a difficult task conscientiously. The attacks that have been made upon it are not deserved, and usually they emanate from attorneys of one of the parties or from zealous advocates who believe that the law should deny due process to the faction they oppose. Any examination of the record will show that the Office of Labor-Management and Welfare-Pension Reports has sought to do a difficult job with concern for the rights of all parties.

14

Fiduciary Responsibilities of Officers of Labor Organizations

It was common knowledge that some union officers were using the funds of their organization for private gain. It had also been established in earlier investigations that some labor leaders were engaging in conflicts of interest when they, directly or through intermediaries, sold goods to employers with whom they were doing business. Such activities, while unethical, were not illegal and could not be restrained.[1]

The McClellan Committee greatly added to knowledge in this area. It showed that thousands of dollars had been used by officers of unions for private investment. Even though these interest free loans were unauthorized, the venal officer was only obligated to return the principal. It was also shown that salaries were raised without approval of the membership or the authorized official bodies of the organization, that expenses were sometimes grossly padded, and that union officers were guilty of conflicts of interest by engaging in business deals with employers

239

of their members. Despite the substantial information gathered by the McClellan Committee on these questions, the Kennedy-Ives bill did not contain provisions for safeguarding union funds, an omission noted by Senator Smith, of New Jersey. He presented an amendment to place those who are responsible for union funds in the position of fiduciaries.[2]

The amendment precipitated a lengthy debate, with Senators Kennedy, Morse and Ervin leading the opposition. In their view, the matter had already been handled by the states and the definition of a fiduciary, with respect to union funds, might be difficult. When Congress renewed consideration of labor reform legislation in 1959 (the Kennedy-Ives bill had failed to pass), it had the report of the McClellan Committee that as union monies are a trust held for the benefit of the members by the officers, "attention should be given to placing certain restrictions on the use of these funds, such as are now imposed on banks and other institutions which act as repositories and administrators for trust funds."[3]

After considerable debate, the Senate adopted proposals for protecting the funds of unions against misuse. The Senate provisions were strengthened in the House, and Congressman Boling, who reported the committee measure, said: "Our committee on Education and Labor, made a major contribution by adding the language now found in Section 501 (a) which language is not in the Senate bill. We wrote a comprehensive statement of the fiduciary duties of union officers. The assets of a labor union belong to the members. In collective bargaining, and the conducting of other business, union officers must place their fiduciary obligations ahead of their personal interest."[4]

It was his view that the failure to recognize the above principles was at the bottom of the evils uncovered by the McClellan Committee. "Therefore, the principle of fiduciary responsibility is violated whenever a union officer acquires an interest in a business concern with which he engages in collective bargaining as the employee representative. The principle has been violated when a relatively few union officers have placed their union's insurance with agencies which paid them money as individuals in return for the favor."

The purpose of this legislation was to prevent the use of the funds of a labor organization for private purposes, and also eliminate, by making them illegal, unauthorized increases in salary or other benefits. As noted above, a union officer who handles the funds of the organization occupies the position of a "fiduciary," similar to other persons who are exercising duties on behalf of others.

Responsibility of a Union Officer

Section 501 (a) defines the duties and responsibilities of union officers. It decrees:

> The officers, agents, shop stewards, and other representatives of a labor organization occupy positions of trust in relation to such organization and its members as a group. It is, therefore, the duty of each such person, taking into account the special problems and functions of a labor organization, to hold its money and property solely for the benefit of the organization and its members and to manage, invest, and expend the same in accordance with its constitution and bylaws and any resolutions of the governing bodies adopted thereunder, to refrain from dealing with such organization as an adverse party or in behalf of an adverse party in any matter connected with his duties and from holding or acquiring any pecuniary or personal interest which conflicts with the interests of such organizations, and to account to the organization for any profit received by him in whatever capacity in connection with transactions conducted by him or under his direction on behalf of the organization. A general exculpatory provision in the constitution and bylaws of such a labor organization or a general exculpatory resolution of a governing body to relieve such person of liability for breach

of the duties declared by this section shall be void as against public policy.

The prohibitions for engaging in business were designed, as indicated, to eliminate the practice of union officers engaging in business which provides goods or services to employers with whom they negotiate on behalf of the members, splitting commissions with brokers handling union pension funds or health and welfare programs, or setting up a business for this purpose. The use of union funds for private investment by a union officer is another practice which this provision sought to eliminate. The McClellan Committee discovered that the head of the Western Conference of Teamsters had borrowed funds for private use from the organization which he headed, and the head of the union was guilty of the same practice. It can be assumed that these were not the only instances. In addition, the provisions sought to eliminate unauthorized increases in payments of salaries or allowances to union officials.

Congress also established a mechanism through which a union member, if he believes that a violation of fiduciary responsibility has occurred, can bring suit for an accounting. At the same time, Congress sought to prevent harassment of union officers by false and unsubstantial charges and claims by discontented or politically ambitious members.

Section 501 (b) states:

When any officer, agent, shop steward, or representative of any labor organization is alleged to have violated the duties declared in subsection (a) and the labor organization or its governing board or officers refuse or fail to sue or recover damages or secure an accounting or other appropriate relief within a reasonable time after being requested to do so by any member of the labor organization, such member may sue such officer, agent, shop steward, or representative in any district court of the United States or in any State court of competent jurisdiction to recover damages or secure an accounting or other appropriate relief for the benefit of the labor organization. No such proceeding shall be brought except upon leave of the court obtained upon verified application and for good cause shown, which application may be made ex parte. The trial judge may allot a reasonable part of the recovery in any action under this subsection to pay the fees of counsel prosecuting the suit at the instance of the member of the labor organization and to compensate such member for any expenses necessarily paid or incurred by him in connection with the litigation.[5]

Responding to the petitions of members of the unions involved, the courts have interpreted Title V as prohibiting a union from paying counsel fees to defend union officers charged with "breaching their fiduciary duty by conspiring to misappropriate union funds." In a case involving the same issue, the Appellate Court of the District of Columbia said: "The treasury of the union is not at the disposal of its officers to bear the cost of their defense against charges of fraudulently depriving the members of their rights as members." Union funds were not available to defend officers charged with wrongdoing, which if true, "would be seriously detrimental to the union and its membership."[6]

This principle was applied in a suit of a group of members of Local 107, Teamsters' Union, Philadelphia. Raymond Cohen and several other officers had been charged with misuse of funds and making sweetheart agreements with favorite employers. They were indicted and brought to trial, and the local union authorized the payment of counsel fees and other expenses required by the defense. The District Court agreed that the payments in behalf of Cohen and his associates were illegal. Cohen appealed. The Appellate Court held that the payments in behalf of a union officer charged with misuse of union funds was "inconsistent with the aims and purposes of the Labor-Management Reporting and Disclosure Act and beyond the powers of the local."[7]

On the ground that there would be a conflict of interest, the federal courts ruled that the attorney for the union could not

represent two officers of Local 70, Bartenders of New York and
Queens counties, who were charged with diverting union welfare
funds to their private use.[8]

The use of union funds to pay the salaries of two port patrolmen by the National Union of Masters, Mates and Pilots, who, it
was alleged, had not been properly appointed,[9] was successfully
contested. One of the locals brought a Title 501 suit, and the
argument of the International Union that the Title was not
intended to be used for such a purpose was rejected by the
courts.

The above suit was only one of a number in which the intervention of the courts was sought by union members against officers
whom they believed guilty of actions harmful to the organization.
Some of the suits raised the question of the scope of Title V. Was it
limited in its application to the use of money and property of the
organization, or did it have wider scope in the sense that other
issues and activities of labor unions might be scrutinized and
adjudicated? In *Nelson* v. *Johnson*, the Appellate Court of the
Eighth Circuit was of the opinion that "Section 501 imposes
fiduciary responsibility in its broadest application and is not con-
fined to union officials only in their handling of money and
property affairs."

The suit was an outgrowth of a controversy within the
Brotherhood of Painters during which Nelson was expelled and
his expulsion voided by the United States District Court.[10] The
charges against Nelson were then dismissed by a union trial
board, and the recommendation by the trial board, which was
approved by a membership vote, was that attorney's fees and
expenses of both sides be paid by the local. The local officers
refused to obey the part of the mandate requiring the payment of
Nelson's counsel fees and expenses. Its position was supported by
the International Union.

In the view of the Appellate Court, "refusal to pay appellees'
attorney's fees and related expenses as duly authorized by a
majority vote of the local members constituted a violation of
appellants' fiduciary responsibility within the meaning of Title V
of the Landrum-Griffin Act—*independent of any action by the Inter-*

national Union." (italics in decision) The International had opposed the payment as well as the local officers. It was the view of the court that the local officers had solicited the support of the International. However, the restraint upon the kind of payments that can be made by local unions is widespread and has been incorporated into union constitutions and by-laws as a protection against financial mismanagement and misuse of funds. There are examples of local unions making donations for a variety of causes, for personal purposes, and for the payment to lawyers and others for services the locals were not authorized to purchase. It may be that the officers solicited the support of the International, but, if such payments were forbidden, they were obligated to inform the International of the decision of the local membership.

The decision also indicated that failure to allow payment of the dissidents' legal fees "would discourage resort to the courts by union members to establish their Title I rights," and the same view was taken with regard to the directive of the International. However, members charging violations of Title I rights have not generally been awarded attorney's fees.[11] Moreover, they frequently could not gain support of the local union in their efforts. Even if that support were usually obtained, it would by no means overcome the long-held objection to giving the local union free reign in the disposal of its finances. The issue is clearly set forth in a trusteeship case involving the International Association of Machinists and one of its local unions in St. Louis, Missouri.[12] The local hired an attorney for aid in a dispute with the district of the union and also with the International. In addition, the attorney was authorized by the local to draw up a program for future activity. His bill for fees and expenses for one year came to more than $60,000, and the insistence of the International Union that the bill not be paid was one of the precipitating causes for the effort of the local to withdraw from the Machinists' Union. It seems to be, irrespective of the merits of *Nelson* v. *Johnson*, that the view taken by the Appellate Court was narrow and did not recognize that local dominance in such matters is not to the larger interest of the organization.

A more narrow view of the meaning of Section 501 was taken in the case involving the Musicians Union, Local 802. The dispute was over the method to be used in the election of officers, the administration favoring a mail referendum ballot, and the dissidents, personal voting. Among the sections cited by the dissidents in support of their position was 501 (a). Rejecting this view, the Court of Appeals Second Circuit said: "It is equally clear that Section 501 of the LMRDA has no application to the present controversy. A simple reading of that section shows that it applies to fiduciary responsibility with respect to the money and property of the union and that it is not a catch-all provision under which union officials can be sued on any ground of misconduct which plaintiffs choose to charge them."[13] Moreover, the court noted:

> The provisions of the LMRDA were not intended by Congress to constitute an invitation to the courts to intervene at will in the internal affairs of unions. Courts have no special experience in the operation of unions which could justify a broad power to interfere. The internal operations of unions are to be left to the officials chosen by the members to manage those operations except in the very limited instances expressly provided by the Act. The conviction of some judges that they are better able to administer a union's affairs than the elected officials is without foundation.

The request to a District Court to invalidate the minimum wage provisions promulgated by the International Executive Board for traveling orchestras, as violative of Section 501, was also rejected, that: "jurisdiction under Section 501 (a) requires a breach of a fiduciary obligation with respect to the money or property of a union and that complaints which do not allege such a breach by union officials are insufficient in law."[14]

As noted above, a member of a union, before filing a request with a competent court for permission to sue, must request the officers of the organization to institute recovery for funds and must show the court good cause for the request. Leave to sue is denied upon failure of a verified application and a showing of good cause.[15] An aggrieved or complaining member must first request the union to sue, to recover funds or secure an accounting or other appropriate relief. Failing to follow this procedure, the court dismisses the suit.[16] For the same reason, the District Court dismissed a suit for an accounting of funds under Section 501 (b), holding that, as a condition to bring suit, the complainants were obligated to make a demand upon the officers to take action to secure an accounting or other appropriate relief.[17] However, the Oregon courts disregarded the requirement because under state law permission of the court was not necessary to sue.[18]

In general, the courts have not required the exhaustion of internal remedies as a condition for bringing suit, although in one of the first Title V cases, this requirement was enforced. A member of the Hod Carriers' Union protested certain payments made by the local union, and also the election of delegates to the building trades council. He sought to bring suit under Section 501. Three requisites for bringing suit under Section 501 (b) were laid down by the court. (1) The suing member must request the union to bring suit; (2) the union or its governing board must refuse to sue; and (3) a showing of good cause must be made. "One factor," said the court, "in determining whether good cause has been shown is the exhaustion requirement." Having failed to meet the third requirement, the suit was dismissed.[19]

The courts have not followed the view just expressed. The United States District Court for Eastern Pennsylvania held that exhaustion of remedies was not a requisite for bringing suit.[20] The view was supported by the Appellate Court. A demand for recovery of misspent funds had been made upon the President of Teamsters' Local No. 69. A committee of inquiry had been appointed, but it did not report its findings to the membership. Consequently, the complaining members had met the requirements of Section 501 (b) for filing a suit.[21]

Exhaustion of internal remedies was held unnecessary in a member's suit over use of pension funds. The court laid down the requirements precedent to a suit under Section 501 (b):

the plaintiff as a member of the labor organization, requests that organization or its governing board or officers to use or recover damages or secure an accounting or other appropriate relief from the asserted violations of fiduciary duties defined in Section 501 (a). The proposed complaint alleges fulfillment of this condition precedent. Section 501 (b) makes reference to no other intraorganizational remedy which must be pursued. It follows that the pursuit of other internal remedies which may be available need not be alleged to show good cause.[22]

The demand for suit must be made to the union or its officers. In a case involving the National Maritime Union, the demand that the National Maritime Union "fully and immediately inquire into the . . . charges and act accordingly" was held to be "not a request that the union bring suit."[23] The complaining members had failed to request that a suit to recover funds be started or take other appropriate action. The demand for an inquiry, made by the complainants, was insufficient to meet the requirement of the suit. The Court of Appeals, Second Circuit, has held that the "request is mandatory . . . An allegation of the futility of such a request will not suffice."

In determining the sufficiency of the complaint, or just cause, it has been held that the court might look beyond the complaint in determining "just cause." It is, furthermore, not appropriate, said the court, to consider "defenses which require the resolution of complex questions of law going to the substance of the case. The requirement of just cause is to prevent harassment of the union and its officers by unfounded charges "and vexation litigation brought without merit or good faith."[24]

The cases that have been brought to court by members of unions under Title V are of two kinds. (1) A number of cases have challenged expenditure of funds or the action of the union in creating offices, pensions, or other payments for officers. (2) Another group has arisen as a result of dissatisfaction with decisions in collective bargaining. In this group are the cases in which agreements with the employer are questioned, the failure of the union to pursue the demands sought by the union are challenged, or the results of an arbitration decision are denounced. A challenge to the election of the former President of the Brotherhood of Railway Clerks to the new post of chief executive officer on the ground that his election was achieved in violation of Title V of the Act failed. It was the argument of the protesting union that Resolution No. 611, under which the vote was held, had been improperly adopted, and that George Harrison, who had been chosen, "notably lacked the candor and honesty which the Statute imposes and which the Brotherhood members had a right to expect from a person so benefited at Union expense and so advantaged by respected and controlling Union office."[25]

While the Court of Appeals ruled that the complainant had failed to request the union to sue for action and had also failed to show good cause for permission from the court to bring suit, it rested its decision on the ground that the complaint had failed to state a cause of action under Title V. It reiterated the views given in *Gurton* v. *Arons*, 58 LRRM 2080, that Section 501 has reference to money and property of the union and not to other allegations of misconduct.

In two cases, the issues raised under Title V involved the disposal of funds held by a seceding local union. In a case involving the secession of a union from the International Brotherhood of Pulp, Sulphite and Paper Mill Workers, a member of the seceding local seeking affiliation with the newly formed Association of Western Pulp and Paper Workers sued to prevent the seizure of the local funds charging a violation of Section 501 (a) and (b). The court held the suing member had no standing to sue as he had unequivocally withdrawn from the local union. Moreover, he could not sue for the additional reason that suit must be brought for the benefit of the organization and not the members. The court said:

> The necessary corollary of the principle that the duties of officers are owed to the organization is that any relief obtained in such litigation shall benefit the corporation as a whole and not the suing individual. Section 501 (b) makes it

clear that the relief granted under Section 501 is for the
benefit of the real party in interest, the union whose officers
are charged with dereliction.[26]

In another secession case involving Local Union 15257, District
50, United Mine Workers of America, the U.S. District Court of
Minnesota found that international representatives who advised
and were active "in servicing the Local, attending its meetings,
advising its officers, and talking directly with the employer . . .
became 'quasi-officers' or at least 'representatives' of Local No.
15257. In any event they occupied a position of trust with regard
to the Local and its members, notwithstanding the fact that someone else paid their salaries."[27]

Another charge of breaching their fiduciary responsibility
arose when officers of the Rochester Independent Workers
Union (RIW) supported the affiliation of their organization with
the International Union of Electrical, Radio and Machine Workers (IUE). It was the contention of the complaining members that
support of a dual union by the officers caused financial losses to
the RIW.[28] The court found that Cassidy, in whose name the suit
had been instituted, had not requested the governing board to
bring suit to recover funds or secure an accounting or other
appropriate relief. The letter that was sent to the officers did not
request suit and there was consequently no refusal.

On the issue of dual unionism, which the officers supported,
the court found that as no monies of RIW were diverted to the
IUE, there was no breach of the fiduciary responsibilities with
respect to money or property. The challenged expenditure of the
officers was found proper and made in good faith. As for loss of
income because of the shift of membership from the RIW to the
IUE, the court held this was the result of voluntary decisions
made by members in an election of the National Labor Relations
Board. The court also held the officers of RIW, who favored
affiliation with the IUE, had not dealt with the RIW as an adverse
party.

The issue of dual unionism raises difficult problems in connection with Title V. The National Labor Relations Act has for its

major purpose the protection of the right of free choice in the selection of bargaining representatives. Local officers may believe that the members would be better served if they affiliated with another International or their interests more closely tied to another union. Since the emergence of the Committee for Industrial Organization, and the enactment of the federal labor relations laws, it has been easier to change a local's affiliation. It may be recalled that the shifting of the company unions in the steel industry to the Steelworkers Organizing Committee, in the mid 1930s, was a major breakthrough for free and uncontrolled unions. There are many examples, since that time, of workers, with the aid and encouragement of their local leaders, shifting their national affiliations.

A local officer may face the charge that he is acting as an adverse party to the union since he is on the payroll of the organization from which he seeks to have his members disaffiliate. As long as his objective is not influenced by personal gain, it would seem that he would be carrying out his fiduciary obligations in the highest sense. The desire to serve the members more effectively, or the affiliation with another International Union because it is more attuned to the needs of the members and is a more effective bargaining representative, cannot be regarded as against the interest of the local union or its members, nor as self-serving activity for personal advantage of the officer. In the three cases dealt with in this group, the courts have shown an appreciation of the problems involved in the change of affiliation by a local union. It would appear that they were correct in their conclusions that Title V was not intended to interfere with the free choice of members of unions with regard to their national affiliation. Whatever incidental conflict may arise between a local officer's position and his conviction that the members would be better served by changing their affiliation, conduct of this kind does not violate his fiduciary obligations or his basic loyalty to his members.

Charges of mismanagement of pensions and health and welfare funds have also been made. A demand for the removal of the trustees of the Alaska Laborers Construction Industry Health and Security Fund was rejected by the District Court because "no mismanagement of the trust fund was found which could conceivably constitute any breach of the fiduciary relationship imposed by this section." The allegations were unsupported and too conjectural "to be entitled to consideration."[29]

The Marine Engineers Beneficial Association (MEBA) established districts in April 1962 which took over the functions formerly performed by the locals. In May 1959, a severance plan for officials was adopted, and it began to make payments in April 1962. No district-wide vote was taken on the adoption of the severance plan, and the protesting members claimed the plan was void because it was not authorized in the manner required by the union constitution and by-laws. The court refused to dismiss the suit. In denying the plea of the union officers, the Appellate Court said that the union officers were not charged "with any misfeasance or malfeasance in connection with the adoption of the plan, or because of any payments made before the Act became effective. They charge only that, after the District was created in April 1, 1962, which was more than a year and a half after the Act became effective, appellees applied District funds under the plan and designated themselves as beneficiaries thereunder, and that this was improper and unauthorized because the plan had never been adopted."[30]

The courts have also refused to allow an international to impose a pension plan upon one of its locals.[31] Local 3, Sheet Metal Workers International Association, concluded an agreement with the unionized contractors in the Omaha-Council Bluffs district, in July 1969, under which a pension plan covering those in the local union would be selected. The local union membership had voted three times for the rejection of the national pension plan sponsored by the International Union since 1966. The members favoring the national plan persisted and in the fourth attempt were successful in securing an affirmative vote on the International's pension plan. The opponents did not surrender, and they succeeded for the fourth time in having the national plan rejected.

Following the fourth rejection, the International Union placed the local under trusteeship, and the local sued, charging a violation of Section 101 (a) (1) and 501 (a). The court held that by ignoring the three votes against the plan cast by the local union, the International had violated the local's right to vote. The court also noted that the vote endorsing the plan had been repudiated in a subsequent vote, which again was in violation of Section 101 (a) (1).

The court also ruled that the International and local officers had violated their fiduciary duties as defined by Section 501 (a) and were jointly and severally liable for the amounts of money deducted from the members' wages on behalf of the pension fund promoted by the International Union. The court directed that the members' vote against the pension plan be observed, and that the International refrain from negotiating a pension provision in the new contract scheduled to be negotiated, and also desist from disbanding the local and distributing its members among local unions.

Morrisey v. *Curran*[32] involved the right of the National Maritime Union to include several office employees in the union's pension program. The suit claimed that in 1961, without constitutional authority or membership approval, the pension plan was amended by the national officers to cover persons not authorized to participate. The action of the officers, it was charged, violated Section 501, LMRDA. The defendants in the case, the national officers and trustees of the pension fund, justified their action by the clause in the constitution which authorized the officers to fix salaries and bargain collectively with the office employees. Consequently, such authority carried with it the power to set up pensions for them.

The District Court found that salaries may include pensions, but that the 1960 NMU constitution distinguished between them as it did between employees and officers. Payments to non-officers of pensions were enjoined, and all monies they had received as pensions were to be returned with interest to the union. Following the decision, the union amended its constitution giving its national officers authority to bring certain employees under the pension program, and validated "retroactively all pensions heretofore paid under the plan." The complaining members charged the amendment constituted an "exculpatory resolution" which contravened Section 501 (a), but the District Court rejected its claim.

In a majority decision, the Appellate Court agreed that under the 1960 NMU constitution only officers were covered by the pension provisions and upheld the trial court's views on this part of the decision. However, it declared the 1969 amendment to the union constitution void. Allowing such a provision to become effective would mean that Section 501 (a) "would be completely emasculated, if every time a court, at the behest of a complaining member of a union, found that the officers had breached their duties, the officers could find sanctuary by putting through a constitutional amendment or bylaw retroactively legitimizing their former dereliction of duty." It also affirmed the District Court's findings that the trustees of the pension fund fall within the group having fiduciary responsibilities of Section 3 (a) and had a duty to see that all the funds improperly spent are returned to the union treasury.

When a union is unresponsive for a year to the request of several members for an accounting of the management of the pension fund, its officers cannot claim that the members have failed to establish good cause. Claiming that the President and Executive Board of the Upholsterers' Union had violated their fiduciary duties as defined in Section 501 in administering the pension funds, several members called on the officers to institute suit for recovering allegedly misspent funds in the health and welfare and pension funds. Instead of suing, the officers of the union appointed a committee to investigate, which showed no undue haste to examine the accuracy of the charges. As a result, the union was unable to have the suit dismissed. In rejecting the union's request, the court ruled that failure to deny the charges made by the members constituted good cause for proceeding with the action. The need to exhaust internal remedies was also denied.[33]

Section 501 has also been used to challenge salary increases, or raises in expenses improperly allowed by the union to its officers.

Members of the International of Bridge, Structural and Ornamental Iron Workers, Local 92, sued to recover unauthorized increases in salary and expenses for several officers. A special master was appointed, and he found that two officials had been paid about $23,000 in unauthorized salaries and expenses. The court ordered the union to recover this sum from the two and directed that, in the event the judgment was not satisfied within sixty days, the union would be liable for about $20,000 in fees for the special master and the counsel and accountant's fees of the complaining members. The net award to the union was approximately $3,000.

The union's liability for the fees of the counsel and accountant of the suing members was affirmed by the Court of Appeals, Fifth Circuit. It based its decision upon the benefits that have been realized by the union as a result of the suit by the members.

Said the court: "So long as the union realizes some substantial benefit as the result of the litigation it stands liable for the fees due the specified persons who secured these benefits . . . In this case, the district court in making the award of attorney's fees stressed the benefits that had been realized by the local through the efforts of counsel employed by the members who instituted the suit." The local union sought to avoid dipping into its treasury to pay the counsel and accountant's fees. Realistically, the local or its members, as a whole, would scarcely look at the assessment upon its treasury as a great boon. The court, however, regarded the award as "merely the allowance of costs fairly attributable to the services performed. From the inception of this suit against the local officials, the only claims which have been asserted have been on behalf of the local, not against it. And it is the benefits to the local that have been secured as a result of such claims which serves as the main basis for allowing fees to those persons through whose efforts such benefits were attained."[34]

The award in the above follows the rule laid down in a dispute over counsel fees in the litigation against the officers of the Bakery and Confectionary Workers International Union. A dissident faction sued for the reorganization of the union and the ouster of its top officers, who had been exposed by the McClellan

Committee as having been guilty of misuse of union funds and the signing of a sweetheart agreement with the employer. Mozart Ratner was retained as counsel, and when the union declined to recognize its responsibility for the dissidents' counsel fees, Ratner resigned. The District Court awarded him a payment for his services, but the Appellate Court held it insufficient and awarded him "reasonable fees, properly earned, based upon the benefits which inured to the union."[35]

A vote by the union's Executive Board to increase the per diem, which was to be treated as salary, without the approval of the membership as required by the union constitution was deemed a breach of fiduciary responsibility.[36] It had been customary in Local 1377 for the two officers to submit itemized vouchers for incurred expenses to the Executive Board for approval. Subsequent to the approval of the Board, the expenditures were submitted to the membership for final approval. In 1959, the method of reimbursement was changed. Instead of reimbursed expenses supported by relevant vouchers, the two officers were given a salary increase. The amounts paid under the latter arrangement were listed as "per diem."

Amendments to the by-laws "legalizing" the payment of the per diem were adopted by the local, but they were rejected by International President Gordon Freeman as improper. After the rejection, the per diem payments were discontinued. A member, Eugene McCabe, sued for the recovery of the per diem payments, and the court ruled that they "were liable to Local 1377 for all per diem payments which they had collected." The District Court refused to allow setoffs until the two officers had obtained approval from the membership of Local 1377 of their alleged expenditures on behalf of Local 1377. In defense of this position the Appellate Court cited the International constitution which requires that claims for reimbursed expenses incurred "must be supported by an itemized expense accounting with receipts attached and must be approved by the Local's membership."[37]

What had happened is that the officers accepted the per diem payments as a wage increase and continued to present vouchers to the union for reimbursed expenses. However, the court noted that an increase in officers' salaries required approval, and such approval, in accordance with the union's constitution and by-laws, had not been obtained.

In another case, *Purcell* v. *Keane*,[38] the charge by several members that officers of Local 169 misused funds and the request by the members for suit to recover went unheeded. The officers appointed a committee to inquire into the charges alleged, but, forty days after the request, no hearings or report had been made by the committee. Thereupon, leave to sue was granted by the court. The court laid down the prerequisite for bringing suit under Title V: The suing member must request the union to sue.

Dissident members sought an injunction to prevent the carrying out of the agreement. It was denied by the court, which held that the decision to accept the reduction in rates of wages had been made democratically and that it would not be reversed by the court.[39] In a dispute among the painters, Martin Rarback, Secretary of Painters' Union District 9, in New York City, was charged with colluding with employers in five woodworking shops to permit them to pay wages lower than required in the trade agreement. Additional charges that the particular employers were favored by being allowed excessive hours of work and lower contributions to the health and welfare funds were also made. "Fiduciary duties," said the court, "extend to such matters as entering into 'sweetheart contracts' or other dealing with parties having interests averse to those of union's membership."[40]

While the case was pending in the courts, the attorney for the protesting members explained to the public that the dissidents in District 9 had unsuccessfully appealed to the AFL-CIO to have Secretary Rarback, who had not had his day in court, removed. Mr. Hall had informed the members that "the federal district court in New York after studying the veritable mountain of evidence submitted by both sides, ruled that the union members had shown a 'wealth of facts and acts' to support their allegations of sweetheart dealings on the part of Rarback."[41] Mr. Hall did not do as well in the trial on the facts. In a long and carefully reasoned opinion, the United States District Court for the Southern District of New York found that the hardwood finishers, twenty-five of whom were involved in this case, received the wages called for in the agreements with the employers' association in the industry. The court noted:

> . . . these agreements, however, inartistically drafted, were genuine. As far as the hourly rate of wages were concerned, these complaining employees received as much as they were entitled to receive. Plaintiffs have not proved that they were entitled to the higher rate for "new work" specified in the painters' Trade Agreement. Moreover, these employees of the Bronx-Manhattan Woodworking shops received an hourly wage distinctly higher than hardwood finishers in Brooklyn and Queens who did similar work.[42]

On the welfare contributions, which the plaintiffs claimed had not been fully paid, the court said: "The evidence on this subject is not clear and convincing enough to justify a finding as to the extent to which any employer failed, if he did fail, to live up to his obligations in this respect. Moreover, there is no proof that defendant was aware of any such deficiencies."[43] The court also found the plaintiffs made no case of favoritism on overtime.

The court noted that District 9 had for years been the scene "of bitter internal strife between rival factions in this union . . . Plaintiffs have charged defendant with deliberate collusion and conspiracy with certain employers. My conclusion is that they have not proved that charge."[44] The situations are not always clear cut. At times, some workers are sacrificed, in the sense that they lose their jobs, or a bargain is made which appears to have neglected their interests. Decisions must, in terms of the economic realities of the situation, sometimes be made which are unfavorable to some of those covered by the agreement. Yet economic necessity may dictate that kind of bargain. It may be either the acceptance of layoffs or other unfavorable conditions for a few to conserve the jobs of the many. For that reason, only certain types of bargains, those which are clearly in contravention of the fiduciary principle, can be attacked. An unfavorable bargain may yet be the best one obtainable under given circumstances.

In a unanimous decision, the Court of Appeals, Second Circuit, rejected the claim that the refusal of a union to challenge the verdict of an arbitrator who had upheld the discharge of several employees for participating in a wildcat strike constituted a violation of Section 501.[45] Against the advice of the union, a wildcat strike was called by Local Lodge 2121, International Association of Machinists. The differences between the workers and the company arose over the interpretation of a seniority clause which the company was willing to submit to arbitration. A large number of strike activists were penalized, and the company's action was in the end submitted to arbitration. The arbitrator reduced the penalties for many, but upheld the discharge of five employees. Those who were discharged claimed that the arbitration violated the evidence and fairness and demanded that the decisions be challenged in the Courts. The union, which had agreed to the arbitration proceedings, refused. As the union's request was necessary for a challenge in the courts, the arbitration decision became effective.

Section 501 was invoked by the discharged employees, who claimed that the refusal to challenge the discharges in the courts constituted a violation of the fiduciary responsibility owed to the union and its members. The Circuit Court disagreed, and noted: "The delineation of the fiduciary duties of union officers applies only to fiduciary responsibility with respect to the money and property of the union and cannot be invoked by union members complaining of loss of employment as the result of a union officer having induced them to participate in a strike in violation of a labor-contract."[46]

The most important case that came before the courts under Title V was the dispute between Local 28, International Brotherhood of Electrical Workers and the parent International. No charge of misuse of funds was involved, but the right of an International Union to insist that its locals follow a specified procedure in its negotiations with its employers was at issue.

Factional rivalries within Baltimore Local 28, International Brotherhood of Electrical Workers, came to the surface in 1958 with the President and financial secretary each leading a rival group. When complaints were made to the International President, Gordon Freeman, the latter placed the local under a trusteeship. Its imposition was justified by the claim that the local had failed to raise sufficient revenue "to pay benefits established," and the local organization faced a threat of insolvency. The local union sued in the United States District Court for the voiding of the trusteeship, and while the suit was pending, its autonomy and self-government were restored.[47]

Soon after the settlement of the trusteeship controversy, the local and the International became involved in a serious dispute over the level of demands to be made on the contractors. Relations between the parties in the electrical contracting industry were governed by the program, devised in 1922 by the National Electrical Contractors Association (NECA) and the International Brotherhood of Electrical Workers (IBEW). The agreement followed a period of stress and strain in the industry, during and immediately after World War I. A number of leading contractors, led by L. D. Comstock, as well as heads and activists in the union, favored the new approach. To facilitate peaceful settlement of differences, the parties established the Council of Industrial Relations, a bipartite body with each side equally represented,[48] which has encouraged adoption of "council clauses" in labor management agreements in the industry.

Under the above "clauses," differences that arise between a local union and NECA chapter are automatically submitted to the council. Agreements remain in effect and can be terminated or modified only with the consent of both parties. The council accepts briefs and other evidence, and its decisions must be unanimous. The agreement under which Local 28 operated had been made on June 1, 1961, and under the rules, it remained in effect "from year to year thereafter from June 1 through May 31 of each year unless changed or terminated in the way provided herein." Local 28 had submitted its first request for a decision to the council in 1958, and it was granted a 15 cent increase. In each of the next two years, the council also considered the demands of Local 28, and granted 17.5 cents in 1959, and 10 cents in 1960.[49] Under the council rules, all differences between the parties which cannot be settled directly must be submitted to the council for final decision.

The agreement between Local 28 and the Maryland chapter of NECA contained a "council clause," which meant that the consent of both parties was required for the termination of the agreement. On January 11, 1961, Local 28 notified the Maryland chapter of its desire to terminate the agreement in force, unless it could be modified to the mutual satisfaction of the parties[50] Negotiations for the renewal of the contract became deadlocked over the wage issue. The local sought a two year contract embodying wage increases of 35 cents for the first year, and an additional 30 cents for the second year. The International believed the demands were excessive, but the local justified its position by pointing to the prevailing rates in Philadelphia, Wilmington, Delaware, and Washington, D.C., the metropolitan labor markets closest to Baltimore, where Local 28 exercised jurisdiction. On the other hand, the International was of the view that the *"increase could not possibly be justified by economic considerations* (italics in original). This is so because of the small degree to which Baltimore has been organized in comparison with neighboring cities . . ."

The Maryland NECA chapter took the same view and claimed that Baltimore had a large and aggressive nonunion contractor association, boasting more than one thousand affiliated firms. It stated that the union had lost ground, and that some of the contractors retained their union connections only because of their interstate operations. "Only through continuous and aggressive bidding," claimed the Maryland NECA, "are the union electrical contractors able to stay in the picture."[51] Perhaps the strongest argument made by the International and the contractors was that the increases would have put the Local 28 members out of line in their wage rates with the comparable building trades in the Baltimore area, such as plumbers, steamfitters and sheet metal workers whose wages have been traditionally regarded as standards for union electricians.

In disregard of the directive of Article XVII, Section 3 of the International constitution,[52] the local called a strike which lasted for two weeks. Negotiations were resumed, after April 1961, but no agreement was reached. The local then challenged the legality of the "council clause." While refusing to rule on the general question of terminability, the court held that the notice given by Local 28 to the Maryland NECA chapter constituted a termination of the agreement.[53]

Despite the interdiction by International President Gordon Freeman, the local voted, on June 13, 1961, by 740 to 79 to call a strike. It was immediately informed by President Freeman that he would not sanction a strike, and that the union constitution must be followed. The same instructions were repeated orally by the International President in his conference at his Washington office, on June 20, 1961, with the two heads of the local and its negotiating committee.[54]

The order of the President was, on the advice of counsel, unanimously rejected in a meeting of members of the local on June 22. President Freeman then sent a letter to every member of the local notifying them of a hearing to show cause why Local 28's charter should not be revoked. Carl R. Schedler, an arbitrator and attorney, was appointed hearing officer. Hearings were held from July 17 to 21. Four days later the referee presented his findings of fact, and oral argument by counsel for the local and for the International was heard. President Freeman announced the revocation of the charter of Local 28 on August 1, 1961, but the members were allowed until August 7 to terminate their stoppage and return to work. In addition the local was required to refer the collective bargaining issues in dispute between the local and Maryland chapter of the NECA "for final and binding decision by the Council of Industrial Relations; it being understood that the Local shall not be required to accept the council clause ruled terminable by . . . the United States District Court for

Maryland."[55] On August 5, 1961, the members voted by 991 to 2 to support their local officers.

The revocation of the charter was carried out, and the jurisdiction of Local 28 transferred to a new local, No. 24. President Freeman also directed that the trust funds of Local 28 be distributed among its members in accordance with legal requirements, and that no per capita payments be accepted from it. An appeal to the International Executive Council was taken by the local, but Freeman's decision was upheld. A suit to reverse the International President's verdict was initiated in the United States District Court. Violations of Section 101 (a) (2) and (5), and also Section 501, were alleged. The hearings before the District Court lasted 22 days and witnesses appeared for the local, the International, and also for the Maryland chapter and national NECA.

The court found that the revocation of the charter was "without a fair hearing and . . . was a breach of the contract between the Local and the International."[56] While agreeing that engaging in an unauthorized strike warranted severe penalties, the court found the "revocation amounted to unreasonable and unjust punishment of the members of Local 28, in violation of their rights under section 101 (a) (5)." The court ordered the restoration of the charter of Local 28 and that the charter of the newly established Local 24 be revoked. The union claimed that in prohibiting the strike, he, the President, was acting in behalf of the entire union and its constitution, and that the officers of the International could not "allow a local to flout the authority of the organization." The court conceded that the principle was a correct one, but only as long as the International President "acted in good faith and not maliciously or in violation of the duty he owed to the members of Local 28, as well as to all other members of the IBEW."

While conceding that the President's conduct was not motivated by "a deliberate intention to commit an injury," the court found that "he did act wilfully and intentionally, for the purpose, inter alia, of imposing severe discipline on the members of Local 28, and without due regard for the duty he owed to them, as well as to the IBEW as a whole."

The decision was reversed.[57] The court found that President Freeman's actions were in harmony with the union constitution. "The broad mandate of power to the International President made by the Union constitution is designed to be used by him to promote such methods of collective bargaining as seem conducive to the interests of the entire organization." The view that revocation of the charter violated Title I rights was rejected. The court also ruled:

> The refusal to sanction the June strike cannot be said to be a breach of a fiduciary duty owed to the plaintiffs under the Constitution. If the International President believed that an appropriate Council clause could be negotiated and that Local 28 was excessive in its demands and "shooting for the moon," it was his prerogative to restrain the Local, and if possible to counteract its headstrong determination to wage a strike that could adversely affect the cause of his international organization. His duty was to 750,000 members, not merely to a few who might gain a short-range advantage that could prove costly to the parent body, the employers, the public and, in the long run, to the plaintiffs themselves. The International was dealing day by day with many chapters of NECA and the International's relations with NECA were important to the welfare of all 150,000 who worked in the construction industry.

The Parks case is significant in that the attempt to compel a local to obey a no-strike provision in a union constitution could not be attacked as a breach of fiduciary duty by the International officers. The agreement between the electrical contractors and the union had been in existence, at the beginning of the dispute, for forty years. By no criterion can it be maintained that the electrical workers have suffered from neglect by their union. Their wages compare favorably with those of other building tradesmen and there is no proof that the agreement has been a means of holding down benefits. The question can always be raised whether the head of the union has acted fairly. Arrangements covering large numbers of workers, as does the agreement in the electrical contracting industry, must take a large number of factors into account. It may be that one local union might be able to improve its position, but consideration for the rest of the industry might require a less favorable settlement. It is for that reason that concentrating merely on local conditions might not provide all the relevant issues in dispute.[58] Nor can we assume that a union leader must be infallible in his judgments on the merits of the question in dispute. His judgment and not his integrity may be defective, and it is within the province of the membership to relieve him of his duties if he demonstrates incapacity. The test of violating his fiduciary duties toward his members must be whether the decision has been made in good faith or whether it is based on personal interest. Prejudice toward one of several alternatives does not demonstrate a violation of fiduciary responsibility, but good or poor judgment. It is therefore of utmost importance that union officials be allowed to make decisions consonant with the authority given to them by the membership and the constitution and by-laws, and as long as no evidence of personal gain or interest is shown, they should not be held to have violated their fiduciary responsibility.

Bonding

Labor organizations have since their beginnings faced the need for protecting their assets. Absconders and embezzlers were present even among the pioneers who appear to have yielded to temptation as readily as their modern counterparts.[59] As a result union leaders have emphasized the necessity for protecting the union against losses by purchase of sureties to cover those in charge of finances or other assets. Such prudent warnings were frequently ignored, and a number of unions faced serious losses. A number of labor organizations, including the Molders, and Railway and Steamship Clerks, tried to compel their locals to cover their officers by purchasing sureties from union-operated bonding departments. Many local unions either refused to bond their officers or neglected to buy adequate coverage. Reasonable bonding requirements must be regarded as an aid rather than an obstacle to effective union administration.

Section 502 (a) as amended by section 1 of Public Law 89-216 requires:

> Every officer, agent, shop steward, or other representative or employee of any labor organization (other than a labor organization whose property and annual financial receipts do not exceed $5,000 in value), or of a trust in which a labor organization is interested, who handles funds or other property thereof shall be bonded to provide protection against loss by reason of acts of fraud or dishonesty on his part or through connivance with others.

The bond of each such person is fixed at the beginning of the union's fiscal year, and must cover at least 10 percent of the funds handled by the person or his predecessor during the preceding fiscal year but in no case more than $500,000. If the labor organization or the trust in which it is interested does not have a preceding fiscal year, the amount of the bond has been set at $1,000 for a local labor organization, and for any other labor organization or trust in which a labor organization is interested at $10,000. "Such bonds shall be individual or schedule in form, and shall have a corporate surety company as surety thereon." Persons not covered by a bond are not permitted to handle funds or property of a labor organization. No bonds can be placed through an agent or broker in which a labor organization has an interest.

A trust established by a labor organization or its officers to provide pensions, health and welfare insurance, or other benefits to members or their beneficiaries also falls under this provision. Profit-sharing programs and strike funds, as well as a business operated by labor organizations, are also included. Brokers or trust administrators are exempt from coverage on the theory that they are bonded as a condition of doing business.

In determining the size of the bond required, unions are permitted to exclude "property of a relatively permanent nature such as land, buildings, furniture, fixtures, and office and delivery equipment or property similarly held for use in the operation of the organization or trust." Items of high convertibility, notes, checks, negotiable instruments, government bonds, and marketable securities, and other property held not for use but for conversion into cash is required as "substantially equivalent to funds," and must be included in the assets covered by the bond.

Who is to be bonded is not always easy to determine. The LMWP believes that the meaning of "handles" in Section 502 (a) "encompasses duties with respect to the receipt, safekeeping and disbursement of funds or other property (regardless of how small the amount of funds or how little the value of the property involved) such that there is a significant risk that the funds or other property would be lost if these duties were not faithfully discharged." Cases are decided on the facts and circumstances.

The LMWP does not regard physical handling of funds as "the controlling criterion" of whether bonding is required. The standard applied is the "access . . . or control, or general powers of custody and safekeeping over funds and other property" is held to be a more effective guide to the need for bonding. Persons were bonded for "faithful discharge" of duties. Here again, the Office has taken the position that "what constitutes faithful discharge in a given situation depends on the facts and circumstances of the case and nature of the duties of the specific position involved." A bond can either be individual or schedule in form. An individual bond lists the person covered for the specific amount purchased; the latter covers specified positions and covers the occupants for a specified amount. The bond allows for "recovery by or for the benefit of that specific organization or trust to the full extent of the coverage."

The statute does not permit the use of bonding companies established by the union or those which are financially unreliable or are influenced by union officials. The bond must be placed with a *corporate* surety which under the Act of July 30, 1947, is "an acceptable surety of Federal bonds." For the purposes of meeting the requirements of the statute, no bond can be placed through an agent or broker or with a surety company in which a labor organization or an officer of a union has an interest.

Originally, the LMRDA required a faithful discharge of duties bond on persons handling funds or other property of a labor union, or of trusts in which labor unions have an interest. Under the 1965 amendments the faithful discharge of duties were eliminated, and as a result unions are permitted to use an honesty bond. Surety companies are required to file annual reports with the Secretary of Labor describing their bonding experience under the Labor-Management Reporting and Disclosure Act. They are not required to indicate the number of persons bonded, bonds in force, bonds upon which losses have been paid, or the name of the defaulter.

Table 10.

Number and Amount of Losses Incurred by
Surety Companies Reporting to the
Department of Labor for Calendar Years 1966-1971[1]

Year	Number of Losses	Amount Paid
1966	71	$ 60,804
1967	133	263,227
1968	149	434,806
1969	194	202,830
1970	209	308,741
1971	154	362,342
Total	910	1,633,342

[1]Compiled from annual reports of the Office of Labor-Management and Welfare-Pension Reports.

Title V is based upon the view that the members of unions are concerned about the assets of their organizations, and will take steps to protect them against the dishonest office holder. Although there have not been an overwhelming number of suits under this Title, it has been useful in preventing unauthorized expenditures and increases in benefits. The courts have allowed suits under Title V in cases where officers were charged with collusion with the employer in the making of a contract. In one instance, the charge was that a union officer had accepted an inferior contract, a so-called sweetheart agreement. On the facts, the court found no basis for the accusation. In the Parks case, originating in the electrical construction industry in Baltimore, a broader issue was raised—whether the International Union by insisting that the local accept a national agreement violated its fiduciary responsibility to the members and the organization.

The Court of Appeals held that the union constitution allowed for the action of the International President, and the claim of the local members was rejected. However, most of the suits initiated deal with finances and their management as it appears that Congress hoped would be the case. No complaints that the provisions place undue burdens on the union have been made, nor is there evidence that it has been used to harass. The latter is unlikely because permission of a court is a necessary condition for bringing suit. Implied in the provisions is the view that the members, or at least a minority among them, would be sufficiently concerned with the assets of the organization to take steps to protect them against irregularities. Members might discover financial improprieties when financial reports are being made to the union's membership. However, successful concealment may be possible in some organizations. Many require that increased compensation for local officers be approved by the parent body, and in one case that came before the courts such approval was refused. When the officer evaded the ruling of his international, a successful suit was started, and the funds were ordered returned.

Borrowing of union funds is not permitted above a relatively small amount. Dipping into the union treasury, à la Beck and Brewster, is forbidden, but the rank and file may not be aware of what is happening. However, the annual report to the Office of Labor-Management and Welfare-Pension Reports may reveal information which can stimulate action for a return of funds improperly diverted from the union treasury.

One of the more important areas in which the interests of the members are paramount is in the use of health and welfare funds. Several suits for accounting or for disqualifying certain claimants have been filed. The courts, when some evidence has been adduced of possible misuse of these monies, have ordered the removal of the improperly assigned claimants from the rolls. It may be that the worst evils of financial malpractice are today in the administration of health and welfare and pension programs. Title V does not provide for regulating administrative costs or consultant's fees, nor does it set up standards of investment that have to be followed by trustees. Some expenditures can be challenged and have been, but those involve the eligibility of certain persons to collect benefits. Congress is wrestling with the problem, but it may regard vesting of pensions and the protection of eligible claimants to their benefits of more importance than the protections that are covered by Title V. Although Title V has been used less frequently than some of the others, it is a useful mechanism for providing protection of the monies and other assets of labor organizations.

15

Summing Up

The decision by Congress to reform the government of trade unions was greatly influenced by the disclosures of the McClellan Committee. Traditional opponents of organized labor, while approving the constraints that might be imposed, were mainly concerned with gaining more stringent limitations on the secondary boycott and a satisfactory definition of recognition picketing. For them the significance of the discussions of the labor reform law by Congress was that it provided a favorable launching pad for amending the National Labor Relations Act. It is difficult to measure precisely the effect of the LMRDA upon the functioning of labor organizations, but it can be said with certainty that it has not inhibited their growth. Unions were obliged to clarify some clauses in their constitutions and by-laws, but these changes appear to have had a minimal effect upon their operations.[1]

Unions have had to give more attention to membership appeals from disciplinary decisions of their subordinate units, and also aid the locals and intermediate bodies to operate their elections so as not to violate the statute. The fears expressed that small locals would not survive because of the burdens imposed, such as filing annual reports, have not materialized. The Department of Labor has shown itself sympathetic to the needs and limitations under

271

which thousands of small local unions operate so that filing places little burden upon the part-time officers.

While there have not been any drastic changes in the manner that unions generally operate, the labor movement has been affected by the reform law. Whether the changes introduced will over time affect the philosophy of the labor movement is an open question, but, on the basis of results of the first fifteen years in which the LMRDA has been in effect, one should not expect many fundamental innovations. It is obvious that union members expect their officers to be honest in matters that have to do with the handling of the assets of the organization. Nevertheless, the reaction of the members to thievery of the union's funds or to extorting payoffs from employers has not always been one of outrage.

The influence of the McClellan Committee is revealed in each of the titles which affect union government, I-VI, and each is a complement of the other. Congress assumed that much of the sordid business revealed by the testimony could only go on because of the ignorance of the membership. In a measure, this point of view is accurate. The best example of this hypothesis is the decision of thousands of members of the Bakery and Confectionary Workers to oust their corrupt officers. The McClellan Committee made a contribution by publicizing the shabby record of the President of the organization and the coterie who supported him. Daniel Conway and Curtis Sims, who were leading the revolt, put their careers on the line, and, had they failed, they would have been expelled from the organization they tried to reform.[2]

Providing the tools is only a first step; there must be members, and perhaps as important, leaders who are willing to use them. The degradation of the Bakery and Confectionary Workers' Union was the work of a clique of venal officials, who were ready to rob the union and to exploit their positions for collusive arrangements with bribe-giving employers. The situation was, however, an accident, and the venal crew never had it completely their own way. The willingness of the second highest officer, Curtis Sims, and several Vice-Presidents to challenge the conduct of the corrupt officers differentiates the union from the others which were expelled by the AFL-CIO. We need not assume that a baker is innately more honest than a truck driver or the man or woman who works in a laundry. However, racketeering in the Bakery and Confectionary Workers' Union might be regarded as a fungus growth, while in the Teamsters' Union it was long-known, established, and tolerated in a number of jurisdictions.

Free Speech and Assembly

Much depends upon the views and reactions of the members to the conduct of the leaders. In support of the proposition that the members should themselves reform their organizations, Congress enacted Title I which protects the reformer or a larger group who might question the policies of the union or the administration of collective bargaining or the health and welfare programs, if such are jointly managed by the union and the employer. Title I has enfranchised groups of workers who had formerly been denied full rights to vote for officers or policies. These provisions have been struck down on the grounds that they violate Section 101 (a) (1) which prescribes that all members must have "equal rights" and privileges to vote and nominate for office, to attend meetings of the organization and to participate in the deliberations of the organization. Under the interpretation of this section, permanent members cannot be granted rights superior to those enjoyed by others.

Such discriminatory provisions arose when some unions of craftsmen expanded into a jurisdiction occupied by workers of lesser skills. The original craft was reluctant to share power with the new recruits who were brought into the organization to strengthen it economically or to prevent another union from occupying a position on the periphery of the original jurisdiction. The justification for lower voting rights was that the new recruits had lower skills, paid lower dues and initiation fees, and were not full beneficiary members—those eligible for mortuary benefits and/or pensions. There was no way that a numerically inferior group could overcome such discrimination if opposition to their full enfranchisement existed. Under the LMRDA these differences in rights cannot be enforced.

The equal rights provision has also been effective in allowing members to appeal to the courts in cases of gross violations of fairness before the election has been completed. Members have challenged union decisions when they were not allowed equal access to the journals of the organization during an election campaign, and when there were attempts to miscount the votes or to substitute the contents of a fraudulent ballot box for the one used in the election. This section is a supplement to Title IV, and it shows Congress's concern with the problem of fair voting. Moreover, it can be used as a basis for challenging in the federal courts arbitrary denial of equal rights flowing out of union membership.

Section 101 (a) (2) grants union members the right to free speech and assembly. Such rights are enjoyed in most organizations of labor, but there are instances when a member who claimed that work was not being fairly distributed through the union hiring hall, or that the business agent was not administering the collective bargaining agreements effectively might be charged with slander or another kind of violation of union rules. Moreover, some state courts might regard certain kinds of speech permissible criticism, while those of another would find they exceeded the limits of fair comment and that the member could be tried on the charges preferred. The free speech provisions guarantee to union members the right to express opinions and to meet in and out of the union hall, and they apply throughout the country. The *Salzhandler* criterion is whether the speech concerns union affairs. If it does, then the union cannot charge the member with violating the union's rules if such prohibitions exist.

While it is always difficult to ascribe behavior which might be influenced by a multitude of factors to a single cause, it would appear that the abolition of restrictions on speech and assembly, as well as other protection given to dissidents by the LMRDA, has increased the number of aspirants for regional and national union office. Election contests have taken place in a number of unions for national office for the first time in a number of years.

unions for national office for the first time in a number of years. Sections (3) and (4) have more limited influence than the other sections in Title I. Section 3 requires that members be given adequate notice of a vote on changes in dues, assessments, and initiation fees, and that such changes be made by a vote of the local membership by secret ballot. In changes voted by an intermediate body or national union affecting the above contributions, they have to be made by a secret referendum ballot or by delegates to a convention who had been elected by a secret ballot.

Evidence of widespread abuses in this area is not voluminous. Even the most popular or powerful officers have found that an increase in dues or assessments without prior notice or explanation is likely to encounter serious membership opposition. In some organizations, however, members have found it risky to complain of the behavior of the officers, and the rank and file will have the opportunity to reject unwantd dues increases.

However, no objection can be raised to the provision as changes in contributions are seldom made under sudden emergencies. Officers who believe the union's finances are dangerously low and their replenishing is necessary have time to inform their members of the needs. Informing the members in advance and giving them notice and an opportunity to vote, as required by the statute, is likely to make acceptance greater. In fact, the requirement under LMRDA is similar to that imposed by many unions. Furthermore, in many organizations, local unions cannot impose assessments without the approval of the parent organization. In others such levies are not allowed. In addition, an assessment by the parent organization may in some unions only be imposed under stipulated conditions: to aid a strike of members of the union in another jurisdiction, to reduce union reserves below a given level; other contingencies may also be covered.

Section (4) spells out a prohibition against a union penalizing a member for appealing for relief to a court or administrative body, or for appearing before a governmental body of any kind on behalf of a public or private cause. It incorporates what has been the view of the courts for a long period of time, that a private organization must not bar its members from access to any unit of government. Normally, a problem would only arise when a union member testified before a legislative body or a law officer and was brought up on charges by the organization when his testimony was disapproved by his organization. However, there arises another type of problem—the right of a member to appeal directly to a government administrative agency such as the National Labor Relations Board, the National Mediation Board, or the Department of Labor when he has been penalized by his union, without exhausting his internal union remedies.

As noted above, unions have established appellate tribunals to which members aggrieved by a decision of a union officer or tribunal can appeal. The LMRDA is aimed at abuses, but it has also sought to promote self-government by labor organizations. One of the evidences of the latter objective is the requirement that a member should exhaust his remedies within the union, not to exceed a four-month lapse of time, before appealing to the courts. A member may, however, believe that the appeal is vain, and therefore will decide to go to the courts without utilizing the union's appellate tribunals. In taking this step the member runs the risk that if his appeal is found without merit, he can be penalized by his union. As noted, the LMRDA moreover places a four-month limit upon the time in which the union may consider an appeal against a penalty.

Section 101 (a) (5) lays down the minimum requirements for a fair trial of a union member charged with a violation of the rules of the union. A member, who is to be tried, must be given written charges, allowed a reasonable time for preparing a defense, and afforded a "full and fair hearing." These specifications must be met, and if evidence has been provided for the charge upon which the accused has been tried, the verdict is likely to stand. The United States Supreme Court has declared that courts, in reviewing the verdicts of union tribunals, cannot substitute their judgments for the one given. Courts can only observe if evidence for the charge exists and whether the complainant has been granted due process as required by the LMRDA.

The sponsors of the labor reform legislation believed that the enactment of Title I would bring a flood of cases by members victimized by oppressive labor organizations. When their expectations were not realized, it was alleged that the necessity for financing the law suits tended to constrain many who would otherwise go to court. Such claims were never accompanied by proof. In *Cole* v. *Hall*, the United States Supreme Court held that it was within the discretion of the judge to grant attorney fees to a suing member. It is too early to determine the accuracy of the claim that unnamed dozens of union members are waiting for a propitious time to sue. It has never been clear why such claims were made. Sometimes it was alleged that members fear to bring charges against their unions, but thousands do so every year to the National Labor Relations Board.[3]

Reporting and Disclosure

The reporting and disclosure requirements were at first regarded with trepidation by a number of leaders of labor organizations, and others feared the sensational revelations that would titilate the public palate. The salary and expense accounts of a few were found substantial, but it was soon found that most union officers were not grossly overpaid. Moreover, thousands of part-time officers gave their services for a nominal amount and tended to their union affairs for what might be called largely psychic income. Nevertheless, the reporting requirements were long overdue as the relatively large sums handled in some organizations should be protected on the basis of the most elementary principle of prudence.

Title II prohibits loans greater than a modest amount out of union funds, and provides that the information in the report must be made available to members. Furthermore, if members find reasons to question the information on the report submitted to the Secretary of Labor, they can request the books, records and accounts to verify it. This request can be enforced providing the suing member is able to show that his suspicion is based upon an alleged discrepancy or other reasons satisfactory to the court. The information that the experience has yielded is interesting and shows that the propensity for diversion of funds is not limited to a particular group or organization. It would appear that an effective auditing service is a better check on embezzlement than principle or philosophy. It has been found that unions that have never been touched by scandal will be harboring a local officer who absconds with the pension premiums or some of the financial reserves belonging to the members.

The provisions in Title II are directed towards protecting the union and its members. Although unions, no more than banks and other institutions, can fully protect themselves against the absconder and embezzler, the periodic checks by a government agency should reduce the inclination to invade the funds of the organization. One of the more interesting results is the discovery that a number of regional officers have been diverting large sums of union money to their private use. Another desirable aspect of Title II is that embezzlement of union monies is a federal crime subject to prosecution in the federal courts. No longer can peculation be hidden by arrangements for partial or complete recovery. The courts have in many of these cases tempered justice with mercy for they recognized that the offenders were not professional criminals, but men and women who temporarily yielded to temptation.

Trusteeships

One of the more successful outcomes of the reform legislation is the elimination of the evils that had developed in the imposition and administration of trusteeships. The procedure is vital if the parent organization is to impose standards agreed to or eliminate evils that had arisen in the subordinate units. Unless the national organization is armed with the power to intervene, there would be no method by which abuses and oppression of the members could be opposed. Self-government means the power to enforce existing rules.

Many unions use the trusteeship sparingly if at all. In reports to conventions, officers of unions have frequently stated that they were reluctant to impose the restrictions upon locals in the form of a trusteeship, and that only the necessities of the situation forced them to act. Considering the few members of unions whose behavior aroused the severe condemnation of the McClellan Committee, such an assertion seems correct. Title III eliminated the abuses that were revealed and at the same time did not weaken the procedure. A union which finds that one of its locals is unable to support itself, or is guilty of severe laxity or misbehavior, can be placed under a trusteeship for the initial period of eighteen months. Upon a showing that the trusteeship should be continued, the union will be allowed a longer period to restore the local to a level at which the causes for intervention have been eliminated. The enforcement of this title has met with no criticism. No trustee can use the funds of the trusteed local except for administering the union under his control and the Department of Labor will not allow a prolongation of a trusteeship except upon proof that it is still necessary. The votes of the trusteed local cannot be used by the appointed officers to serve their own needs. The remedy has been effective.

Elections

The protection of election appears to have had the highest priority because the enforcement of the provisions have been delegated to the Secretary of Labor. This delegation of authority is in line with the Congressional view that democratic unions would be the most effective antidote to the evils exposed by the McClellan Committee. An immediate result was the holding of elections by a number of independent organizations which had regarded such activities as unnecessary. They were not a large number. The main activity of the LMWP has been directed to eliminating burdensome qualifications for candidacy, although much time has been spent investigating violations which dilute the fairness of an election. Persistent campaigns in the courts have been successful in eliminating clauses which are discriminatory or difficult to meet, and its persistent efforts have compelled a number of unions to abolish such restrictions.

What has been the effect of these changes? Some important ones are evident. One of the best examples of the effectiveness of the LMRDA is Local 825, International Union of Operating Engineers, in New Jersey. This is a powerful organization which at one time was the base for Joseph Fay's nefarious operations. When Fay was removed from the scene as a result of a conviction of extortion, he was succeeded by Peter Weber who followed in the footsteps of his predecessor and ended up in a federal jail. Weber's imprisonment was the direct result of the LMRDA. After the enactment of the reform labor law, an opposition ticket came to the surface in Local 825. Elections with an opposition candidate were held for the first time by the local. More significant was the persistence of the opposition over time, persistence which was finally rewarded in the defeat of the business manager, a brother of Peter Weber. It is doubtful if this change would have been possible without the protecting shield of the LMRDA. The experience in this local may indicate that the members are not as complacent about corruption as one assumes. At least in New Jersey they voted to end it.

Of equal significance is the ability of candidates to challenge an incumbent for national office in a labor organization. Such challenges are not numerous, and very likely will not be too plentiful in the future. Some writers emphasize that the top office holders in labor unions tend to serve over long periods of time, and moreover they are not often opposed for reelection.[4] The situation in the United States is not different from the one prevailing in England or in the unions on the continent. Once the organization becomes stabilized, contests for union office diminish, except in unions such as the International Typographical Union, the American Newspaper Guild, and a few others. The reasons are lack of acquaintance of local and even regional leaders with the national constituency, the difficulty of achieving success against the incumbent whose duties bring him in contact with a large number of members through meetings, the publications of the union, or the reports submitted on the state of the organization. In addition, a candidate must run on a platform and must be willing to spend his own and his followers' money on behalf of his candidacy.

Writers who have no experience with unions will, as Robert Michels did in Germany prior to World War I, discover that such a tendency is a manifestation of the "iron law of oligarchy," but the writers do not usually inquire what the purpose of sheer opposition might be.[5] Whatever the reasons, a continuing struggle for union office has not been characteristic of American unions. Usually it is implied that persistence in office is a vice of "conservative" organizations, but the late Sidney Hillman, Philip Murray, and Walter Reuther held office in their unions for lengthy periods of time, and the conclusion would inevitably be that the members showed very good judgment in keeping them in office.

Unions are not and have never been organizations which are concerned with a wide variety of problems. Resolutions on many topics are adopted at conventions, but the work of a labor organization is mainly dealing with the employer over the terms of employment. State or national federations concern themselves with a wider range of issues, but they are exempt from the provisions of the Landrum-Griffin Act. Even though not always used, the ability to mount a campaign of challenge should always be open so that a venal or incompetent officer can be eliminated. In that respect the LMRDA is significant because it allows for the setting up of opposition to an administration in those instances in which the members or some of them are dissatisfied with the performance of the incumbents. It is not subject to proof but it would seem that the LMRDA was significant in the elections in the unions of steelworkers, electrical workers, miners and allied workers.

The Secretary of Labor was attacked for not having investigated the denial of rights by the administration led by President W. A. Boyle to the opposition headed by Joseph A. Yablonski. As a result of the agitation, the Senate Sub-Committee on Labor looked into the matter. Mr. Joseph L. Rauh, the attorney for Yablonski, requested on July 9 and 18, 1969, that the Secretary order an investigation of "events and activities involved in the forthcoming election of International officers to be conducted by the United Mine Workers of America." In reply, Secretary of Labor George P. Shultz stated the position of the Department: "Although the Secretary of Labor does have the power under Section 601 (a) of the Labor-Management Reporting and Disclosure Act of 1959 (LMRDA) to investigate election irregularities at any time, it is the Department of Labor's long-established policy not to undertake one of this kind without having a valid complaint under Section 402 (a) after an election has been completed. In the absence of such complaint the Secretary of Labor lacks enforcement authority prescribed in Section 402 (b)."[6]

Mr. Rauh was further informed: "The Department of Labor, as a matter of policy, has never initiated or conducted an investigation of an election prior to the actual conduct of the election. In those very few situations where investigations have been conducted prior to the receipt of a valid complaint under Section 402 (a), the Department acted only after the election had been completed or a request for intervention had been received from both parties involved."[7]

Mr. Rauh was not satisfied with the decision, and in a meeting with Secretary Shultz and in the letter of July 25, 1969, he listed a number of additional violations that the Boyle faction had committed. Shultz would not move from his position.[8] Because of the propaganda campaign and the tragedy that followed the election, the murder of Joseph Yablonski, his wife and daughter, the position of the Department of Labor has been obscured. Secretary Shultz, in his testimony, claimed that the requests for an investigation were rejected because of the "longstanding policy" of the Department not to investigate before the balloting takes place. "That has been the policy of the Department since the enactment of the statute, and it was adopted despite the seemingly broad language of Section 601 of the statute authorizing investigations in general."[9]

Title IV contains a three-stage procedure for curing violations of the election provisions: (1) An appeal to the appellate tribunals of the union; (2) investigation by the Secretary; (3) court action to set aside the election and the holding of a new one under the supervision of the Secretary. "The statute gives the Secretary no authority to challenge violations occurring before the election is held or before the internal remedies have been exhausted."[10] Section 601, upon which Mr. Rauh replied, only gives the Secretary the power to investigate; it has no enforcement power. Moreover, the Secretary stated: "From 1959 until today, the sole use of Section 601 investigatory authority in election cases has been to collect or preserve evidence regarding elections which have already been held, and, therefore, in circumstances in which the outcome of the election could not be affected."[11] The Secretary was willing to do that "if we had received any persuasive indication that evidence was likely to be destroyed."[12] The Department used its investigatory authority only after the balloting was finished "but before the procedural requirements for a Title IV investigation had been met. Under these circumstances our investigation cannot affect the outcome of the election."[13]

It has been the view of the Secretary, supported by the legislative history of the statute, that Congress sought to promote self-government by the unions. The Secretary declared: "The Department should not, as a matter of policy, and I believe may not, as a matter of sound statutory construction, investigate and publicize the activities of one faction in an election in order to assist the campaign of the other."[14]

An assessment of the position of the Department of Labor, actually the Office of Labor-Management and Welfare-Pension Reports, should be made independent of the Yablonski policy. The attorneys for the dissident group were able to set in motion a nationwide campaign of pressure upon the Department.[15] The attorneys for Boyle, as well as those for Yablonski, criticized the Office of Labor-Management and Welfare-Pension Reports for its conduct during the vote. However, "Mr. Yablonski's attorney not only asked for the Department's assistance in Mr. Yablonski's campaign but stated that an early investigation was necessary to maintain the campaign's momentum."[16]

Safeguards for Labor Organizations

As noted in the discussion on this section, the purpose of Title V is to allow members to challenge unauthorized expenditures or the misuse of funds through a suit in the federal or state courts. The suits have involved the pension programs of several unions, and claims have been made that beneficiaries were being assigned who were ineligible or that other kinds of violations of fiduciary responsibility have occurred. In some cases, the increases in salary or expenses were challenged. The small number of cases may indicate that the finances in the unions are generally handled properly. Moreover, in order to challenge the use of funds, the challenger must show that there is a reasonable suspicion of an impropriety. Only if an organized group is challenging the leadership which exists is such evidence likely to be assembled. Even if it is not widely utilized, the provisions can be of assistance in protecting the integrity of union funds.

Protection Against Violence

Section 610 aims to eliminate the use of violence in connection with a union member exercising his rights under the act. Assaults against dissidents for expressing unpopular views during an election campaign might fall under these provisions. Many charges are made during political campaigns of unions, but frequently they are not supported by the kind of evidence that justifies intervention. In enacting this provision, Congress believed that it would protect members against intimidation and strong-arm tactics. It has not been used extensively because the kinds of situation envisaged by the proponents of the legislation are not frequent.

The LMRDA has not had any harmful effect upon the labor movement, or upon the organizations against which many suits have been directed. Section 609 repeats the prohibition against penalizing a member for exercising his rights given to him under the LMRDA. It adds that in addition a union may not "otherwise discipline" a member for exercising his rights under the statute. The statement refers to punishment through adverse changes imposed on the job, through the administration of collective bargaining and in any related manner ostensibly for a reason different from the actual one, the opposition of the member to the officers or policies of the organization.

Since the enactment of the law, union membership has risen by several millions. Among the unions which have gained substantial increases in membership, the Teamsters' Union heads the list. The substantial gains are a tribute to its organizing prowess and not to its virtue. It does, however, show that the American worker was not overimpressed by the revelations of the McClellan Committee. Another sign of this attitude was the late Walter Reuther's joining his organization in a joint effort to improve the American labor movement.

There is another aspect of this issue which should be noted. The McClellan Committee recognized in its reports that the evils exposed affected only a few organizations, and in some instances only a few units within a larger whole. American labor has a long history. It has operated in times of prosperity and adversity. Aside from its adaptability to new situations, the changes, other than the attention and expense necessary to perform some of the requirements, do not affect the majority of unions. Others have had to make greater changes, but, even in these instances, the basic activities carried on by the organizations were neither impaired nor made excessively burdensome. The law and the changes in the National Labor Relations Board have increased the dependence of labor organizations upon members of the bar, but the LMRDA made a minor addition to a well-established trend that goes back to the 1930s. In return, the LMRDA has compelled an improvement in the keeping of accounts. It has also been the basis for exposing a number of embezzlers in strategically lucrative places and for uncovering others operating on a smaller scale.

Appendix I

Federal Cases

Addison v. Grand Lodge Machinists, 300 F. 2d 863 (C.A.9, 1963) 318 F. 2d 504 (C.A.9, 1963)

Aho v. Bintz, 58 L.C. 13,016 (D.C. Minn., 1968)

Air Line Stewards v. Transport Union, 49 L.C. 18,850 (C.A. 9, 1960)

Allen v. Armored Car etc., 185 F. Supp. 492 (D.C.N.J., 1960)

Allen v. Local 92 Iron Workers, 41 L.C. 16,697 (D.C.N. Ala., 1960)

Allen v. Stage Employees, 338 F. 2d 309 (C.A. 5, 1960)

Altman v. Wirtz, 56 LRRM 2651 (D.C. D.C., 1964)

Ames v. Musicians, 251 F. Supp. (D.C.S. N.Y., 1968)

Anderson v. Carpenters, 47 L.C. 18,400 (D.C. Minn., 1968)

Anthal v. Mine Workers, 54 L.C. 11,621 (D.C. Pa., 1966)

Archibald v. Operating Engineers, 276 F. Supp. 326 (D.C. R.I., 1967)

Arthur v. Musicians Local 802, 278 F. Supp. 400 (D.C. N.Y., 1967)

Associated Orchestra Leaders v. Philadelphia Musical Society, 203 F. Supp. 755 (D.C.E. Pa., 1962)

Avise v. Carpenters District Council of Denver, 44 L.C. 17,499 (D.C. Col., 1962)

Bakery and Confectionery Workers v. Ratner, 335 F. 2d 152 (C.A., 1960)

Barbour v. Sheet Metal Workers, 401 F. 2d 152 (C.A.,6, 1968)

Baron v. Newspaper Guild, Local 173, 224 F. Supp. 85 (1963), reversed 342 F. 2d 523 (C.A. 3, 1963)

Baruncia v. Hatters, 321 F. 2d 764 (C.A.8, 1963)

Beauchamp v. Local 761, 43 L.C. 17,196 (D.C.S. Cal., 1961)

Beckman v. Local 49, Iron Workers, 314 F. 2d 848 (C.A.7, 1963)

Bennett v. Hoisting Engineers, Local 701, 207 F. Supp. 361 (D.C. Ore., 1963)

Berman v. Local 107, Teamsters, 237 F. Supp. 767 (D.C.E. Pa., 1964)

Besom v. Transport Workers, 46 L.C. 18,102 (D.C.W. Pa., 1963)

Bey v. Muldoon, 223 F. Supp. 489 (D.C.E. Pa., 1963)

Blackmarr v. Teamsters 64 L.C. (D.C. Central Cal., 1966)

Blassie v. Poole, 51 L.C. 510 (D.C.E. Mo, 1965)

Blue v. Carpenters Local No. 7, 50 L.C. 19,099 (D.C. Minn., 1964)

Boggia v. Hoffa, 40 L.C. 16,731 (D.C.S. N.Y., 1961), (41 L.C. 16,732) (C.A. 2, 1961)

Boggs Electrical Workers (IBEW), 326 F. Supp. (D.C. Mont., 1971)

Boilermakers v. Hardeman, 401 U.S. 223 (1971)

Boilermakers Local 42 v. Boilermakers, 324 F. 2d (C.A. 6, 1963) cert. denied, 376 U.S. 913 (1964)

Boilermakers v. Raferty, 348 F. 2d 367 (C.A. 9, 1965)

Boling v. Teamsters, 224 F. Supp. 18 (D.C.E. Tenn., 1963)

Bougie v. Carpenters Local 599, 67 LRRM 2402 (D.C.N. Tenn., 1968)

Bradley v. Electrical Workers (IUE), 236 F. Supp. 724 (D.C.E. Pa., 1964)

Braswell v. Boilermakers, 388 F. 2d 193 (C.A. 5, 1968), cert. denied 391 U.S. 935 (1968)

Britt v. Penninsula Shipbuilders, 62 L.C. 10,609 (D.C.E. Va., 1969)

Brooks v. Tile Workers, 187 F. Supp. 365 (D.C.E. Pa., 1960)

Broomer v. Schultz, 239 F. Supp. 699 (D.C.E. Pa., 1965), 356 F. 2d 384 (C.A. 3, 1966)

Burke v. Boilermakers, 57 L.C. 12,496 (D.C.S. Cal., 1968)

Burns v. Carpenters Local 626, 204 F. Supp. 599 (D.C. Del., 1962)

Burris v. Teamsters, 224 F. Supp. 277 (D.C.W. N.C., 1963)

Burroughs v. Operating Engineers, Local 3, 54 L.C. 11,454 (D.C.S. Cal., 1960)

Byrd v. Archer, 38 L.C. 66,083 (D.C.S. Cal., 1959)

Calabrese v. United Association, 211 F. Supp. 609 (D.C. N.J., 1962), 324 (C.A. 3, 1963) 955.

Calhoon v. Harvey, 379 U.S. 134 (1964)

Caraballo v. Union De Operadores Canteros, 49 L.C. 18,784 (D.C. P.R., 1964)

Carpenter v. Brady, 241 F. Supp. 679 (D.C. Minn., 1964)

Carpenters Local 201 v. Brown, 343 F. 2d 862 (C.A. 10, 1965)

Carroll v. Associated Musicians of Greater New York, 284 F. 2d (C.A. 2, 196)

Cassidy v. Horan, 56 L.C. 12,280 (D.C.W. N.Y., 1967)

Catanzaro v. Soft Drink Workers, 55 L.C. 11,821 (D.C.S. N.Y., 1960)

Charles v. Musicians, 241 F. Supp. 595 (D.C.S. N.Y., 1965)

Cisney v. Carpenters Local 413, 51 L.C. 2749 (D.C.N. Ind., 1965)

Cleveland Orchestra Comm. v. Musicians Local 4, 303 F. 2d 229 (C.A. 6, 1962)

Clinton v. Hueston, 308 F. 2d 908 (C.A. 5, 1962)

Cole v. Hall, 339 F. 2d 88 (C.A. 2, 1964)

Cole v. Hall, 93 S. Ct. 1943 (1973)

Colella v. United States, 360 F. 2d 792 (C.A. 2, 1966) cert. denied 385 U.S., 1966.

Coleman v. Railway and Steamship Clerks, 340 F. 2d 206 (C.A. 2, 1965)

Conley v. Aiello, 56 L.C. 12,397 (D.C.S. N.Y., 1967)

Connor v. Teamsters Local 560, 39 L.C. 66,115 (D.C. N.J., 1959)

Coratella v. Roberta, 49 L.C. 18,939 (D.C. Conn., 1964), set aside 50 L.C. 18,939 (D.C. Conn., 1964)

Cornelio v. Carpenters District Council, 348 F. 2d 728 (C.A. 3, 1966)

Cox v. Hutcheson, 49 LRRM 2990 (C.A. 3, 1960)

Cunningham v. English, 269 F. 2d 517 (C.A. D.C., 1958), cert. denied 361 U.S. 897 (1959)

Cutler v. Musicians, 316 F. 2d 546 (C.A. 2, 1963)

Dave v. Tobacco Workers, 234 F. Supp. 815 (D.C. D.C., 1964)

Deacon v. Operating Engineers Local 12, 378 F. 2d 245 (C.A. 10, 1967)

Deluhery v. Marine Cooks and Stewards, 199 F. Supp. 270 (D.C.S. Cal., 1962)

Denov v. Davis, 51 L.C. 18,449 (D.C.N. Ill., 1966)

Detroy v. American Guild of Variety Artists, 286 F. 2d 75 (C.A. 3, 1961), cert. denied 306 U.S. 929 (1961)

De Vito v. Shultz, 300 F. Supp. 381 (D.C. D.C., 1969)

De Vito v. Schultz, 61 L.C. 10,465 (D.C. D.C., 1969)

Doyle v. United States, 318 F. 2d 419 (C.A. 9, 1963)

Duncan v. Penninsula Shipbuilders, 394 F. 2d 237 (C.A. 4, 1968)

Durandetti v. Chrysler Corp. 195 F. Supp. 653 (D.C.E. Mich., 1961)

Echols v. Cook, 50 L.C. 187 (D.C.N. Ga., 1962)

Electrical Workers Local 28 v. Electrical Workers (IBEW) 184 F. Supp. 649 (D.C. Md., 1960)

Farowitz v. Musicians Local 802, 330 F. 2d 999 (C.A. 2, 1964)

Falcone v. Dantine, 58 L.C. 12,959 (D.C.E. Pa., 1969)

Ferger v. Local 483, Iron Workers 356 F. 2d 854 (C.A. 3, 1966), 94 N.J. Super. 554 (1967)

Figueroa v. Maritime Union, 342 F. 2d 946 (C.A. 2, 1965)

Flaherty v. McDonald, 183 F. Supp. 300 (D.C.S. Cal., 1960)

Flight Engineers v. Continental Airlines, 209 F. 2d 397 (C.A. 9, 1961)

Fogg v. Randolph, 244 F. Supp. 885 (D.C.S. N.Y., 1962)

Fogle v. Steelworkers, 230 F. Supp. 797 (D.C.S. Pa., 1964)

Ford v. Kammerer 58 L.C. 12,909 (D.C.E. Pa., 1968)

Fruit Packers Local 760 v. Morly, 378 F. 2d 738 (C.A. 9, 1967)

Gammon v. Machinists, 199 F. Supp. 433 (D.C.N. Ga., 1961)

Gartner v. Solner, 384 F. 2d 348 (C.A. 3, 1967), cert denied 390 U.S. 1,040 (1968)

George v. Bricklayers, 255 F. Supp. 239 (D.C.E. Wis., 1966)

Gilbert v. Hoisting Engineers, Local 701, 48 L.C. 50,901 (Ore. Sup. Ct., 1963), cert. denied 376 U.S. 963 (1964)

Giordani v. Hoffman, 277 F. Supp. 722 (D.C.E. Pa., 1967)

Giordani v. Upholsterers, 69 LRRM 2548 (D.C. 2, 1968)

Gleason v. Chair Service Restaurants Local 11, 60 L.C. 1065 (D.C.S. N.Y., 1969)

Goldberg v. Amalgamated Local 355, 202 F. Supp. 844 (D.C.E. N.Y., 1962)

Goldberg v. Truck Drivers Local 299, 293 F. 2d 807 (C.A. 6, 1961)

Gordon v. Laborers International, 315 F. Supp. 824 (D.C. Ok., 1972)

Graham v. Solner, 220 F. Supp. 711 (D.C.E. Pa., 1963)

Grasso v. Phillips, 45 L.C. 50,535 (D.C.S. N.Y., 1962)

Green v. Hotel and Restaurant Local 705, 220 F. Supp. 505 (D.C.E. Mich., 1963)

Gross v. Kennedy, 183 F. Supp. 750 (D.C.S. N.Y., 1960)

Gulickson v. Forrest, 58 L.C. 12,763 (D.C.E. N.Y., 1968)

Gurton v. Arons, 339 F. 2d 371 (C.A. 2, 1964)

Gurton v. Manuiti, 339 F. 2d 371 (C.A. 3, 1964)

Haiduk v. Atlantic Independent Union, 46 L.C. 17,941 (D.C.E. Pa., 1962)

Hall v. Pacific Coast Maritime Asn., 281 F. Supp. 54 (D.C.N. Cal., 1968)

Hamilton v. Guinan, 199 F. Supp. 562 (D.C.S. N.Y., 1961)

Harris v. Local 1291, Longshoremen, 205 F. Supp. 45 (D.C.E. Pa., 1962) 210 F. Supp. 4 (D.C.E. Pa., 1963), 321 F. 2d 801 (C.A. 3, 1963)

Henderson v. Sarle, 197 N.Y.S. 920 (N.Y. Sup. Ct., 1960)

High Truck Drivers Local 107 v. Cohen, 182 F. 2d 688 (C.A. 3, 1960), cert. denied 365 U.S. 833 (1961)

Hill v. Aro Corp., 275 F. Supp. 482 (D.C.N. Ohio, 1967)

Hodgson v. Local Union, 76 LRRM 3025 (C.A. 6, 1971)

Hodgson v. Local 582, Plumbers, 350 F. Supp. 16 (D.C. D.C., 1972)

Hodgson v. Local 610, United Electrical Workers, 342 F. Supp. 1345 (D.C.W. Pa., 1972)

Hodgson v. Local 734, Teamsters, 336 F. Supp. 1234 (D.C.N. Ill., 1972)

Hodgson v. Local 1291, International Longshoremen's Association (D.C.E. Pa., 1972)

Hodgson v. Mine Workers, 344 F. Supp. 17 (D.C. D.C., 1972)

Hodgson v. Steelworkers, 403 U.S. 33 (1971)

Holdeman v. Sheldon, 311 F. 2d 304 (C.A. 2, 1967)
Holton v. McFarland, 215 F. Supp. 372 (D.C. Alaska, 1963)
Horn v. Amal. Street Electric Railway Employees, Div. 1303, 194 F. Supp. 560 (D.C.S. Mich., 1961)
Horner v. Feron, 362 F. 2d 224 (C.A. 9, 1966), cert. denied, 54 L.C. 11,567 (1966)
Humphrey v. Moore, 375 U.S. 335 (1964)
Inland Steel Corp. v. National Labor Relations Board, 170 F. 2d 247 (C.A. 7, 1949)
International Brotherhood of Electrical Workers v. Eli, 307 F. Supp. 495 (D.C. Hawaii, 1969)
Jackson v. Longshoremen's Association, 212 F. Supp. 79 (D.C. La., 1962)
Jackson v. Marine Engineers Ben. Assn., 221 Supp. 347 (D.C.S. N.Y., 1963)
Jackson v. Martin Co., 180 F. Supp. 475 (D.C. Md., 1962)
Jackson v. Local 2496, Steelworkers, 50 L.C. 19,120 (D.C.S. N.Y., 1964)
Jacques v. Local 14, Longshoremen, 246 F. Supp. 57 (D.C.E. La., 1965)
Jennette v. Amons, 51 L.C. 16,804 (D.C.M. Tenn., 1965)
Jennings v. Carey, 51 L.C. 19,423 (D.C. D.C., 1964)
Johnson v. Electrical Workers Local 58, 181 F. Supp. 734 (D.C.E. Mich., 1960)
Johnson v. Nelson, 325 F. 2d 646 (C.A. 8, 1963)
Johnson v. San Diego Waiters, Local 500, 190 F. Supp. 444 (D.C.S. Cal., 1961)
Jolly v. Gorman, 70 LRRM 3119 (D.C.S. Miss., 1969)
Jones v. American Guild of Variety Artists, 190 F. Supp. 840 (D.C.E. Pa., 1961)
Kalish v. Hosier, 364 F. 2d 829 (C.A. 10, 1966), cert. denied, 386 U.S. 944 (1967)
Kelly v. Streho, 42 L.C. 16,843 (D.C.E. Mich., 1961)
Kelsey v. Local 8, Stage Employees, 491 F. 2d 491 (C.A. 3, 1969)
King v. Machinists, 335 F. 2d 340 (C.A. 9, 1964), cert. denied 372 U.S. 917 (1964)
King v. Randazo, 346 F. 2d 307 (C.A. 2, 1965)
Knox v. United Automobile Workers, 223 F. Supp. 1009 (D.C.E. Mich., 1963)
Kolmon v. Hod Carriers 1191, 215 F. Supp. 703 (D.C.E. Mich., 1964)
Krilkowski v. Carpenters District Council, 212 F. Supp. 338 (D.C.E. Pa., 1962)
Kuykendall v. Carpenters Local 1763, 49 L.C. 19,040 (D.C. Wyo., 1964)
Lamb v. Carpenters Local 1292, 51 L.C. 19,682 (D.C.E. N.Y., 1965)

Lanigan v. Local Union 9, Electrical Workers, 327 F. 2d 627 (C.A. 7, 1964), cert. denied, 379 U.S. 979 (1964), subnom *Reese* v. *Electrical Workers*.

Lankford v. International Bro. of Electrical Workers, 196 F. Supp. 661 (D.C.N. Ala., 1961), 293 F. 2d 928 (C.A. 5, 1961), cert. denied 368 U.S. 1004 (1962)

Leonard v. M.I.T. Employees Union, 198 F. Supp. 212 (D.C. Mass., 1964)

Letter Carriers v. Sombrotto, 449 F. 2d 915 (C.A. 2, 1971)

Levinson v. Perry, 60 L.C. 10,107 (D.C.S. N.Y., 1969)

Lewis v. American Fed. of State and County Employees, 407 F. 2d 1185 (C.A. 3, 1969)

Libutti v. DiBrizzi, 337 F. 2d 216 (C.A. 2, 1964), 343 F. 2d 460 (C.A. 2, 1965)

Local 2 v. Telephone Workers, 261 F. Supp. 433 (D.C. Mass., 1966), 362 F. 2d 891 (C.A. 1, 1966)

Local 28 v. Electrical Workers, 184 F. Supp. 649 (D.C. Md., 1960)

Local 10 v. Musicians, 57 LRRM 2227 (D.C.N. Ill., 1964)

Local 42 Boilermakers v. Boilermakers, 324 F. 2d 201 (1963)

Local 115 v. Carpenters, 247 F. Supp. 660 (D.C. Conn., 1965)

Local 33 v. Mason Tenders v. Hod Carriers, 186 F. Supp. 737 (D.C.S. N.Y., 1960)

Local 92 Iron Workers v. Norris, 383 F. 2d 735 (C.A. 5, 1967)

Local 1419, Longshoremen v. Smith, 301 F. 2d 791 (C.A. 5, 1963)

Lucas v. Kenny, 220 F. Supp. 188 (D.C.N. Ill., 1963)

Luggage Workers v. Leather Goods Workers, 316 F. Supp. 500 (D.C. Del., 1971)

Lynch v. Railway Clerks, 51 L.C. 19,782 (D.C.S. N.Y., 1965)

McArty v. District Lodge Machinists, 252 F. Supp. 350 (D.C.E. Mo., 1966)

McCabe v. Electrical Workers (IBEW), 60 L.C. 10,297 (C.A. 6, 1969)

McCraw v. United Association, 341 F. 2d 705 (C.A. 6, 1965)

McDonough v. Johnson, 49 L.C. 19,042 (D.C.N. Ohio, 1964), 54 L.C. 11,386 (C.A. 6, 1965) vacated and dismissed.

McDonough v. Operating Engineers Local 805, 66 L.C. 12,243 (D.C. N.J., 1972), 69 L.C. 13,208 (C.A. 3, 1972)

McFarland v. Building Material Teamsters Local 262, 180 F. Supp. 806 (D.C.S. N.Y., 1960)

McKeon v. Highway Truck Drivers Local 107, 223 F. Supp. 341, (D.C. Del., 1963)

Magelssen v. Local 518, Plasterers, 233 F. Supp. 459 (D.C.W. Mo., 1964), 240 F. Supp. 259 (D.C.W. Mo., 1965)

Mamula v. Local 1211, Steelworkers, 198 Supp. 652 (D.C.W. Pa., 1962), 304 F. 2d 108 (C.A. 3, 1962)

Martin v. Boilermakers. Lodge 636, 245 F. Supp. 375 (D.C.W. Pa., 1963)

Martire v. Laborers Local 1058, 410 F. 2d 32 (C.A. 3, 1969)

Milone v. English, 306 F. 2d 814 (C.A. D.C., 1962)

Morrisey v. Curran, 423 F. 2d 339 (C.A. 2, 1970)

Moscheta v. Cross, 354 F. 2d 504 (C.A. D.C., 1965)

Moss v. Davis, 198 F. Supp. 441 (D.C.M. Fla., 1963)

Navarro v. Gannon, 65 LRRM 2071 (D.C.S. N.Y., 1967), 385 F. 2d 512 (C.A. 2, 1967), cert. denied 390 U.S. 987 (1968)

Nelms v. Plumbers Union, 405 F. 2d 70 (1968)

Nelson v. Painters, Local 386, 212 F. Supp. 233 (D.C. Minn., 1961), sub nom Johnson v. Nelson, 325 F. 2d 646 (C.A., 1963)

Nix v. Fulton Lodge No. 2, Machinists, 71 LRRM

Null v. Carpenters District Council, 239 F. Supp. 809 (D.C.S. Tex., 1965) (C.A. 5, 1969)

Operating Engineers Local 3 v. Burroughs, 417 F. 2d 370 (C.A., 1969)

Paige v. Maritime Union, 54 L.C. 11,503 (D.C.S. N.Y. 1965)

Painters Union v. District Council 15, 67 LRRM 2459 (D.C.N. Cal., 1968)

Paley v. Greenberg, 62 L.C. 10,677 (D.C.S. N.Y., 1970)

Parker v. Teamsters Local 172, 229 F. Supp. 172 (D.C.W. N.C., 1964)

Parks v. Electrical Workers, 314 F. 2d 897 (C.A. 4, 1963)

Parrish v. Legion, 450 F. 2d 821 (C.A. 9, 1971)

Peck v. Food Distributors, 237 F. Supp. 113 (D.C. Mass., 1965)

Penuelas v. Moreno, 198 F. Supp. 441 (D.C.S. Cal., 1961)

Persico v. Daley, 51 L.C. 19,480 (D.C.S. N.Y., 1965)

Phillips v. Osborne, 403 F. 2d 826 (C.A. 9, 1968)

Phillips v. Teamsters Local 560, 209 F. Supp. 768 (D.C. N.J., 1962)

Pignotti v. Local 3, Sheet Metal Workers, 343 F. Supp. 236 (D.C. Neb., 1972)

Pittman v. Carpenters, 251 F. Supp. 323 (D.C.M. Fla., 1966)

Plant v. Local 199 Laborers, 331 F. Supp. 736 (D.C. Del., 1971)

Plenty v. Laborers, 77 LRRM 2305 (D.C.E. Pa., 1969), 77 LRRM 2429 (D.C.E. Pa., 1969)

Postma v. Teamsters Local 294, 337 F. 2d 609 (C.A. 2, 1964)

Pucell v. Keane, 277 F. Supp. 252 (D.C.E. Pa., 1967), 406 F. 2d 1195 (C.A. 3, 1969)

Ragland v. United Mine Workers, 188 F. Supp. 131 (D.C.N. Ala., 1960)

Ranes v. Office Employees, Local 28, 317 F. 2d 915 (C.A. 7, 1963)
Rekant v. Meat Cutters Local 446, 320 F. 2d 271 (C.A. 3, 1963)
Rekant v. Rabinowitz, 194 F. Supp. 194 (D.C.E. Pa., 1961)
Rinker v. Local 24, Lithographers, 313 F. 2d 956 (C.A. 3, 1963)
Rizzo v. Almond, 40 L.C. 66,506 (D.C. N.J., 1960)
Robbins v. Rarback, 325 F. 2d 929 (C.A. 2, 1962), cert. denied 379 U.S.
    974 (1965)
Robinson v. Weir, 277 F. Supp. 581 (D.C. Neb., 1967)
Rosen v. Painters District Council, No. 9, 326 F. 2d 400 (C.A. 2, 1964)
Rothstein v. Manuti, 235 F. Supp. 48 (D.C.S. N.Y., 1963)
Ryan v. Local 134, Electrical Workers, 361 F. 2d 942 (C.A. 7, 1966), cert.
    denied 387 U.S. 935 (1966)
Salzhandler v. Caputo, 316 F. 2d 445 (C.A. 2, 1963), cert. denied 375
    U.S. 946 (1963)
Sanders v. Iron Workers, 235 F. 2d 271 (C.A. 6, 1966)
Sands v. Abeli, 58 L.C. 12,924 (D.C.S. N.Y., 1968)
Santos v. Bonanno, 369 F. 2d 369 (C.A. 2, 1966)
Sawyers v. Machinists, 279 F. Supp. 747 (D.C.E. Mo., 1967)
Schonfeld v. Raftery, 271 F. Supp. 128 (D.C.S. N.Y., 1967), 381 F. 2d 446
    (C.A. 2, 167)
Schonfeld v. Rarback, 54 L.C. 11,440 (D.C.S. N.Y., 1966)
Scoville v. Watson, 338 F. 2d 678 (C.A. 7, 1964), cert. denied 380 U.S. 963
    (1965)
Schuchardt v. Millwrights and Machinery Erectors Local 380, 380 F. 2d
    795 (C.A. 10, 1967)
Schwartz v. Musicians Local 802, 340 F. 2d 228 (C.A. 2, 1964)
Seeley v. Painters, 308 F. 2d 52 (C.A. 5, 1962)
Serio v. Liss, 300 F. 2d 386 (C.A. 3, 1961)
Sertic v. Carpenters Council, 423 F. 2d 515 (C.A. 6, 1972)
Sewell v. Machinists, 445 F. 2d 545 (C.A. 5, 1971)
Sheridan v. Carpenters Local 626, 197 F. Supp. 347 (D.C. Del., 1961)
    reversed 306 F. 2d 152 (C.A. 3, 1962)
Simons v. Avisco, 350 F. 2d 1012 (C.A. 4, 1965)
Sordillo v. Local Union 63, Sheet Metal Workers, 47 L.C. 18,384 (D.C.
    Mass., 1963)
Spivey v. Grievance Comm., 69 LRRM 2709 (D.C.N. Ga., 1969)
Stark v. Twin City Carpenters, 219 F. Supp. 528 (D.C. Minn., 1963)
Stein v. Wirtz, 366 F. 2d 189 (C.A. 10, 1966)
Stettner v. Printing Pressmen, 278 F. Supp. 675 (D.C.E. Tenn., 1967)
Stout v. Laborers, 226 F. Supp. 673 (D.C.N. Ill., 1963)
Strauss v. Teamsters, 179 F. Supp. 297 (D.C.E. Pa., 1959)

Sylvia v. Lopez, 51 L.C. 19,741 (D.C. P.R., 1964)

Textile Workers v. Lincoln Mills, 353 (U.S. 448, 1957)

Thompson v. New York Central Railroad, 361 F. 2d 137 (C.A. 2, 1966)

Trbovich v. Mine Workers, 404 U.S. 528 (1972)

Tucker v. Local 70, Bartenders, 236 F. Supp. 233 (D.C.E. N.Y., 1964)

Tucker v. Shaw, 378 F. 2d 304 (C.A. 2, 1967)

United States v. Brown, 381 U.S. 437 (1965)

United States v. Budzanoski, 462 F. 2d 443 (C.A. 3, 1972)

United States v. DiBrizzi, 393 F. 2d 642 (C.A. 2, 1968)

United States v. Hartsough, 54 L.C. 516 (D.C.E. Pa., 1966)

United States v. Ferrara, 451 F. 2d 91 (C.A. 2, 1971)

United States v. Ford, 426 F. 2d 199 (C.A. 2, 1972)

United States v. Franco, 434 F. 2d 956 (C.A. 6, 1970), cert. denied 91 S.Ct., 1375 (1971)

United States v. Green, 350 U.S. 415 (1956)

United States v. Lynch, 464 F. 2d 909 (C.A. 3, 1972)

United States v. Haggerty, 61 L.C. 651 (C.A. 7, 1969)

United States v. McCarthy, 422 F. 2d 160 (C.A. 2, 1970)

United States v. Stubin, 446 F. 2d 4657 (C.A. 3, 1971)

Vars v. Boilermakers, 320 F. 2d 576 (C.A. 2, 1963)

Verbiscus v. Marine and Industrial Workers, 314 F. 2d 848 (C.A. 3, 1963)

Vestal v. Teamsters Local 327, 245 F. Supp. 823 (D.C.N. Tenn., 1965)

Weirauch v. Electrical Workers (IUE), 272 F. Supp. 472 (D.C. N.J., 1967)

Wesling v. Waitresses Union 305, 63 L.C. 11,148 (D.C. Ore., 1970)

White v. King, 64 L.C. 11,273 (D.C.E. La., 1972)

Williams v. Typographical Union, 423 F. 2d 1295 (C.A. 9, 1970)

Wingate v. Highway Truck Drivers Local 107, 51 L.C. 19,643 (D.C. Del., 1970)

Wirtz v. General Drivers 577, 214 G. Supp. 74 (D.C.N. Tex., 1963)

Wirtz v. Edmonds, 51 L.C. 12,410 (D.C. Colo., 1965)

Wirtz v. Carpenters Local 559, 61 LRRM 2618 (D.C.W. Ky., 1966)

Wirtz v. Carpenters Local 1622, 285 F. Supp. 455 (D.C. Cal., 1968)

Wirtz v. Glass Blowers Local 153, 389 U.S. 463 (1968)

Wirtz v. Great Lake District, Masters, Mates and Pilots, 240 F. Supp. 829 (D.C. Ohio, 1965)

Wirtz v. Hod Carriers Local 11, 211 F. Supp. 468 (D.C.W. Pa., 1964)

Wirtz v. Hotel, Motel and Club Employees Local 6, 391 U.S. 492 (1968)

Wirtz v. Independent Service Employees, 52 L.C. 16,759 (D.C.E. N.Y., 1965)

Wirtz v. Independent Workers of Fla., 272 F. Supp. 31 (D.C.M. Fla., 1967)

Appendix II

State Cases Up To 1959: 363 State Cases
Involving Discipline of Membership*

Abdon v. Wallace, 165 N.E. 147 (Ind. App., 1929)
Aggripponi v. Perrotti, 270 Mass. 55 (1929)
Alexion v. Holingsworth, 288 N.Y. 1 (1940)
Allen v. Carpenters, 337 P. 2d 457, 457 Cal. App. 1 (1959)
Allnut v. High Court of Foresters, 61 Mich. 110 (1886)
Ames v. Dubinsky, 70 NYS 2d (1947)
Anderson v. Painters, 330 S.W. 2d 541 (Texas Civil App., 1959)
Andrews v. Local No. 13, Plumbers, 234 N.Y.S. (1929)
Angrisani v. Stearn, 8 N.Y.S. 2d 998 (1938)
Armstrong v. Duffy, 90 Ohio App. 122 (1951)
Arrell v. Brotherhood of Trainmen, 79 Pa. D. & C. 581 (1951)
Ash v. Holdeman, 175 N.Y.S. 2d 135 (1958)
Attig v. Teamsters, 231 Iowa 1 (1942)
Austin v. Dutcher, 56 N.Y. App. 393 (1900)
Babrick v. Huddell, 245 Mass. 429 (1923)
Bachman v. Harrington, 102 N.Y.S. 406 (1906)
Bacon v. Paradise, 318 Mass. 649 (1945)
Baltimore Lodge No. 450 v. Machinists, 106 A. 692 (Md. App., 1919)
Barry v. Frascona, 28 LRRM 2480 (N.Y. App., 1951)
Barnhart v. United Automobile Workers, 10 N.J. Super. 357 (1959)
Bartone v. Di Pietro, 18 N.Y.S. 178 (1939)
Becker v. Calman, 331 Mass. 625 (1942)
Belkin v. Spiegel, 3 LRRM 800 N.Y. Sup. Ct. Special Term (1938)
Beneficial Association of Brotherly Unity, 38 Pa. 298 (1868)
Benson v. Screwmen's Benefit Ass. 76 Texas Sup. Ct. 554 (1890), 3 Texas
  Civil App. 66 (1893)
Berkowitz v. Robelack 73 N.Y.S. 2d 534 (1947)
Bernstein v. Robinson, 63 N.Y.S. 2d 300 (1946)
*358 cases involving unions; 5, fraternal organizations

Bertucci v. United Cement, Etc., 249 N.Y.S. 635 (1931)
Bianco v. Eisen 75 N.Y.S. 2d 914 (1944)
Bires v. Barney, 277 P. 2d 751 (Sup. Ct. Oregon, 1954)
Blek v. Wilson, 262 N.Y.S. 417 (1913), 237 N.Y. App. 712 (1933) reversing.
Bloom v. Nann, 41 N.Y.S. 852 (1943)
Bobbit v. Cleveland, Cincinnati and St. Louis RR, 73 Ohio App., 339 (1943)
Bonham v. Trainmen, 146 Ark., 117 (1920)
Brennan v. Hatters, Local 17, 73 N.J.L. 729 (1906)
Bricklayers Local 39 v. Bowen, 183 N.Y.S. 850 (1920)
Brooks v. Edgar, 19 N.Y.S. 2d 114 (1940)
Brotherhood v. Cook, 221 S.W. 1041 (Texas Civil App., 1920)
Brown v. Hook, 180 Pa. 2d (Cal. App., 1947)
Brown v. Lehman, 15 A 2d 513 (Pa. Super., 1940)
Browne v. Hibbets, 290 N.Y.S. 459 (1943)
Bucko v. Murray, 11 N.Y.S. 2d 402 (1939)
Burns v. Bricklayers, 14 N.Y.S. 361 (1891)
Buscarello v. Gugielmelli, 43 LRRM (N.Y. County Sup. Ct., 1959)
Bush v. Stage Employees, 130 P. 2d 788 (Cal. App., 1942)
Caliendo v. McFarland, 175 N.Y.S. 868 (1958)
Cameron v. Durkin, 321 Mass. 590 (1947)
Cameron v. International Alliance, 49 N.J. Eq. (1935)
Campbell v. Industrial Union of Marine, 52 Pa. D.C. 597 (1944)
Canfield v. Moreschi, 48 N.Y.S. 2d (1944)
Carey v. Brotherhood of Paper Makers, 206 N.Y.S. 730 (1924)
Carpenters Union v. Backman, 86 P. 2d 456 (Oregon Sup. Ct., 1939)
Cason v. Glass Bottle Blowers, 231 P. 2d (Cal. Sup. Ct., 1950)
Cavanaugh v. Hutchinson, 250 N.Y.S. 127 (1931)
Chagian v. Local 117, 14 N.J. Eq. 497 (1933)
Cheetham v. United Garment Workers Local 242, 55 Pa. D. & C. 38 (1945)
Chew v. Manhattan Laundries, 133 N.J. Eq. 326 (1943)
Clark v. Morgan, 271 Mass. 164 (1930)
Clarke v. Corr, 145 N.Y.S. 125 (1955)
Coleman v. O'Leary, 38 N.Y.S. 2d 812 (1945)
Collins v. International Alliance, 49 N.J. Eq. 230 (1935)
Connell v. Stalker, 48 N.Y.S. 77 (1897)
Constantino v. Moreschi, 9 Wash. 2d 638 (1941)
Cook v. Collins, 131 W.Va. 475 (1948)
Cook v. Mathis, 1 N.J. Super. 335 (1948)

Corregan v. Hay, 94 N.Y. App. 71 (1904)
Cotton Jammers v. Longshoremen's Assn. No. 2, 23 Tex. Civil App. 367 (1900)
Couie v. Local 1849 Carpenters, 316 P. 2d 473 (Wash. Sup. Ct., 1957)
Cox v. Carpenters, 190 Wash., 511 (1937)
Crawford v. Newman, 175 N.Y.S. 2d 903 (1958)
Cromwell v. Morrin, 91 N.Y.S. 2d 176 (1949)
Crossen v. Duffy, 90 Ohio App. 252 (1951)
Crutcher v. Order of Ry. Conductors, 151 Mo. App. 622 (1910)
Cunningham v. Milk Drivers, 148 N.Y.S. 2d 114 (1955)
Curtatella v. Heide, 20 LRRM 2347 (N.Y. Sup. Ct. Special Term, 1947)
Dachoylous v. Hotel and Restaurant Employees, 118 N.Y.S. 2d 455 (1952)
Daley v. Stickel, 6 N.Y. App., 951 (1958)
Dallas Photo-Engravers No. 38 v. Lemmon, 148 S.W. 954 (Tex. Civ. App.) (1941)
Dame v. LeFavre, 251 Wis. 146 (1946)
Davis v. Bioff, 141 P. 2d 486 (Cal. App., 1951)
Davis v. Inter. Alliance, 60 Cal. App. 2d 713 (1943)
Degonia v. Building Material Drivers, 318 P. 2d 486 (Cal. App., 1957)
DeMille v. Am. Fed. of Radio Artists, 31 Cal. 2d 139 (1947)
DeMonbrun v. Sheet Metal Workers, 295 P. 2d 881 (1956)
DeMotte v. Meat Cutters, 320 P. 2d 50 (Cal. App. 1958)
Deverell v. Musical Mutual Protective Union, 118 N.Y. 101 (1889)
DiBucci v. Uhrich, 189 N.Y.S. 2d 717 (1959)
Dickman v. Simons, 26 N.Y.S. 2d 889 (1941)
Dingwall v. Street Railway Union, 88 P. 597 (Cal. App. 1906)
Dixon v. Sheridan, 161 N.Y.S. 475 (1957)
Dodson v. International Alliance, 210 P. 2d 5 (Cal. Sup. Ct., 1949)
Donahue v. Kenney, 327 Mass. 409 (1951)
Dorrington v. Manning, 135 Pa. Super. 194 (Pa. Super., 1939)
Dragarva v. Federal Labor Union 23070, 136 N.J. Eq. 172 (1945)
Drazen v. Curby, 158 N.Y.S. 507 (1916)
Drummond v. Curran, 27 LRRM 2488 (Sup. Ct. N.Y. County, 1951)
Duffy v. Kelly, 91 N.W. 2d 916 (Sup. Ct. Mich., 1959)
Dusing v. Nuzzo, 31 N.Y.S. 2d (1941)
Edwards v. Teamsters Local 318, 8 Wash. 2d 492 (1941)
Eimans v. Gallagher, 185 N.Y.S. 2d 77 (1959)
Elfer v. Marine Engineers, 179 La. 383 (1934)
Ellis v. American Federation of Labor, 48 Cal. App. 440 (1941)
Engel v. Walsh, 101 N.E. 222 (Ill. Sup. Ct., 1913)

Harper v. Hoerchel, 14 So. 2d 179 (Sup. Ct. Fla., 1943)
Harris v. Detroit Typographical Union, 108 N.W. (Mich. Sup. Ct., 1906)
Harris v. Geier, 112 N.J. Eq. 99 (1932)
Harris v. Marine Cooks and Stewards, 221 P. 2d 336 (1950), 116 Cal. App. (1953)
Harrison v. O'Neil, 26 LRRM 2294 (N.Y. App., 1950)
Hartley v. Brotherhood of Rd. Trainmen, 283 Mich. 201 (1938)
Hatch v. Grand Lodge Trainmen, 233 Ill. 495 App. (1924)
Havens v. King, 224 N.Y.S. 193 (1927)
Havens v. Local 19, 338 Mich. 418 (1953)
Heasley v. Operative Plasterers No. 31, 384 Pa. 257 (1936)
Hickey v. Baine, 193 Mass. 446 (1907)
Hickman v. Kline, 270 P. 2d 662 (Sup. Ct. Nev., 1955)
Hod Carriers Local 426 v. Hod Carriers, 101 N.J. Eq. 474 (1929)
Hogan v. Faber, 89 N.Y.S. 2d 746 (1950)
Holdeman v. National Org. of Masters, Mates and Pilots, 7 N.Y. App. 2d 1021 (1958)
Holderby v. Operating Engineers, 45 Cal. 2d 843 (Cal. Sup. Ct., 1955)
Holmes v. Brown, 146 Ga. 402 (1916)
Holstrom v. Independent Dock Builders, 149 N.Y.S. 771 (1919)
Hopson v. Marine Cooks and Stewards, 253 P. 2d 136 (Cal. App., 1950)
International Union v. Owens, 119 Ohio St. 94 (1928)
Inter. Union of Brewery Workers v. Becherer, 4 N.J. Super. 456 (1948)
Irwin v. Posehl, 257 N.Y.S. 597 (1932)
Johnson v. Petrillo, 123 N.Y.S. 2d 1 (1953)
Johnston v. Carpenters, Union No. 971, 52 Nev. 400 (1930)
Jones v. Harmon, 220 La. 673 (1952)
Jose v. Savage, 205 N.Y.S. 6 (1924)
Junkins v. Local Union 6313, Communications Workers, 271 S.W. 71 (Mo. App. 1954)
Kanzler v. Linoleum Carpet and Soft Tile Workers, 149 P. 2d 276 (Sup. Ct. Wash., 1948)
Kaplan v. Elliott, 261 N.Y.S. 112 (1932)
Kehoe v. Leonard, 65 N.Y.S. 357 (1917)
Kehoe v. Sokol, 82 N.Y.S. 196 (1948)
Keller v. Lindelof, 50 N.Y.S. 705 (1943)
Kelman v. Kaplan, 91 N.Y.S. 2d 165 (1949)
Kennedy v. Schroder, 35 N.Y.S. 2d 835 (1942)
Kennedy v. Teamsters, 140 N.Y.S. 2d 899 (1955)
Killen v. Hotel and Restaurant Local 560, 190 P. 2d 30 (Cal. App., 1948)
King v. Inter. U. of Operating Engineers, 25 P. 2d 11 (Cal. App., 1952)

Kinnane v. Fay, 168 A 724 (N.J. Eq., 1933)
Kiser v. International Alliance, 26 Ohio App. 284 (1929)
Klein v. Morin, 248 N.Y. App., 253 (1937)
Kouky v. Canavan, 277 N.Y.S. 28 (1935)
Krause v. Sandler, 122 N.Y.S. 554 (1910)
Kunze v. Weber, 188 N.Y.S. 644 (1941)
Lafferty v. Fremd, 36 LRRM 2674 (N.Y. County Super. 1954)
LaRose v. Posehl, 282 N.Y.S. 332 (1935)
Leahigh v. Beyer, 116 N.E. 458 (Common Pleas, Ohio, 1953)
Le Bianco v. Cushing, 117 N.J. Eq. 593 (1935)
Leventhal v. Jennings, 311 Mass. 622 (1942)
Leo v. Local Union 612, Operating Engineers, 174 P. 2d 523 (Sup. Ct.
    Wash., 1946)
Licamel v. Weinstock, 3 LRRM 799 (N.Y. County Sup., 1938)
Ligget v. Koivunen, 34 N.W. 345 (Sup. Ct. Minn., 1948)
Liming v. Maloney, 32 Tenn. 632 (1949)
Litvin v. Novak, 45 LRRM 2021 (N.Y. App. 1959)
Local No. 2 v. Reinlib, 133 N.J. Eq. 572 (1943)
Local Iron Workers v. Iron Workers, 114 N.J. Eq. 555 (1933)
Local Union 57 v. Boyd, 245 Ala. 227 (1943)
Local Union No. 76 v. Carpenters, 116 La. 270 (1918)
Local Lodge 104 v. Boilermakers, 158 Wash. 480 (1930)
Local Union 118 v. Utility Workers, 162 N.E. 524 (Ohio App., 1958)
Local 273 Iron Workers v. Inter. Assoc. of Iron Workers, 120 N.J. Eq.
    220 (1936)
Locomotive Engineers v. Higgs, 79 Ind. App. 427 (1922)
Longo v. Reilly, 35 N.J. Super. 405 (1955)
Longshoremen's Association Local 909 v. Graham, 175 S.W. 2d 255
    (Tex. Civ. App., 1943)
Love v. Grand International Division, Locomotive Engineers, 139 Ark.
    375 (1919)
Lundine v. McKinney, 183 S.W. 2d 165 (Civil Appeal, Texas, 1944)
McBride v. Shultz, 39 D. & C. Pa., 425 (1940)
McCantz v. Brotherhood of Painters, 138 S.W. 902 (Civil App., Texas,
    1929)
McCarver v. Severino, 249 N.Y. App. 112 (1936)
McConville v. Milk Wagon Drivers, 106 Cal. App. 696 (1930)
McGinley v. Milk and Ice Cream Salesmen, 351 Pa. 47 (1951)
McGrath v. Dillion, 262 N.Y.S. 90 (1932)
McPherson v. Green, 72 N.Y.S. 790 (1947)
Madden v. Atkins, 147 N.Y.S. 2d 19 (1947)

Maddoc v. Reul, 256 N.Y.S. 915 (1932)
Maglio v. Moving Picture Machine Operators of Essex County, 119 N.J. Eq. 230 (1935)
Maguire v. Buckley, 301 Mass. 355 (1938)
Mahoney v. Sailors Union of the Pacific, 275 P. 2d 440 (Sup. Court of Washington, 1954)
Malloy v. Carroll, 272 Mass. 524 (1930)
Maloney v. United Mine Workers, 308 Pa. 251 (1932)
Maltese v. Dubinsky, 108 N.E. 2d 604 (Court of Appeals, New York, 1952)
Mandracio v. Bartenders Union Local 41, 256 P. 2d 927 (Cal. App., 1953)
Manicoff v. Robinson, 189 N.Y.S. 712 (1958)
Manning v. Kennedy, 320 Ill. 11 (1943)
Margolis v. Burke, 53 N.Y.S. 157 (1945)
Martin v. Curran, 303 N.Y. 276 (1951)
Martin v. Favell, 344 Mich. 215 (1955)
Martin v. United Roofers, 196 Md. 428 (1950)
Marvin v. Manath, 175 Oregon 311 (1944)
Mayer v. Hansen, 260 N.Y. App., 150 (1940)
Mayo v. Great Lakes Greyhound, 333 Mich., 205 (1952)
Merscheim v. Musical Union, 37 N.Y. Hun. 273 (1888)
Metzler v. Gleason, 276 N.Y. App. 865 (1949)
Meurer v. Detroit Musicians Benevolent Association, 95 Mich. 451 (1893)
Minch v. Local 370, Operating Engineers, 265 P. 2d 286 (1953)
Mixed Local v. Hotel and Restaurant Employees, 212 Minn. 587 (1942)
Mogelever v. Newark Newspaper Guild, 124 N.J. Eq. 60 (1938)
Monroe v. Colored Screwmen's Benevolent Assoc., 135 La. 894 (1914)
Montgomery v. Richards, 275 Mass., 553 (1950)
Moody v. Farrington, 227 Ill. App. 40 (1922)
Mooney v. Bartenders Local Union 284, 313 P. 2d 857 (Sup. Ct. Cal., 1957)
Moore v. Moreschi, 291 N.Y. 81 (1943)
Morgan v. Local 1150, United Electrical, Radio and Machine Workers, 311 Ill. App. 21 (1947)
Mulcay v. Huddell, 272 Mass., 539 (1930)
Mulhern v. Dock Builders Benevolent Union, 164 N.Y. App. 271 (1914)
Mullen v. Segers, 220 Mo. App. 847 (1927)
Mulroy v. Knights of Honor, 28 Mo. App. 298 (1888)
Mursener v. Fort, 205 P. 2d 568 (1949)

Musical Mutual Protective Union v. Weber, 205 N.Y.S. 599 (1924)
Musicians Protective Assoc., v. Semon, 254 S.W. 2d 211 (Texas Court of Civil Appeal, 1952)
Naylor v. Askins, 32 N.J. Super. 558 (954)
Neal v. Hutchinson, 106 N.Y.S. 1007 (1916)
Nilan v. Colleran, 283 N.Y. 84 (1940)
Nissen v. Teamsters Local 650, 295 N.W. 858 (Iowa Sup. Ct., 1941)
Nyland v. Carpenters Local 1960, 156 La. 604 (1924)
O'Brien v. Matual, 144 N.E. 2d 446 (Ill. App., 1958)
O'Brien v. Musical Mutual Protective and Benevolent Assoc., 64 N.J. Eq. 525, (1903)
O'Brien v. Pappas, 49 N.Y.S. 2d 521 (1944)
O'Connell v. O'Leary, 3 N.Y.S. 2d 833 (1938)
O'Connor v. Morrin, 179 N.Y.S. 599 (1919)
O'Grady v. McFetridge, 324 Ill. App. 390 (1948)
O'Grady v. Suffridge, 84 N.Y.S. 211 (1948)
O'Keefe v. United Association, Local 463, 14 N.E. 2d 77 (N.Y. Court of Appeals, 1938)
O'Neil v. United Association, 348 Pa. 531 (1931)
Otto v. Journeymen Tailors, 75 Cal. 308 (1889)
Overton-Bey v. Jacobs, 131 N.Y.S. 2d 31 (1954)
Pabone v. Curran, 44 LRRM (N.Y. Sup. Ct., 1959)
Peabody v. Kaufman, 61 N.Y.S. 313 (1946)
People v. Medical Society, 32 N.Y. 187 (1865)
Petrie v. Ruehl, 22 N.Y.S. 2d 549 (1940)
Pfoh v. Whitney, 62 N.E. 2d 744 (Ohio App., 1945)
Pizer v. Trade Union Service, 276 N.Y. App., 1071 (1950)
Polin v. Kaplan, 290 N.Y. 257 (1931)
Porth v. Local 201, Carpenters, 231 P. 2d 252 (Kas. Sup. Ct., 1952)
Powell v. United Association, 148 N.E. 728 (Court of Appeals, N.Y., 1925)
Pratt v. Rudisvle, 292 N.Y.S. 68 (1936)
Pratt v. Amalgamated Association, 50 Utah 473 (1917)
Quinlan v. Machinists Local 1653, 56 Pa. D.&C., 341 (1946)
Raevsky v. Upholsterers, 38 Pa. D.&C. 187 (1939)
Ray v. Brotherhood of Railroad Trainmen, 44 P. 2d 787 (Sup. Ct., Washington, 1935)
Real v. Curran, 138 N.Y.S. 2d 809 (1955)
Redler v. Sangriani, 5 LRRM 954 (N.Y. Sup. Ct., 1940)
Reichert v. Carpenters, 183 A. 72, N.J. Eq., 72 (1936)

Spitzer v. Ernst, 72 N.Y.S. 2d 570 (1947)

Stanton v. Harris, 152 Fla. 736 (1943)

Steenert v. Carpenters, 91 Minn., 189 (1893)

Stenzel v. Cavanaugh, 189 N.Y.S. 883 (1921)

Stoica v. International Alliance, 178 P. 2d 21 (Cal. App., 1947)

Strobel v. Irving, 14 N.Y.S. 2d 864 (1939)

Sullivan v. Barrows, 303 Mass., 197 (1939)

Sullivan v. McFetridge, 50 N.Y.S. 2d 385 (1944)

Swaine v. Miller, 7 Mo. App. 446 (1897)

Sweetman v. Barrows, 263 Mass., 349 (1928)

Taussig v. Weber, 205 N.Y.S. 605 (1924)

Taxicab Drivers Local 889 v. Pittman, 302 P. 2d 159 (Sup. Ct. Okla., 1958)

Taylor v. Favorito, 74 N.E. 2d 768 (Ohio App., 1947)

Taylor v. Marine Cooks and Stewards, 256 P. 2d 595 (Cal. App., 1953)

Thomas v. Musical Mutual Protective Union, 121 N.Y. 45 (1890)

Thompson v. Brotherhood of Locomotive Engineers, 41 Tex. Civ. 176 (1905)

Tobacco Workers Inter. v. Weyler, 280 Ky. 355 (1939)

Trainer v. Inter. Alliance of Stage Employees, No. 516, 353 Pa. 487 (1946)

Tserio v. Miller, 88 N.Y.S. 2d (1949)

United Brotherhood of Carpenters v. Local 14, 178 S.W. 2d 559 (Texas Ct. of Civil Appeals, 1944)

Vacaro v. Gentile, 138 N.Y.S. 2d 872 (1955)

Waldman v. Ladinsky, 101 N.Y.S. 2d 87 (1950)

Walker v. Grand Inter. Brotherhood of Locomotive Engineers, 186 Ga. 811 (1938)

Walsche v. Sherlock, 110 N.J. Eq. 223 (1932)

Walsh v. International Alliance, 37 A 2d 667 N.J. Eq. (1944)

Walsh v. Judge, 188 N.E. 280 (Mass. Supreme Ct., 1933)

Walsh v. Reardon, 274 Mass. 530 (1930)

Washington Local 104, Boilermakers v. Boilermakers, 33 Wash. 2d 1 (1949)

Way v. Paton, 241 P. 2d 895 (Oregon Sup. Ct., 1952)

Weber v. Marine Cooks and Stewards, 93 Cal. App. 2d 327 (1954)

Webster v. Rankin, 50 S.W. 2d 746 (Mo. App., 1932)

Weinstock v. Ladinsky, 98 N.Y.S. 2d 85 (1950)

Weiss v. Musical Protective Union, 189 Pa. 446 (1898)

Werner v. Machinists District 108, 337 N.E. 100 (Ill. App., 1956)

Williams v. District Executive Board, United Mine Workers, 1 Pa. D.&C. 31 (1942)

Williams v. Masters, Mates and Pilots, 384 Pa. 413 (1956)

Willis v. General Longshoremen, 202 La. 278 (1942)

Zacharias v. Siegel, 165 N.Y.S. 925 (1957)

Zalnerovich v. Van Ausdal, 65 N.Y.S. 2d 650 (1946).

Notes

Chapter 1

[1]Quote is from the decision on *Legislative History of Labor Management Reporting and Disclosure Act, Titles I-IV* (Washington, D.C.: U.S. Labor Department, Office of Labor-Management and Welfare-Pension Reports), p. 17.

[2]John L. McClellan, *Crime Without Punishment* (New York: Duell, Sloan and Pearce, 1962), pp. 13-18, 208; Sar A. Levithan, "The Politics and Provisions of the Landrum-Griffin Act," *Regulating Union Government*, edited by Marten S. Estey, Philip Taft, and Martin Wagner (New York: Harper and Row), 1964, p. 35.

[3]Philip Taft, *Corruption and Racketeering in the Labor Movement*, Bulletin of the New York State School of Industrial and Labor Relations, No. 38 (2d edition, 1970). John Hutchinson, *The Imperfect Union* (New York: E. P. Dutton, 1970), is the most complete study of labor racketeering.

[4]Joel Seidman, *Democracy in the Labor Movement*, Bulletin of the New York State School of Industrial and Labor Relations, No. 39 (2d edition, 1969). William Stafford, "Disputes Within Trade Unions," *Yale Law Journal*, May 1935, pp. 1249-1271; Copal Mintz, "Trade Union Abuses," *St. John's Law Review*, pp. 272-313; Richard Witmer, "Civil Liberties and Trade Unions," *Yale Law Journal*, February 1941, p. 635; Benjamin Aaron and Michael Komaroff, "Statutory Regulation of Trade Unions," *Illinois Law Review Northwestern University*, September-October 1949, pp. 425-465, November-December 1949, pp. 631-674; Joseph Kovner, "The Legal Protection of Civil Liberties Within Unions," *Wisconsin Law Review*, 1948, pp. 18-27; Clyde W. Summers, "Union Powers and Workers' Rights," *Michigan Law Review*, April 1951, pp. 805-838; Clyde W. Summers, "Legal Limitations on Union Discipline," *Harvard Law Review*, May 1951, pp. 1049-1102, Philip Taft, *The Structure and Government of Labor Unions* (Cambridge: Harvard University Press, 1954).

[5]For a discussion of this issue, see Theodore W. Glocker, *The Government of American Trade Unions* (Baltimore: The Johns Hopkins Press,

1913), pp. 103-131; George E. Barnett, "The Dominance of the National Union in American Labor," *Quarterly Journal of Economics*, May 1913, pp. 458-460; and Lloyd Ulman, *The Rise of the National Trade Union* (Cambridge: Harvard University Press, 1955).

[6]*Democracy in Trade Unions* (New York: The American Civil Liberties Union, 1943). The author was one of the twenty-six signers.

[7]*Amendments to the National Labor Relations Act*. Hearings Before the Committee on Education and Labor, House of Representatives, on Bills to Amend and Repeal the National Labor Relations Act, Vol. V, pp. 3633-3638, 3639.

[8]*Legislative History of the Labor Management Relations Act, 1947* (Washington D.C.: National Labor Relations Board, 1948), p. 298.

[9]Benjamin Aaron and Michael Komaroff, "Statutory Regulation of Internal Union Affairs," *Illinois Law Review Northwestern University*, November-December 1949, pp. 631-643.

[10]The preliminary report noted: "It was expected that the public announcement of this pilot study would bring a large number of complaints from trade union members and other interested persons. But only a relatively small number of complaints were received—not all of which had even *prima facie* merit." This report was made by the author.

[11]*A Report and Statement of Policy*, American Civil Liberties Union, June 1952, New York. The report was prepared by Professor Clyde W. Summers. The report notes that its recommendations were based upon what others have done in detailing "specific union abuses." The works cited cannot adequately serve as a factual foundation on the prevalence of union abuses, since they consist largely of legal analysis of case law and studies of union procedures.

[12]*A Labor Union "Bill of Rights,"* Democracy in Labor Unions, the Kennedy-Ives Bill, a statement of the American Civil Liberties Union, New York, September 1958, p. 16. The statement can be found in *Union Financial and Administrative Practices and Procedures*, Hearings Before the Sub-Committee on Labor of the Committee on Labor and Public Welfare, United States Senate, 85th Congress, 2d Session, 1958, pp. 115-1127.

[13]*Inland Steel Company v. National Labor Board*, 170 F. 2d 247 (1949).

[14]*Welfare and Pension Plans Investigations*, Final Report of the Committee on Labor and Public Welfare Submitted by the Sub-Committee on Welfare and Pension Funds Pursuant to S. Res. 225 (83d Congress) and S. Res. 40 as extended by S. Res. 200 and 232, 84th Congress, p. 3. *Investigation of Welfare and Pension Funds*, Interim Report of a Special Subcommittee to the Committee on Education and Labor Pursuant to H. Res. 115, 1953. *Welfare and Pension Plans Investigation*, Interim Report

Submitted to the Committee on Labor and Public Welfare by its Sub-committe on Welfare and Pension Funds Pursuant to S. Res. 40, 84th Congress, 1st Session. See also *Final Report* of the Committee on Labor Public Welfare Submitted by Its Subcommittee on Welfare and Pension Funds Pursuant to S. Res. 225 (84th Congress) and S. Res. 40 as extended by S. Res. 200 and 232, 84th Congress, 1956. The report was based on hearings before the above committee, and has been examined.

[15]*Welfare and Pension Plans Investigation,* op. cit., p. 41.

[16]Section 420 (d) reads: "That no court shall construe or apply any of the provisions of this Act in such a manner as to impair, diminish, or in any manner affect the rights of a bona fide labor organization in lawfully carrying out the legitimate object thereof, as such rights are expressed in existing statutes of the United States.

[17]*Local 807* v. *United States,* 315 U.S. 521 (1942).

[18]350 U.S. 415 (1956).

[19]*Congressional Record* (Senate), May 20, 1959, pp. 1276-1278.

[20]*Report of the Proceedings of Eighteenth Annual Convention of the American Federation of Labor,* 1898, p. 55; ibid. (Nineteenth Convention), 1899, p. 155.

[21]*AFL Codes of Ethical Practices* (Washington D.C.: American Federation of Labor-Congress of Industrial Organizations, 1957), p. 12.

[22]*Proceedings of the 2nd AFL-CIO Constitutional Convention,* 1957, Vol. II, pp. 407-409.

[23]Ibid., pp. 405-422.

[24]*Proceedings AFL-CIO Convention,* 1957.

Chapter 2

[1]Theodore W. Glocker, *The Government of American Trade Unions* (Baltimore: Johns Hopkins Press, 1913), p. 132.

[2]Ibid., pp. 135-144.

[3]The most exhaustive examination of disciplinary clauses in union constitutions is *Disciplinary Powers and Procedures in Union Constitutions,* U.S. Department of Labor Bulletin No. 1350, 1963.

[4]*Constitution of the United Association of Journeymen and Apprentices of the Plumbing and Pipe Fitting Industry of the United States and Canada,* 1966, pp. 104, 105.

[5]*Constitution of International Union United Steelworkers of America,* 1964, pp. 65-67.

[6]*Constitution of the United Association,* p. 108.

[7]*Constitution of International Union United Steelworkers,* p. 69.

[8]*Constitution of the United Association*, p. 110.

[9]Such a case is described in Philip Taft, *The Structure and Government of Labor Unions* (Cambridge: Harvard University Press, 1954), p. 168.

[10]Frederick H. Bacon, *A Treatise on the Law of Benefit Societies and Life Insurance* (St. Louis: The T. H. Thomas Law Book Co., 1894), p. 97. The same view was expressed by William C. Niblack, *The Law of Voluntary Societies and Mutual Benefit Associations and Accident Insurance* (Chicago: Callaghan & Co., 1894), pp. 80 and seq. Consult the following: *Roehler* v. *Mechanics Aid Society*, 22 Mich. 86 (1870); *Bartlett* v. *Medical Society*, 32 N.Y. 187 (1865); *Fuller* v. *Plainfield Academy*, 6 Conn. 298 (1829); *Butchers Beneficial Association*, 38 Pa. 298 (1868); *Mulroy* v. *Knights of Honor*, 28 Mo. 472 (1888); *Allnutt* v. *High Court of Forresters*, 61 Mich. 110 (1886). In the last case the court said: "Under the common law, the mere fact of defamation of another member is no cause of discipline. Any other doctrine would be monstrous, and it cannot be held that a corporation shall deprive a member of his rights unless he is himself at fault. Neither can anyone be called upon to meet vague and uncertain charges."

[11]Bacon, op. cit., 97. See also Niblack, op. cit., p. 80 and seq.

[12]*Holmstrom* v. *Independent Dock Builders and Benevolent Union*, 149 N.Y.S. 771 (1906).

[13]*Congressional Record*, April 22, 1959, pp. 6492-6493.

[14]*Legislative History of the Labor-Management Reporting and Disclosure Act, Titles I-VI* (Office of Labor-Management and Welfare-Pension Reports, U.S. Department of Labor, p. 283). *Congressional Record*, April 24, 1959, for Senator Johnston's statement, Senator Kuchel, pp. 6693-6694.

[15]Ibid.

[16]*Legislative History*, p. 363, *Congressional Record*, April 25, 1959, p. 6727.

Chapter 3

[1]Title IV requires elections at specified periods, and specifies some of the requirements. Section 402 allows an aggrieved member to appeal to the Secretary of Labor against failure to offer adequate opportunity to nominate and vote and empower the Secretary to appeal for remedial measures to the courts.

[2]304 F. 2d 108 (C.A., 3, 1962), cert. denied, reversing 202 F. Supp. 348 (D.W. Pa., 1961).

[3]*Byrd* v. *Archer*, 45 LRRM 2289 (D.C.S. Cal. 1959).

[4]*Johnson* v. *San Diego Waiters and Bartenders Local No. 500*, 190 F. Supp. 444 (D.C.S. Cal., 1961).

[5]*Kolmon* v. *Hod Carriers*, 215 F. Supp. 703 (D.C.W. Mich., 1963).
[6]*Robins* v. *Rarback*, 325 F. 2d 929 (C.A. 2, 1962), cert. denied 55 LRRM 2027 (1963).
[7]*McKeon* v. *Highway Truck Drivers*, 223 F. Supp. 341 (D.C. Del., 1961).
[8]*Colpo* v. *Highway Truck Drivers and Helpers*, 201 F. Supp. 307 (D.C. Del., 1961), 305 F. 2d 363 (C.A. 3, 1962), cert. denied 46 L.C. 17,889 (1962).
[9]*Martin* v. *Boilermakers*, 55 LRRM 2576 (D.C.W. Pa., 1963). See also *Verbiscus* v. *Industrial Union of Marine and Shipbuilding Workers of America*, Local 49, 58 LRRM 2029 (D.C.E. Mich., 1964).
[10]*Beckman* v. *Iron Workers*, 314 F. 2d 848 (C.A. 7, 1963).
[11]*Calhoon* v. *Harvey*, 379 U.S. 134 (1964), rehearing denied. The Supreme Court had reversed the Second Circuit Court of Appeals, 324 F. 2d 486 (1963). The C.A. had reversed the District Court, 211 F. Supp. 545 (D.C.S.N.Y., 1963).
[12]*Code of Federal Regulations.*
[13]In the Supreme Court of the United States, October Term 1964, *Calhoon* v. *Harvey*, et al. Memorandum for the United States Filed September 10, 1964.
[14]*Gurton* v. *Atons*, 339 F 2d 371 (C. A. 2, 1964).
[15]*Williams* v. *Typographical Union*, 423 F 2d 1295 (C.A. 10, 1970).
[16]*O'Brien* v. *Paddock*, 246 F. Supp. 809 (D.C.S. N.Y., 1965).
[17]*Acevedo* v. *Book Binders and Machine Operators Local* No. 25, 196 F Supp. 308 (D.C.S. N.Y., 1961).
[18]*Depew* v. *Edmundston*, 386 F. 2d 710 (C.A. 3, 1967).
[19]*Stettner* v. *International Printing Pressman*, 278 F. Supp. 675 (E.D. Tenn., 1967).
[20]*Vestal* v. *Teamsters Local 237*, 245 F. Supp. 623 (M.D. Tenn., 1965).
[21]*Ferger* v. *Iron Workers*, 342 F. 2d 430 (C.A. 3, 1965), Affirming 238 F. Supp. 1016 (D.C. N.J., 1964), 356 F. 2d 854 (C.A. 3, 1966), 94 N.J. Super (Court of Chancery, 1967), affirmed in 66 LRRM 2685 (Super. App. Div.) See also *Hughes* v. *Iron Workers*, 287 F. 2d 430 (C.A. 3, 1964).
[22]*Santos* v. *Bonanno*, 53 L.C. 11,337 (D.C.S. N.Y., 1966). District Judge Sidney Sugarman noted: "I am ignoring the invective laden charges of the parties as to motives which prompted the plaintiff's attempts to transfer to Local 1011 and defendants' motives in barring. . . ."
[23]*Parrish* v. *Legion*, 450 F. 2d 821 (C.A. 9, 1971).
[24]*Axelrod* v. *Stoltz*, 264 F. Supp. 546 (D.C.E. Pa., 1967), 391 F. 549 (C.A. 3, 1968).
[25]*Hurwitz* v. *Directors Guild*, 364 F. 2d (C.A. 2, 1966) , cert. denied 385 U.S. 871 (1966).
[26]*Williams* v. *Tyopgraphical Union*, 293 F. Supp. 1346 (D.C. Colo., 1969),

affirmed in 62 L.C. 10, 751 (C.A. 10, 1970). The quotation in the discussion of Williams is from the decision of the Court of Appeals.

[27]*Spivey* v. *Grievance Committee*, 69 LRRM 2709 (D.C. N. Ga., 1968).

[28]*Young* v. *Hayes*, 195 F. Supp. 911 (D.C. D.C., 1961).

[29]*Britt* v. *Peninsula Shipbuilders Association*, 62 L.C. 10,609 (C.E. Va., 1969).

[30]*Local 2* v. *Telephone Workers*, 300 F. Supp. 910 (D. Mass., 1969).

[31]*Rank and File Committee* v. *Clothing Workers*, 334 F. Supp. 760 (D.C.E. Pa., 1971).

Chapter 4

[1]*Salzhandler* v. *Caputo*, 316 F. 2d 445 (C.A. 2, 1961), cert. denied 375 U.S. 946 (1963).

[2]*Solomon* v. *Brotherhood of Painters*, 112 N.E. 752 (New York Court of Appeals, 1916) came out of District No. 9. See also Philip Zausner, *Unvarnished* (New York: Brotherhood Publishers, 1941), which tells of the factional warfare in District 9 by a former secretary.

[3]A business agent who had been charged with seeking to burn down the home of a member of the union sued for libel in the Queens County New York, Supreme Court. The member sought to enjoin the suit in the United States District Court on the ground that his business agent had not exhausted his internal remedies. The court rejected the plea and cited *Salzhandler* as a justification for the direction taken. *Johnson* v. *Rockhold*, 293 F. Supp. 1016 (D.C.S. N.Y., 1968).

[4]Salzhandler died and his estate sued the union and was awarded $23,520, which included $6,000 in exemplary damages, and $5,000 for counsel fees. *Sands* v. *Abeli*, 290 F. Supp. 677 (D.C.S. N.Y., 1968).

[5]*Cole* v. *Hall*, 339 F. 2d 681 (C.A. 2, 1961).

[6]*Boilermakers* v. *Raferty*, 348 F. 2d 367 (C.A. 9, 1965).

[7]*Leonard* v. *MIT Employees*, 55 LRRM 2691 (D.C. Mass., 1961).

[8]*Farowitz* v. *American Federation of Musicians 802*, 330 F. 2d (C.A. 2, 1964).

[9]*Gartner* v. *Solon*, 220 F. Supp. 115 (D.C.E., Pa., 1963).

[10]*Archibald* v. *Local 57, Operating Engineers*, 65 LRRM 2745 (D.C. R.I., 1967).

[11]*Giordani* v. *Upholsters*, 58 L.C. 755 (D.C.S. N.Y., 1968), 58 L.C. 13,012 (C.A. 2, 1968).

[12]*Sawyers* v. *Grand Lodge International Association of Machinists*, 279 F. Supp. 747 (D.C.E. Mo., 1967).

[13]*Airline Maintenance Lodge 702, International Association of Machinists* v. *Lowdermilk*, 442 F. 2d 719 (C.A. 5, 1971).

[14]*National Labor Relations Board* v. *International Molders Union*, 442 F. 2d 92 (C.A. 7, 1971).

[15]Ibid.

[16]*Salzhandler* v. *Caputo*, 316 F. 2d 445 (C.A. 2, 1961) cert. denied 375 U.S. 946 (1963).

[17]*Deacon* v. *Operating Engineers, Local 12*, 59 LRRM 2706 (D.C.S. Cal., 1965).

[18]*Deacon* v. *Operating Engineers, Local 12*, 273 F. Supp. 169 (D.C.S. Cal., 1967).

[19]*Stark* v. *Twin City Carpenters District Council*, 219 F. Supp. 528 (D.C. Minn., 1963).

[20]*Bailey* v. *Netter*, 64 LRRM 2752 (C.E. La., 1967).

[21]*Navarro* v. *Gannon*, 66 LRRM 2668 (C.A. 2, 1967).

[22]*Yanity* v. *Benware*, 65 LRRM 2019 (C.A. 2, 1967). The reading of the arbitrator's decision showed that the union sought to prevent the wildcat strike because the company was acting in a layoff in accordance with its rights under the contract. The union had succeeded in canceling and reducing the penalties of many of the strikers, and the arbitrator also reduced the number. It would have been difficult for the union to challenge the award without committing an act of bad faith.

[23]*Carballe* v. *Operadores do Ponce*, 55 LRRM 49 L.C. P 18784 (D.C. P.R., 1964).

[24]*Johnson* v. *Local 58, Electrical Workers*, 181 F. Supp. 785 (D.C.E. Mich., 1960).

[25]*Stuart* v. *Carpenters District Council of Chicago*, 226 F. Supp. 341 (N.D. Ill., 1963).

[26]*Cefalo* v. *District 50, United Mine Workers*, 311 F. Supp. 946 (D.D.C.C., 1970).

[27]*Sheridan* v. *Local 2, Liquor Salesmen's Union*, 303 F. Supp. 999 (D.C.S. N.Y., 1969).

[28]*Semancik* v. *Mine Workers*, 324 F. Supp. 1292 (D.C. W. Pa., 1971); 446 F. 2d 144 (C.A. 3, 1972).

[29]*Reyes* v. *Laborers Union*, 327 F. Supp. 978 (D. N.M., 1971).

[30]*Harris* v. *International Longshoremen's Association*, Local 1291, 205 F. Supp. 45 (D.C.E. Pa., 1961), 210 F. Supp. 4 (D.C.E. Pa., 1962), affirmed in 334 F. 2d 801 (C.A. 3, 1963).

[31]*Broomer* v. *Schultz*, 239 F. Supp. 699 (E.D. Pa., 1965), affirmed in 356 F. 2d 984 (C.A. 3, 1966).

[32]*Philips* v. *Local 560, Teamsters*, 209 F. Supp. 768 (D.C.N.J., 1962).

[33]*McGraw* v. *United Association of Journeymen Apprentices of the Plumbing and Pipefitting Industry*, 341 F. 2d (C.A. 6, 1965).

[34]*Gartner* v. *Solon*, 384 F. 2d 348 (C.A. 3, 1967).

[35]*Cole* v. *Hall*, 93 S. Ct., 1943 (1973) The plaintiff was denied damages, but the attorney was awarded $10,500 for his services. *Cole* v. *Hall*, 85 LRRM 2305 (1974).

[36]In *U.S.* v. *Brown*, 381 U.S. 437, the Supreme Court ruled that Section 504 could not be applied to members of the Communist Party because the prohibition constituted a bill of attainder which could not be maintained. The weeding out of those who threaten security must be accomplished by rules of general applicability, and cannot specify the ones "upon whom the sanction it prescribes is to be levied."

[37]*Jackson* v. *The Martin Co.*, 180 F. Supp. 475 (D.C. Md., 1960).

[38]*Strauss* v. *Teamsters Local 596*, 179 F. Supp. 297 (D.C.E.D. Pa., 1959), *Postma* v. *Teamsters Local 294*, 337 F. 2d 609 (C.A. 2, 1964).

[39]*Kelly* v. *Streno*, 47 LRRM 2609 K,C. 46,843 (D.C.E. Mich., 1961).

[40]*Hamilton* v. *Guinan*, 199 F. Supp. 562 (D.C. Md., 1960).

[41]*Bennett* v. *Hoisting Engineers Local 701*, 204 F. Supp. 361 (1960), *Mirra* v. *Teamsters*, 49 L.C. 19,076 (D.C. N.J., 1964), dealt with the removal of a steward who was also suspended from membership. He was reinstated before his trial and the issue was held moot. The court ruled officers were unprotected.

[42]In *Myers* v. *Blok*, 57 L.C. 12,553 (D.C.E. Mich., 1968), a business agent was denied relief because the business manager presented evidence that he had neglected his duties. The court rejected the charge that his removal was influenced by his announcement of candidacy for business manager.

[43]*Sheridan* v. *Carpenters*, Local 626, 306 F. 2d 152 (C.A. 3, 1962).

[44]*Vars* v. *International Brotherhood of Boilermakers*, 215 F. Supp. 943 (D.C. Conn., 1963), affirmed in 320 F. 2d 576 (C.A. 2, 1963). Vars was also penalized for padding his expense account, an offense as an officer, but the court found no evidence to support the charge.

[45]*Nix* v. *Fulton Lodge*, IAM, 262 F. Supp. 1000 (D.C.N. Ga., 1967); 415 F. 2d 212 (C.A. 5, 1969); 452 F. 2d 794 (C.A. 5, 1971).

[46]*Martire* v. *Laborers Local 1058*, 410 F. 2d 32 (C.A. 3, 1968).

[47]*Barbour* v. *Sheet Metal Workers*, 401 F. 2d 152 (1968), reversing 263 F. Supp. 724 (D.C.E. Mich., 1966). The decision raises a question on Salzhandler: "Notwithstanding the limitations upon the exercise of *free speech* contained in the proviso. . . . and that nowhere in the Act are libel and

slander spelled out as protected activities, it has been held that libel of a union officer is a permissible and unpunishable exercise of the right of free speech." *Salzhandler* v. *Caputo*, 316 F. 2d 445, 446 (2d Cir., 1963). We, however, need not pass upon the question here.

[48]*Bragg* v. *Local 653, International Union of Operating Engineers*, 63 L.C. 10,983 (D.C.S. Ala., 1970).

[49]*King* v. *Grand Lodge, International Association of Machinists*, 215 F. Supp. 351 (D.C. N. Cal., 1963), affirmed in 335 F. 2d 340 (C.A. 3, 1964), cert. denied 372 U.S. 917 (1964). *The Grand Lodge of the International Association of Machinists* v. *King*, No. 18542, Transcript of Record. The argument of counsel is on pp. 105-151.

[50]In the United States District Court for the District of Columbia, *Retail Clerks Union Local 648* v. *Retail Clerks International Association*, Civil Action No. 1322-68, Memorandum Opinion, p. 11. 60 L.C. P. 10,031 299 F. Supp. 1012.

[51]*Wambles* v. *Teamsters*, 85 LRRM 2328 (C.A. 5, 1974).

[52]*George* v. *Bricklayers, Masons and Plasterers International*, 255 F. Supp. 239 (D.C.E.D. Wis., 1966).

[53]In *Paley* v. *Greenberg*, 62 L.C. 10,677 (D.C.S. N.Y., 1970), the District Court ordered the reinstatement of Paley because he had been discharged for opposing the views of the International Executive Board at a meeting. However, Greenberg was charged with administering and even making policy between conventions.

[54]*Sewell* v. *International Association of Machinists*, 445 F. 2d 545 (C.A. 5, 1971).

[55]*Witte* v. *Myers*, 343 F. Supp. 873 (D.C.W. Mich., 1971).

[56]*DeCampli* v. *Greeley*, 293 F. Supp. 746 (D. N.J., 1968).

Chapter 5

[1]Initiation fees are paid by new entrants. Dues are regular contributions and are generally made on a monthly or quarterly basis. Their level is related to the pay scale of the affected members. Assessments are irregular levies made for a special cause or other purpose by the local union, a district council, or an international union. The conditions under which these charges can be made are usually specified in the constitution of the organization.

[2]Philip Taft, *The Structure and Government of Labor Unions* (Cambridge: Harvard University Press, 1954), pp. 65-85, deals with membership contributions and their division between the local and international.

[3]Unions in the maritime industry do not pay per capita because the locals have no independent existence and are administrative units. Port delegates are elected by the entire membership in the unlicensed seamen's unions.

[4]*Ranes* v. *Office Employees Local 28*, 51 LRRM 2620 (D.C. N. Ill., 1962), affirmed in 317 F. 2d (C.A. 7, 1963).

[5]*Cole* v. *UAW, Local No. 509*, 68 LRRM 2097 (D.C. Cal., 1968).

[6]*Brooks* v. *Local Union No. 30, United Slate, Tile, Etc.*, 187 F. Supp. 365 (D.C.E. Pa., 1960).

[7]*Sertic* v. *Carpenters Council*, 423 F. 2d 515 (C.A. 6, 1972).

[8]*King* v. *Randoazzo*, 234 F. Supp. 388 (D.C.E. N.Y., 1964), affirmed in 346 F. 2d 307 (C.A. 2, 1965).

[9]*King* v. *Randazzo*, 346 F. 2d 307 (C.A. 2, 1965).

[10]*Sourcebook of Union Government Structure and Procedures* (New York: National Industrial Conference Board, 1956), p. 223.

[11]Ibid., p. 213. The statement is from the constitution of the United Association of Journeymen and Apprentices of the Plumbing and Pipe Fitting Industry.

[12]*Sawyers* v. *Machinists*, 57 L.C. 12, 478 (D.C. Mo., 1967).

[13]*Telephone Workers Local 2* v. *Telephone Workers*, 362 F. 2d 891 (C.A. 1, 1966) vacating 61 LRRM 2198 (D.C. Mass., 1965).

[14]64 L.C. 11, 409 (D.C.E. La., 1970), upheld 436 F. 2d 1101 (C.A. 5, 1971), per curiam.

[15]*White* v. *King*, 64 L.C. 11, 273 (D.C.E. La., 1970).

[16]*Wesling* v. *Waitresses Union No. 305*, 63 L.C. 11, 148, (D.C. Oregon, 1970).

[17]*Cutler* v. *Local 802, American Federation of Musicians*, 211 F. 433, affirmed in 316 F. 2d 546 (C.A. 2, 1963), cert. denied 375 U.S. 941 (1963).

[18]*Zentner* v. *Musicians*, 237 F. Supp. 457 (D.C.S. N.Y., 1965), affirmed in 343 F. 2d 758 (C.A. 2, 1965).

[19]*Denov* v. *Davis*, 61 LRRM 2203 (D.C. N.Ill., 1966).

[20]United States Court of Appeal for the Second Circuit, *Wittstein* v. *American Federation of Musicians, Appendix to Appellants Brief*, p. 491a.

[21]*Wittstein* v. *Musicians*, 223 F. Supp. 27 (D.C.S. N.Y., 1963), affirmed in 326 F. 2d 26 (C.A. 2, 1963), reversed 370 U.S. 171 (1964).

[22]*Kalish* v. *Hosier*, 265 F. 2 Supp. 853 62 LRRM 2749 (D.C. Colo., 1965); affirmed in 364 F. 2d 829 (C.A. 9, 1966). Cert. denied 55 LC 11747 (1966).

[23]*Peck* v. *Food Distributors*, 237 F. Supp. 113 (D.C. Mass., 1965).

[24]*Painters Union Local 127* v. *District Council No. 16*, 278 F. Supp. 830 (D.C. N. Cal., 1968).

Chapter 6

[1]*Detroy* v. *American Guild of Variety Artists*, 286 F. 2d 75 (C.A. 2, 1961).

[2]William C. Niblack, *The Law of Voluntaries, Mutual Insurance and Accident Insurance* (Chicago: Callaghan and Co., 1894), p. 101. For a similar view, see Frederick H. Bacon, *A Treatise on the Law of Benefit Societies and Life Insurance* (St. Louis: The H. F. Thomas Law Book Company, 1894), p. 181.

[3]*Holderby* v. *Operating Engineers*, 291 P. 2d 463 (Cal. Sup. Ct., 1955).

[4]*McCraw* v. *United Association*, 216 F. Supp. 655 (D.C.E. Tenn., 1963); 341 F. 2d 705 (C.A. 6, 1965).

[5]241 F. Supp. 489 (D.C.N. Ill., 1965).

[6]*Ryan* v. *International Brotherhood of Electrical Workers*, 361 F. 2d 942 (C.A. 7, 1966). The three plaintiffs were subsequently awarded damages for lost wages between $23,086 and $24,000, 387 F. 2d (C.A. 7, 1967).

[7]*National Labor Relations Board* v. *Marine Workers*, 319 U.S. 418 (1968) reversing 379 F. 2d 702 (C.A. 3, 1967).

[8]Ibid.

[9]*Operating Engineers Local 3* v. *Burroughs*, 417 F. 2d 370 (C.A. 9, 1969).

[10]*Parks* v. *International Brotherhood of Electrical Workers*, 203 F. Supp. 288 (D. Md., 1962), 304 F. 2d 886 (C.A. 4, 1963), cert. denied 372 U.S. 976 (1963).

[11]*Allen* v. *International Alliance of Theatrical Stage Employees*, Ets., 338 F. 2d 309 (C.A. 5, 1964); *Lewis* v. *American Federation of State, County and Municipal Employees*, 294 F. Supp. 834 (D.C.E. Pa., 1968), held that the "penal provisions are to be strictly constituted against the union." The Fourth Circuit in *Simmons* v. *Avisco*, 350 F. 2d 1012 (1965), held that failure to comply strictly with the provisions of the union's constitution did not render the action of the union void so long as it satisfied the "due process requirements of the LMRDA." The same view expressed by the court in *Null* v. *Carpenters' District Council*, 239 F. Supp. 809 (D.C.S. Tex., 1965).

[12]*Buresch* v. *International Brotherhood of Electrical Workers, Local 24* 77 LRRM 2932 (D.C. Md., 1971).

[13]Ibid.

Chapter 7

[1]*Gleason* v. *Chair Service Restaurant Employees*, Local 11, 300 F. Supp. 1241, affirmed in 422 F. 2d 346 (C.A. 2, 1970).

[2]*Bougle* v. *Carpenters Lake County District Council*, 67 LRRM 2402, 57 LC

12435, (D.C. N. Ind., 1968). Union constitutions generally prescribe a "reprimand," a public scolding or censure administered at a business meeting of the organization.

[3]*Tirino* v. *Hotel and Restaurant Employees Local 599*, 282 F. Supp. 809 (E.D. N.Y., 1968).

[4]*Pittman* v. *Carpenters*, 251 F. Supp. 323 (M.D. Fla., 1966).

[5]*Allen* v. *Local 92, Bridge, Structural and Ornamental Iron Workers*, 41 L.C. 16,697, 47 LRRM 2214 (D.C. N. Ala., 1960).

[6]*Ford* v. *Kammerer*, 287 F. Supp. (D.C.E. Pa., 1968).

[7]*Jacques* v. *Local No. 1418, International Longshoremen's Association*, 246 F. Supp. 857 (1965).

[8]*Null* v. *Carpenters District Council of Houston*, 239 F. Supp. 809 (D.C.S. Texas, 1965).

[9]*Boggs* v. *Electrical Workers* (BEW), 326 F. Supp. (D.C. Mont., 1971).

[10]*Gleason* v. *Hotel and Restaurant Employees, Local 11*, 300 F. Supp. 1241 (D.C.S. N.Y., 1969).

[11]*Magelson* v. *Local Union 518, Operative Plasterers*, 233 F. Supp. 459 (D.C.W. Mo., 1964). Magelson was awarded back pay for lost wages, 240 F. Supp. 259 (D.C.W. Mo., 1965).

[12]*Allen* v. *International Alliance of Theatrical Stage Employees*, 338 F. 2d 309 (C.A. 5, 1964).

[13]*Simmons* v. *Avisco Local 713, Textile Workers*, 350 F. 2d 1012 (C.A. 4, 1965). Simmons was awarded $15,000 in damages for the effect of his suspension on his reputation and the mental anguish he had suffered.

[14]*Boilermakers* v. *Braswell*, 388 F. 2d 193 (C. 5, 1965), cert. denied 391 U.S. 935 (1968).

[15]*International Brotherhood of Boilermakers* v. *Hardeman*, 420 F. 2d 485 (C.A. 5, 1969) per curiam, reversed 401 U.S. 233 (1971).

[16]*Kelsey* v. *Local 8*, 419 F. 2d 491 (C.A. 3, 1969).

[17]*Nelms* v. *Plumbers' Union*, 405 F. 2d 70 (C.A. 5, 1968).

[18]*Falcone* v. *Dentine*, 288 F. Supp. 719 (D.C.E. Pa., 1968), reversed 420 F. 2d 1157 (C.A. 3, 1969).

[19]*Lewis* v. *State, County and Municipal Employees*, 295 F. Supp. (E.D. Pa., 1968), reversed 407 F. 2d 1185 (C.A. 3, 1969).

[20]*Anderson* v. *Brotherhood of Carpenters*, 53 LRRM 2793 (D.C. Minn., 1963).

[21]*Anderson* v. *Brotherhood of Carpenters*, 59 LRRM 2684 (D.C. Minn., 1965).

[22]*Burke* v. *Boilermakers*, 57 L.C. 12,496 (N.C. Cal., 1967), upheld per curiam 61 L.C. 10,423 (C.A. 9, 1969).

[23]*Schuchardt* v. *Local 2834, Carpenters*, 380 F. 2d 795 (C.A. 10, 1967).

Chapter 8

[1]*Rekant* v. *Meat Cutters Local 446*, 194 F. Supp. 187 (E.D. Pa., 1963), reversed 320 F. 2d 271 (C.A. 3, 1963).

[2]*Rinker* v. *Local 24, Lithographers*, 201 F. Supp. 204 (W.D. Pa., 1962), appeal dismissed, 313 F. 32d 956 (C.A. 3, 1963).

[3]*Stout* v. *Construction and General Laborers District Council, of Chicago*, 226 F. Supp. 673 (N.D. 111., 1963).

[4]*Baruncia* v. *Hatters and Millinery Workers, Local 55*, 321 F. 2d 764 (C.A. 8, 1963).

[5]*Seeley* v. *Brotherhood of Painters*, 308 F. 2d 52 (C.A. 5, 1962).

[6]*Duncan* v. *Peninsula Shipbuilders Association*, 394 F. 2d 237 (C.A. 4, 1968).

[7]*Figueroa* v. *National Maritime Union*, 198 F. Supp. 946 (D.C.S. N.Y., 1964), reversed in 324 F. 2d 400 (C.A. 2, 1965). See also *Paige* v. *Maritime Union*, 63 LRRM 2505 (D.C.S. N.Y., 1966) for the same ruling involving the use of narcotics.

[8]*Hall* v. *Pacific Maritime Association*, 281 F. Supp. 54 (D.C. N. Cal., 1968).

[9]*Allen* v. *Armored Car Chauffeurs and Guards, Local 820*, 185 F. Supp. 492 (D.C. N.J., 1960). In *Yaca* v. *Sipes* (389 U.S. 171, [1967]), the U.S. Supreme Court held: "A breach of the statutory duty of fair representation occurs only when a union's conduct toward a member of the collective bargaining unit is arbitrary, discriminatory or in bad faith."

[10]*Scovile* v. *Watson*, 338 F. 2d (C.A., 7, 1964), cert. denied 380 U.S. 963 (1965).

[11]*Gross* v. *Kennedy*, 40 L.C. 66, 432 (S.D. N.Y., 1960), held that Gross had a cause of action under Title I. The issue was decided in United States District Court for the Southern District of New York, 60 Civ. 526, from which the above quotation came, p. 17. Hon. Fred L. Wham, district judge, tried the suit.

[12]The defendant in the case was interviewed by me.

[13]*Gross* v. *Kennedy*, above, p. 18.

[14]*Supra* from Judge Wham's decision.

[15]*Rekant* v. *Meat Cutters Local 446*, 320 F. 2d 271 (C.A. 3, 1963).

[16]*Lucas* v. *Keeney*, 220 F. Supp. 189 (N.D. Ill., 1963).

[17]*Green* v. *Hotel and Restaurant Employees*, Local 750, 220 F. Supp. 505 (E.D. Mich. S.D., 1963). The charge of unfair representation was almost made in *Durandetti* v. *Chrysler Corporation*, 195 F. Supp. 653, but the events took place in 1957, before the enactment of the LMRDA. On the other hand, a suit for lost wages during the period of expulsion was

upheld when it was shown the plaintiff could not find a job. *Burns* v. *Carpenters Local 626*, 50 LRRM 2196 (D.C. Del., 1962).

[18]*Calabrese* v. *United Association of Journeymen and Apprentice Plumbers and Pipe Fitting of the United States and Canada*, 211 F. Supp. 609 (D.C. N.J., 1962); affirmed in 324 F. 2d 955 (C.A. 3, 1963).

[19]*Heasley* v. *Operative Plasters*, 324 Pa., 257 (1936); also *Simmons* v. *Berry*, 240 N.Y. 463 (1925).

[20]*Parks* v. *Electrical Workers*, 203 F. Supp. 288 (D.C. Md., 1962), reversed in 314 F. 2d 886 (C.A. 4, 1963), also involves the revocation of a local charter and the replacement by another in the same jurisdiction, Baltimore, Maryland. The internecine dispute started over the level of demands to be made by the union in its negotiations for a new contract, and its obligations to use the machinery established by the International and the contractors' association. The basic charge made by the local was that the International had breached its fiduciary responsibility. The case is discussed below.

[21]*Thompson* v. *New York Central Railroad Company*, 361 F. 2d 137 (C.A. 2, 1966), affirming 53 L.C. 11, 034 (D.C. S. N.Y., 1966). *Carpenter* v. *Brady*, 241 F. Supp. 679 (D.C.S. N.Y., 1962), *Fog* v. *Randolph*, 52 LRRM 2216 (D.C.S. N.Y., 1962).

[22]*Cleveland Orchestra Committee* v. *Musicians Local 4*, Cleveland Federation of Musicians, 193 F. Supp. 647 (U.S.D.C.N.D. Ohio, 1961), affirmed in 303 F. 2d 229 (C.A. 6, 1962).

[23]*Detroy* v. *American Guild of Variety Artists*, 189 F. Supp. 575 (D.C.S. N.Y., 1960), reversed in 286 F. 2d 75 (C.A. 2, 1961), cert. denied, 306 U.S. 929 (1961).

[24]Actually, the union failed to collect the fine. Detroy suffered no loss of employment during his suspension.

[25]*Catanzaro* v. *Soft Drink Workers Union*, 55 L.C. 11,821 (E.D. N.Y., 1967). In *Hill* v. *Aro Corp.*, 275 F. Supp. 482 (D.C. N. Ohio, 1967), the removal of a committeeman who refused to change shifts and his eventual removal from the job did not constitute discipline because Title I rights apply to union members and not union officers.

Chapter 9

[1]*Hearings Before the Committee on Labor and Public Welfare United States Senate*, 85th Congress, 2d Session on Union Financial Aid and Administrative Practices and Procedures, 1958, pp. 49-50 (testimony of George Meany); pp. 531-532 (testimony of President Hayes of Machinists'

Union); pp. 1185-1187 (testimony of George Harrison, President of Brotherhood of Railway and Steamship Clerks.).

[2]A. M. Sakolski, "The Finances of the Iron Molders Union," *Studies in American Trade Unionism*, edited by Jacob H. Hollander and George E. Barnett (New York: Henry Holt, 1906), p. 104.

[3]John B. Kennedy, "The Beneficiary Features of the Railway Unions," ibid., p. 345.

[4]Sakolski, op.cit., p. 104.

[5]Ibid., pp. 345-346.

[6]Philip Taft, *The Structure and Government of Labor Unions* (Cambridge: Harvard University Press, 1954), pp. 112-116. The data were obtained from the proceedings of the unions' conventions.

[7]Hutchinson, *The Imperfect Union*, p. 371.

[8]The large number of names on the delinquent delegates list of the Industrial Workers of the World (IWW) shows that revolutionary organizations are not immune to this problem. Lists of delinquent delegates were issued for those who (1) failed to report supplies held, (2) had withheld cash, or (3) had withheld cash and supplies. The delegates were volunteers who were given credentials to organize new members and to collect dues from those in the organization. The monies collected were to be sent to the headquarters of the union to which the delegate belonged. Among the delinquent were also an occasional stationary delegate and local secretary who were full-time officers. As an example there were forty delinquent delegates in Lumber Workers Industrial Union No. 120 who in 1919 failed to send in cash, and forty-seven who failed to account for supplies and cash. Seventy-seven delinquent delegates are listed by the same union in 1920. Other IWW unions also report delinquents and there are several hundred in the lists. *Lists of Delinquent Industrial Union Delegates* (Chicago: Industrial Workers of the World, 1922).

[9]A summation of *Goldberg* v. *Truck Drivers Local No. 299*, 293 F. 2d 807 (C.A. 6, 1961), cert. denied 368 U.S. 938 (1961).

[10]*Summary of Operations Bureau of Labor-Management Reports*, Fiscal Year 1961, p. 3.

[11]*Compliance, Enforcement on 1972 Under the Labor-Management Reporting and Enforcement Act* (Washington, D.C.: U.S. Department of Labor, 1973), p. 10.

[12]The indictments were for violating Section 501 (c), and Section 209 (a) (b). The figures do not include all who might have been prosecuted because the agency does not keep a record of the prosecutions by the Department of Justice. Data have been collected from annual reports and releases of the Office.

¹³The information has been compiled from releases and bulletins of the LMWP.

¹⁴See Philip Taft, "The Response of the Bakers, Longshoremen and Teamsters to Public Exposure," *Quarterly Journal of Economics*, August 1960, pp. 393-394.

¹⁵*Summary of Operations*, 1969, pp. 24-25.

¹⁶*Henderson* v. *Sarle*, 197 N.Y.S. 2d 920, 45 LRRM 3037 (N.Y. Sup. Ct., 1960).

¹⁷*Zastrow* v. *Teamsters, Local 200*, 50 L.C. 19,177 56 LRRM 2873 (Wisconsin Circuit Court, Milwaukee County, 1961).

¹⁸*Coratella* v. *Roberto*, 56 LRRM 2068, 49 L.C. 18,939 (D.C. Conn., 1964).

¹⁹*Coratella* v. *Roberto*, 56 LRRM 2668 50 L.C. 19,147 (D.C. Conn., 1964).

²⁰*Rekant* v. *Rabinowitz*, 194 F. Supp. 194 (D.C.E.D. Pa., 1961), 48 LRRM 2157 42 L.C. P. 16974.

²¹*Allen* v. *Local 92, Bridge, Structural and Ornamental Iron Workers*, 41 L.C. P. 16,697 47 LRRM 2214 (D.C.N. Ala., 1960).

²²Ibid.

²³*Local 1419 Longshoremen* v. *Smith*, 301 F. 2d 791 (C.A. 5, 1963).

²⁴*Deacon* v. *Operating Engineers, Local 12*, 47 Cal. Rper. 11, 60 LRRM 2045 (Cal. Dist. App., 1965), cert. denied, 383 U.S. 103 (1966).

²⁵*McCraw* v. *United Association*, Local 43, 26 F. Supp. 655 (D.C.E.D. Tenn., 1963), affirmed in 341 F. 2d 705 (C.A. 6, 1965).

²⁶*Fruit Packers Local 760* v. *Morley*, 64 LRRM 2364, 54 L.C. 11, 632 (D.C.E. Wash., 1966). affirmed as modified 378 F. 2d 738 (C.A. 9, 1967).

²⁷*Fruit Packers Local 760* v. *Morley*, 378 F. 2d 738 65 LRRM 2424 (C.A. 9, 1967).

Chapter 10

¹*Local 39* v. *Bowen*, 183 N.Y.S. 850 (1920); *Kehoe* v. *Leonard*, 65 N.Y.S. 357 (1917); *Ellis* v. *American Federation of Labor*, 48 Cal. App. 2d 440 (1941); *Hickman* v. *Kline*, 279 P. 2d 662 (Sup. Ct. Nevada, 1955); *Local 11 Iron Workers* v. *Iron Workers*, 114 N.J. Eq. 555 (1933); *International Union* v. *Becherer*, 61 A. 2d 835 N.Y. Chancery (1948). *Kennedy* v. *Schroder*, 35 N.Y.S. 2d 835 (1942); *United Brotherhood of Carpenters* v. *Local 14*, 178 S.W. 559 (Texas Court of Appeal, 1944).

²*Robinson* v. *Nick*, 235 Mo. App. 461 (1940); *Moore* v. *Moreschi*, 39 N.Y.S. 2d (Sup. Ct., 1942); *Dussing* v. *Nuzzo*, 262 N.Y. App. Div. 781

(1941); *Canfield* v. *Moreschi*, 262 N.Y. App. Div. 64 (1943). *Local 373* v. *Iron Workers*, 120 N.J. Eq. 220 (1936).

[3]*Interim Report of the Select Committee on Improper Activities in the Labor or Management Field United States Senate*, 85th Congress, 2d Session, Report No. 1417, p. 130.

[4]Ibid., p. 371.

[5]Ibid., pp. 477-448.

[6]*Compliance, Enforcement and Reporting in 1972 under the Labor-Management Reporting and Disclosure Act*, p. 3.

[7]*A Report of the Bureau of Labor-Management Reports, Fiscal Year, 1960*, pp. 32-33.

[8]*Summary of Operations, Bureau of Labor-Management Reports, Fiscal Year, 1961* p. 8.

[9]*1965 Summary of Operations, Labor-Management Reporting and Disclosure Act*, Office of Labor-Management and Welfare-Pension Reports.

[10]*Hodgson* v. *Mine Workers*, 344 F. Supp. 990 (D.C.D.C., 1972). See also *Monborne* v. *Mine Workers*, 342 F. Supp. 718 (D.C. W. Pa., 1972).

[11]Ibid., p. 6.

[12]*Summary of Operations*, 1963, p. 6.

[13]Ibid., p. 60.

[14]Ibid., p. 61.

[15]Ibid.

[16]Ibid., p. 69.

[17]Ibid.

[18]Ibid., p. 71, for the last quotation.

[19]Ibid.

[20]Ibid., p. 79.

Chapter 11

[1]178 F. Supp. 544 LRRM 2938 (D.C.S. Cal., 1959), also 183 F. Supp. 300, 45 LRRM 2690 (D.C.S. Cal., 1960).

[2]*Rizzo* v. *Ammond*, 40 L.C. 66,506, 45 LRRM 3159 (D.C. N.J., 1960).

[3]*Executive Board Local No. 28* v. *Electrical Workers*, 194 F. Supp. 649, 46 LRRM 2159 (D.C. Md., 1960).

[4]*Vars* v. *Boilermakers*, 204 F. Supp. 245 (D.C. Conn., 1962). However, *Cox* v. *Hutcheson*, 49 LRRM 2990 (D.C. Ind., 1960) takes an opposite view.

[5]*Flight Engineers' Cal Chapter* v. *Continental Airlines*, 209 F. 2d 397, 49 LRRM 2951 (C.A. 9, 1961).

[6]*Air Line Stewards and Stewardesses* v. *Transport Workers*, 55 LRRM 2711 (D.C. N. 111., 1963), 49 L.C. 18,850 (C.A. 3, 1964).

[7]*Carpenters* v. *Brown*, 343 F. 2d 872 (C.A. 10, 1965).

[8]*Dave* v. *Tobacco Workers Union*, 234 F. Supp. 815, 57 LRRM 2397 (D.C. D.C., 1964).

[9]*Parker* v. *International Brotherhood of Teamsters*, 229 F. Supp. 172 (W.D. N.C., 1964).

[10]*Blackmarr* v. *International Brotherhood of Teamsters*, 64 L.C. 11,446 (D.C. Central Cal., 1970).

[11]*Local 2, Telephone Workers* v. *Telephone Workers*, 261 F. Supp. 433, 64 LRRM (D.C. Mass., 1966).

[12]*Luggage Workers* v. *Leather Goods Workers*, 316 F. Supp. 500 (D.C. Del., 1971).

[13]*Schonfeld* v. *Raferty*, 271 F. Supp. 128, 65 LRRM 2689 (D.C.S. N.Y., 1967), affirmed in 381 F. 2d 446 (C.A. 2, 1967).

[14]*Sawyers* v. *Grand Lodge International Association of Machinists*, 279 F. Supp. 747 (D.C.E. Mo., 1967).

[15]*Weihrauch* v. *Electrical Workers* (IUE), 272 F. Supp. 472, 67 LRRM 2170 (D.C. N.J., 1967).

[16]*Plenty* v. *Laborers' Union*, 72 LRRM 2305 (D.C.E. Pa., 1969).

[17]*Plenty* v. *Laborers' Union*, 72 LRRM 2429 (E.D. Pa., 1969).

[18]*Jolly* v. *Gorman*, 305 F. Supp. 15 (D.C. Miss., 1969), 74 LRRM 2706 (C.A. 5, 1970).

[19]Ibid.

[20]*IBEW Local 1186* v. *Eli*, 307 F. Supp. 495 (D.C. Hawaii, 1969).

[21]*Local 10* v. *American Federation of Musicians*, 57 LRRM 2227 (D.C. N. Ill., 1964).

[22]*Letter Carriers* v. *Sombrotto*, 449 F. 2d 915 (C.A. 2, 1971).

[23]*Gordon* v. *Laborers International Union of North America*, 351 F. Supp. 824 (D.C. W. Okla., 1972).

Chapter 12

[1]*Interim Report of the Select Committee on Improper Activities in the Labor or Management Field*, 85th Congress, 2d Session, Senate Report No. 1,417, p. 371.

[2]Ibid., p. 439.

[3]Ibid., p. 443.

[4]Ibid., p. 444.

[5]*Legislative History of the Labor-Management Reporting and Disclosure Act, Titles I-VI* (Washington, D.C.: U.S. Department of Labor), p. 669.

[6]Ibid., p. 669.

[7]Ibid., p. 705.

[8]A federation of national or international labor organizations is not covered by the election provisions.

[9]*Altman* v. *Wirtz*, 56 LRRM 2651 (D.C. D.C., 1964).

[10]*Wirtz* v. *Local 191, Teamsters*, 218 F. Supp. (D.C. Conn., 1963), affirmed in 321 F. 2d 445 (C.A. 2, 1963).

[11]*A Report of the Bureau of Labor-Management Reports, Fiscal Year, 1960*, p. 38.

[12]*Summary of Operations, Bureau of Labor-Management Reports, Fiscal Year, 1961*, p. 3.

[13]*Wirtz* v. *Local 30, Operating Engineers*, 242 F. Supp. 631 (D.C.S. N.Y., 1965); *Wirtz* v. *Local 9, Operating Engineers*, 254 F. Supp. 980 (D.C. Col., 1965); 366 F. 2d 911 (C.A. 10, 1967); *Wirtz* v. *Local 545*, 381 F. 2d 448 (C.A. 2, 1967); *Wirtz* v. *Local 406, Operating Engineers*, 254 F. Supp. 962 (D.C.E. La., 1966).

[14]*Hodgson* v. *Local Union No. 18, Operating Engineers*, 66 L.C. 10,111 (D.C.N. Ohio, 1969); 440 F. 2d 485 (C.A. 6, 1971).

[15]*Hodgson* v. *Local 18, Operating Engineers*, 440 F. 2d 485 (C.A. 6, 1971), certiorari denied.

[16]*McDonough* v. *International Union of Operating Engineers, Local 805*, 66 L.C. 12,243 (D.C.N.J., 1972), 69 L.C. 13,208 (C.A. 3, 1972).

[17]*The Hudson Record* (a daily published in Jersey City), December 8, 1965, said: "At no time in Local 560's history have its members afforded such a chance to vote conscience. It is generally agreed that the Labor Department, the Honest Ballot Association, and the Seacaucus police enforced a proper polling procedure."

Chapter 13

[1]The case was not reported. Information from the public files of the Department of Labor.

[2]*Goldberg* v. *Amalgamated Local Union No. 355*, 242 F. Supp. 844 (D.C.E. N.Y., 1962).

[3]*Wirtz* v. *Independent Service Employees Union*, 52 L.C. 16, 759 (D.C.E. N.Y., 1965).

[4]*Wirtz* v. *Longshoremen's Local 1752* (D.C. Miss., 1964).

[5]*Wirtz* v. *Local No. 1622, Carpenters*, 285 F. Supp. 455 (D.C.M. Cal., 1968).

[6]*Wirtz* v. *Local 125, Laborers*, 1389 U.S. 477 (1968).

[7]*Wirtz* v. *Hod Carriers Local No. 11*, 211 F. Supp. 408 (D.C.W. Pa.).

[8]*Wirtz* v. *Hod Carriers Local 169*, 52 L.C. 16,752 (D.C. Nev., 1965).

[9]*Wirtz* v. *American Guild of Variety Artists*, 267 F. Supp. 527 (D.C.S. N.Y., 1967).

[10]*Anthal* v. *United Mine Workers*, 54 L.C. 11,621 (D.C.W. Pa., 1966).

[11]*Conley* v. *Aiello*, 56 L.C. 12,327 (D.C.S. N.Y., 1967).

[12]*Wirtz* v. *Independent Workers Union of Florida*, 272 F. Supp. 31 (Mic. D. Fla., Jacksonville, Div., 1967).

[13]*Hodgson* v. *Local 129, International Longshoremen's Association*, 338 F. Supp. 1204 (D.C.E. Pa., 1972).

[14]*Hodgson* v. *Local 610, United Electrical, Radio and Machine Workers*, 342 F. Supp. 1345 (D.C. W. Pa., 1972).

[15]*Wirtz* v. *Amarillo General Drivers Local 577*, 214 F. Supp. 74 (D.C.N. Tex., 1963).

[16]*Wirtz* v. *Teamsters 191*, 226 F. Supp. 179 (D.C. Conn., 1964).

[17]*Goldberg* v. *Marine Cooks and Stewards*, 204 F. Supp. 844 (D.C. Cal., 1962).

[18]*Wirtz* v. *Local Unions 9, 9A, 9B*, 254 F. Supp. 980 (D.C. Colo., 1965), affirmed in 366 F. 2d 911 (C.A. 10, 1966), cert. granted, 387 U.S. 96 (1967). The judgments were vacated and the case remanded to the District Court with directions to dismiss complaint as moot. The course of action was suggested by the parties, who agreed that the 1967 election would be conducted under the supervision of the Secretary under newly accepted rules.

[19]A question is "moot" requiring "dismissal of appeal, when it involves no actual controversy, interests or rights of parties or where issues have ceased to exist." *Chicago City Bank* v. *Board of Education*, 306 Ill. 508, *Words and Phrases* (St. Paul, Minn., 1961), Vol. 27A, p. 156.

[20]*Wirtz* v. *Local Unions 545*, etc., 366 F. 2d 435 (C.A. 2, 1966), *Wirtz* v. *Local 406*, etc., 254 F. Supp. 962 (D.C.E. La., 1966), held unreasonable a rule which required members to pay all dues on the first day of each month during the year preceding the election. It upheld the union's rule that only members of the parent body could be candidates. However, it ruled that members complaining did not exhaust the internal remedies.

[21]*Wirtz* v. *Local 153, Glass Bottle Blowers Association*, 244 F. Supp. 75 (D.C.W. Pa., 1965).

[22]*Wirtz* v. *Local 153, Glass Bottle Blowers Association*, 372 F. 2d 86 (C.A. 3, 1966).

[23]*Wirtz* v. *Local 153, Glass Bottle Blowers Association*, 389 U.S. (1968).

[24]*Wirtz* v. *Local 125, Laborers*, 231 F. Supp. 590 (D.C.N. Ohio, 1964).

[25]*Wirtz* v. *Local 125, Laborers*, 270 F. Supp. (D.C.N. Ohio, 1966).

[26]*Wirtz* v. *Local 125, Laborers*, 375 F. 2d 921 (C.A. 6, 1966).

[27]*Wirtz* v. *Local 125, Laborers,* 387 U. S. 904 (1968).

[28]*Wirtz* v. *Local 6799, Steelworkers,* 71 LRRM 2821 (D.C.M. Cal., 1969). In *Berman* v. *Steelworkers Local 3724,* 85 LRRM 2001 (C.A. 6, 1974), the Sixth Circuit Court of Appeals also upheld the attendance rule and said: "To satisfy the minimum requirements of the Steelworkers' rule, all any member had to do was to devote approximately two hours to union affairs every other month during the three year period between elections. The obligation thus imposed upon a member was to spend thirty-six hours at union meetings every three years. Further it should be emphasized that the meetings followed a set pattern. They were conducted on the second Thursday of each month and were scheduled at the most desirable time for purposes of accommodating a majority of members (30 minutes after the day shift ended). In addition the meeting hall was conveniently located within a fifteen minute automobile drive from the plant."

The Appellate Court found that "not only does the Secretary mistakenly fail to look to the real cause of the disqualification here, but he also misinterprets the Supreme Court's decision on Hotel Employees and our decision on local Union 18." The two cases are treated below.

[29]*Hodgson* v. *Local Union 6799 Steelworkers,* 426 F. 2d 969, (D.C.M. Cal., 1970).

[30]*Hodgson* v. *Steelworkers,* 403 U.S. 333 (1971), at 338.

[31]Ibid., p. 340.

[32]Ibid.

[33]Ibid., p. 341.

[34]*Hodgson* v. *Local 734, Teamsters,* 336 F, Supp. 1243 (D.C.N. Ill., 1972).

[35]*Compliance, Enforcement and Reporting in 1972 Under the Labor-Management Reporting and Disclosure Act,* p. 12.

[36]*Wirtz* v. *Office Employees Association,* 60 LRRM 2215 (D.C.N. Ill., 1965).

[37]*Wirtz* v. *Local 174, American Federation of Musicians,* 272 F. Supp. 294 (E.D. La., 1967). "It is apparent that in the case of a union the size of Local 174, American Federation of Musicians, possessing a gross annual income of approximately $700,000 and representing a varied cross-section of local musicians, the offices of president and vice-president must be held by persons both experienced and responsible if the union is to possess the qualities of stability and continuity upon which its existence may depend."

[38]*Wirtz* v. *National Maritime Union of America,* 284 F. Supp. 47 (D.C.S. N.Y., 1968), affirmed in 399 F. 2d 544 (C.A. 2, 1968).

[39]*Wirtz* v. *Hotel, Motel and Club Employees Union, Local 6*, 265 F. Supp. 510 (D.C.S. N.Y., 1967), affirmed as modified 381 F. 2d 500 (C.A. 2, 1967), rehearing denied, reversed 391 U.S. 492 (1968).

[40]*Wirtz* v. *Local 18, Etc., Operating Engineers*, 71 LRRM 2305, (D.C.N. Ohio, 1969).

[41]*Hodgson* v. *Local Unions*, 76 LRRM 3025 (C.A. 6, 1971).

[42]Information from the public file of the LMWP and the IBEW.

[43]*Stein* v. *Wirtz*, 366 F. 2d 188 (C.A. 10, 1966), cert. denied. 336 U.S. 996 (1966).

[44]*Wirtz* v. *Carpenters Local Union No. 559*, 61 LRRM 2618 (D.C.W. Ky., 1966).

[45]*Sanders* v. *International Association of Bridge, Structural and Ornamental Iron Workers* 130 F. Supp. 253 (D.C. Ky., 1955), affirmed in 235 F. 2d 271 (C.A. 6, 1956).

[46]*Sanders* v. *Iron Workers*, 235 F. 2d 271 (C.A. 6, 1966).

[47]*Hodgson* v. *Local Union 582, Plumbers*, 350 F. Supp. 16 (1972).

[48]*Wirtz* v. *Local Union No. 1377, IBEW*, 299 F. Supp. 641 (D.C.N. Ohio, 1969).

[49]*Jennings* v. *Carey* (D.C. D.C., 1967).

[50]*Book of Laws of the International Typographical Union*, 1967, Article XI, Sec. 5, pp. 49-50.

[51]*Wirtz* v. *Edmonds*, 51 L.C. 12, 410 (D.C. Colo., 1965).

[52]*Edmonds* v. *Wirtz*, Civil Action No. 8887, United States District Court for Colorado (1965). Judge William E. Doyle enjoined the Secretary "from disclosing to the public the information so obtained without first obtaining an order of this court."

[53]Letter from Frank M. Kleiler, Director, Office of Labor-Management and Welfare Pension Reports to Mozart Ratner, an un-dated letter delivered on January 10, 1969.

[54]*De Vito* v. *Shultz*, 300 F. Supp. 381 (D.C. D.C., 1969).

[55]*De Vito* v. *Shultz*, 61 L.C. 10,465 (D.C. D.C., 1969).

[56]*Compliance, Enforcement Reporting in 170 Under the Labor-Management Reporting and Disclosure Act*, p. 12.

[57]*Yablonski* v. *Mine Workers*, 305 F. Supp. 868 (D.C. D.C., 1969), 61 L.C. 10,488 (C.A. D.C., 1969).

[58]*Yablonski* v. *Mine Workers*, 61 L.C. 10,516 (D.C. D.C., 1969).

[59]*Yablonski* v. *Mine Workers*, 60 L.C. 10,312 (D.C. D.C., 1969).

[60]*Yablonski* v. *Mine Workers*, 60 L.C. 10,204 (D.C. D.C., 1969).

[61]*Compliance, Enforcement and Reporting in 1970 Under the Labor-Management Reporting and Disclosure Act*, p. 13.

[62]Last two quotations are from Ibid.

[63]*Trbovich* v. *Mine Workers*, 404 U.S. 528 (1972).

[64]*Hodgson* v. *Mine Workers*, 344 F. Supp. 17 (D.C. D.C., 1972).

[65]*Compliance, Enforcement and Reporting in 1971 Under the Labor-Management Reporting and Disclosure Act*, pp. 14, 33. *Cefalo* v. *Moffett*, 449 F. 2d 1193 (C.A. D.C., 1971). The court suggested a referendum on merger. It also held that failure of officers to inform members of benefits to them from merger was a breach of fiduciary responsibility.

Chapter 14

[1]John Hutchinson, *The Imperfect Union* (New York: E. P. Dutton & Co., 1970), p. 45.

[2]*Legislative History of the Labor-Management Reporting and Disclosure Act* (Washington, D.C.: U.S. Department of Labor), p. 861.

[3]Ibid., p. 997.

[4]*Congressional Record*, August 11, 1959, 14,213.

[5]*Moscheta* v. *Cross*, 241 F. Supp. 347 (D.C. D.C., 1965); *Alvino* v. *Bakery and Confectionery Workers Union*, 43 L.C. 17,058 (D.C. D.C., 1962).

[6]*Milone* v. *English*, 306 F. 2d 814 (C.A. D.C., 1962).

[7]*Highway Truck Drivers Local 107* v. *Cohen*, 182 F. 2d 608, (D.C.E. Pa., 1960); 284 F. 2d 162 (C.A. 3, 1960), cert. denied 365 U.S. 833 (1961).

[8]*Tucker* v. *Shaw*, 378 F. 2d 304 (C.A. 2, 1967).

[9]*Holdeman* v. *Sheldon*, 204 F. Supp. 890 (D.C.S. N.Y., 1962), 311 F. 2d 304 (C.A. 2, 1967).

[10]*Nelson* v. *Brotherhood of Painters, Decorators and Paperhangers, Local 386*, (D.C. Minn., 1961). *Nelson* v. *Johnson* 325 F. 2d 646 (C.A. 6, 1963).

[11]*Cole* v. *Hall*, 93 S. Ct. 1943 (1973) overruled the view; federal courts can now award counsel fees to a member suing for a Title I violation.

[12]*Sawyers* v. *Grand Lodge International Association of Machinists*, 67 LRRM 2375 (D.C. Mo., 1967).

[13]*Gurton* v. *Arons*, 339 F. 2d 371 (C.A. 2, 1964).

[14]*Charles* v. *Musicians*, 51 L.C. 19,647 (D.C.S. N.Y., 1965).

[15]*Addison* v. *International Association of Machinists*, 300 F. 2d 363, 49 LRRM 2756 (C.A. 9, 1962).

[16]*Moss* v. *Davis*, 49 L.C. 18,941 (D.C.M. Fla., 1963).

[17]*Persico* v. *Daley*, 51 L.C. 19,480 (D.C.S. N.Y., 1965).

[18]*Gilbert* v. *Hoisting Engineers*, Local Union 701, 384 p. 2d 701, 48 L.C. 50,901 (Oregon Supreme Court, 1963), cert. denied 376 U.S. 963 (1964).

[19]*Penuelas* v. *Moreno*, 198 F. Supp. 441, 43 L.C. 17,231 (D.C.S. Cal., 1961).

[20]*Purcell* v. *Keane*, 277 F. Supp. 252 (D.C.E. Pa., 1967).

[21]*Purcell* v. *Keane*, 70 LRRM 3167 (C.A. 3, 1969); the same view was

expressed in *Ahov* v. *Bintz*, 58 L.C. 13,016 (D.C. Minn., 1968). See also *Coleman* v. *Brotherhood of Railway Clerks*, 228 F. Supp. (D.C.S. N.Y., 1964), affirmed on other grounds in 340 F. 2d 206 (C.A. 2, 1965).

[22]*Horner* v. *Feron*, 362 F. 2d 224 (C.A. 9, 1966), rehearing denied.

[23]*Levinson* v. *Perry*, 60 L.C. 10,107 (D.C.S. N.Y., 1969). The view was in harmony with the majority decision of the Second Circuit in *Cassidy* v. *Horan*, 405 F. 2d 230 (C.A. 2, 1968). The last quotation is from *Coleman* v. *Brotherhood*, 340 F. 2d 206.

[24]*Horner* v. *Feron*, see above.

[25]*Coleman* v. *Brotherhood of Railway Clerks*, 228 F. Supp. 276 (S.D. N.Y., 1964), affirmed in 340 F. 2d 206 (C.A. 2, 1965). Quote is from decision of Appellate Court.

[26]*Phillips* v. *Osborne*, 403 F. 2d 826 (C.A. 9, 1968).

[27]*Aho* v. *Bintz*, 69 LRRM 2440.

[28]*Cassidy* v. *Horan*, 66 LRRM 2521, 56 L.C. 12,280 (D.C. W. N.Y., 1967).

[29]*Holton* v. *McFarland*, 215 F. Supp. 372, 47 LRRM (D.C. Alaska, 1963).

[30]*Horner* v. *Feron*, 362 F. 2d 224 (C.A. 9, 1966), rehearing denied.

[31]*Pignotti* v. *Local 3, Sheet Metal Workers International Association*, 343 F. Supp. 236 (D.C. Neb., 1972).

[32]*Morrissey* v. *Curran*, 423 F. 2d 393 (C.A. 2, 1970), affirming in part and reversing in part 302 F. Supp. 32 (D.C.S. N.Y., 1970).

[33]*Giordani* v. *Hoffman*, 57 L.C. 12,550 (D.C.E. Pa., 1967), 227 F. Supp. 722 (E.D. Pa., 1967), *Giordani* v. *Upholsterers*, 69 LRRM 2434 (D.C.S. N.Y., 1968), affirmed in 69 LRRM 2548 (C.A. 2, 1968).

[34]*Local 92, Iron Workers* v. *Norris*, 383 F. 2d 735, 66 LRRM 2297 (C.A. 5, 1967).

[35]*Moschetta* v. *Cross*, 241 F. Supp. 347, 60 LRRM 2425 (D.D.C., 1964), affirmed in *Ratner* v. *Bakery and Confectionery Workers*, 354 F. 2d, 60 LRRM 2455 (D.C. Cir., 1965).

[36]*McCabe* v. *International Brotherhood of Electrical Workers, Local 1377*, 60 L.C. 10,297 (C.A. 6, 1969).

[37]Constitution quoted in Ibid.

[38]277 F. Supp. 252 (D.C.E. Pa., 1967).

[39]*Echols* v. *Cook*, 50 L.C. 19,187 (D.C. Ga., 1962).

[40]*Schonfeld* v. *Rarback*, 52 L.C. 16,722 (D.C.S. N.Y., 1965).

[41]Burton Hall, "Painters and the Dictatorship of Bureaucrats," *New Politics*, vol. V, no. 3, p. 26.

[42]*Schonfeld* v. *Rarback*, 62 L.C. 10,689 (D.C.S. N.Y., 1970). In an interview with Mr. Rarback, after I had read the affidavits and the papers

submitted by his and the dissidents' lawyers, he explained that the few woodworkers who were members of District 9 had always received more than those who were affiliated with the Carpenters' Union, and that the contractors with which he dealt always complained of the differential.

[43]Ibid., p. 18, 278.

[44]Last two quotes are from Ibid.

[45]*Yanity* v. *Benware*, 65 LRRM 202 (C.A. 2, 1967).

[46]Ibid.

[47]*Electrical Workers Local No. 28* v. *Electrical Workers*, 40 L.C. (D.C. Md., 1960).

[48]Marion H. Hedges, *A Strikeless Industry* (New York: John Day Company, 1937), p. 13; *Council on Industrial Relations for the Electrical Contracting Industry* (Washington, D.C.: Council on Industrial Relations, 1964), p. 210.

[49]In the U.S. Court of Appeal for the Fourth Circuit, *Parks* v. *International Brotherhood of Electrical Workers*, Joint Appendix, vol. 2, p. 657.

[50]Ibid., p. 669.

[51]Ibid., p. 811.

[52]The article states: "No Local Union shall cause or allow a stoppage of work in any controversy of a general nature before obtaining consent of the International President. The International President, or his representative, has the power at any time to enter any situation or controversy involving a Local Union or any of its members, and the decision of the International President, direct or through his represenatatives, shall be accepted by the Local Union and its officers, subject to appeal to the International Executive Council or International Council."

[53]*Local No. 28* v. *Maryland Chapter, National Electrical Contractors Association*, 194 F. Supp. 494 (D.C. Md., 1961).

[54]*Transcript of Proceedings in the Matter of a Hearing Between the International Brotherhood of Electrical Workers, AFL-CIO and Local No. 28*, Washington, D.C., July 1961, Book II. The hearings were before Carl R. Schedler.

[55]*Parks* v. *IBEW*, joint Appendix, pp. 759-760.

[56]*Parks* v. *Electrical Workers*, 203 F. Supp. 288 (D.C. Md., 1962).

[57]*Parks* v. *Electrical Workers*, 314 F. 2d 897 (C.A. 3, 1962), cert. denied 377 U.S. 976 (1963).

[58]See *Textile Workers* v. *Loncoln Mills*, 353 U.S. 448 (1957); *United Steelworkers of America* v. *American Manufacturing Co.*, 363 U.S. 564 (1960); *United States Steelworkers of America* v. *Warrior and Gulf Navigation Co.*, 363 U.S. 574 (1960); *United Steelworkers of America* v. *Enterprise Wheel and Car*

Co., 363 U.S. 593 (1960); *Humphrey* v. *Moore*, 375 U.S. 335 (1964); *Vaca* v. *Sipes*, 386 U.S. 171 (1967).

[59] See Philip Taft, *Corruption and Racketeering in the Labor Movement* (Ithaca, New York, 1970), pp. 56-70; see also Hutchinson, op. cit.

Chapter 15

[1] Phillip Ross and Philip Taft, "The Effect of the LMRDA Upon Union Constitutions," *New York University Law Review*, April 1968, pp. 305-323.

[2] Philip Taft, "The Responses of the Bakers, Longshoremen and Teamsters," *Quarterly Journal of Economics*, August 1960, pp. 393-412.

[3] Ross and Taft, op. cit., p. 321. Former President Maurice Hutchinson of the Carpenters' Union claimed that some locals were overzealous in bringing members up on charges, and others were lax. He claimed that there was little the central organization could do except reverse the verdict if a case came up on appeal. More recently, an officer of the Chicago Carpenters District Council informed me that the council seldom brought anyone up on charges, and the members take care of violators on the job. He was surprised when I informed him about the large number charged in the 1920s.

[4] Philip Taft, *The Structure and Government of Labor Unions* (Cambridge: Harvard University Press, 1954), chapter 2.

[5] Robert Michels, *Political Parties* (New York: Hearst's International Library Co., 1915), pp. 377-392. Michels' study was of the German Social Democratic Party, but his conclusions have been applied to labor unions.

[6] Secretary of Labor George P. Shultz to Joseph L. Rauh, July 23, 1969, in *Miners Election*, Hearings by the Sub-Committee on Labor, 91st Congress, 2d Session, Report 1471, 1970, p. 48.

[7] Ibid.

[8] The letters of Rauh to Shultz, July 23, 1969, and Shultz to Rauh, July 25, 1969 are in ibid., pp. 51-55.

[9] Ibid., p. 339.

[10] Ibid.

[11] Ibid., p. 340.

[12] Ibid.

[13] Ibid.

[14] Ibid.

[15] I recall a member of the University of Chicago's English Department asking me "what has happened to Shultz?".

[16] *Miners Election*, p. 342.

Index

elections not to be evaded, 211;
defective, 211-212; definition of
secret ballot, 201; denial of right
to vote, 202-203; disadvantages
of opponents, 280;
disqualification of temporary
workers from voting, 207;
disqualified candidates, 223;
effect of LMRDA on, 237-238;
exhaustion requirements,
216-217; failure to give
adequate notice, 200, 201;
federal courts and, 186-187;
Hotel, Motel and Club
Employees, 220-223;
independent unions directed to
hold, 200; inspection of
membership lists, and, 184;
investigated, 188; limitation of
office holding, 223; Maritime
Union, National, 219; member's
complaint to Secretary of Labor,
186; method of challenging,
32-34; miscounting of ballots,
200; nature of complaints to
Secretary, 192; nature of court
cases, 199; number of cases
investigated by Department of
Labor, 188-189; offices not
limited to certain groups, 204;
opposition candidates and, 280;
power of Secretary of Labor to
investigate, 186-187, 227; prior
office holding as a requisite for
candidacy, 217-223; procedure
for appealing in, 282-283; racial
clause challenged, 204; right to
be a candidate, and, 185; secret
ballot necessary, 183; Secretary
of Labor and, 279; supervised in
Carpenters Local 559, 227;

Supreme Court and, 211-212,
213-214; tampering with ballots,
34-35; unequal voting in
districts, 37, 42-43; use of union
funds and, 185
Electrical Contractors Association,
National (NECA), 260-262;
Council of Industrial Relations,
"council clauses," 260;
Maryland Chapter, 261
Electrical, Radio and Machine
Workers, International Union
(IUE), 144, 173, 229; attempt to
steal the national election, 229;
election to presidency, 195;
Section 501 suit, 250; vote in
1964 election, 229
Electrical Workers, International
Brotherhood of (IBEW), 88-89,
260; Council of Industrial
Relations, 260; "council
clauses," 260; embezzlement of
funds, 125; internal procedures,
90; Local 28, 166; calls strike in
violation of President Gordon
Freeman's order, 262; demands
wage increases, 261; dispute
over wage demands, 261;
factional rivalries, 260; placed
under trusteeship, 260; Section
501 suit, 259-265; Local 34,
election dispute, 225;
incumbents win 12 out of 13
offices, 225; member charged
with slander, 225; Local 611,
dissident candidate defeated,
226; member denied right to
intervene in Secretary's suit,
226; member expelled for
slander, 225; Secretary
supervises election, 226; Local

Suspended members and
readmission to the union, 40-41
Sweetheart agreements, 257;
hardwood finishers, 257-258
Switchmen's Union of North
America, defaulting officers,
124
Symphony Orchestra, Cleveland,
117

Taft-Hartley Act, 13, 28
Teamsters, Chauffeurs,
Warehousemen and Helpers of
America, International
Brotherhood of, 16, 112; and
democracy, 182; and
trusteeships, 149-150; elections
in, 197; Local No. 69, Section
501 suit, 247; Local 71, 169;
Local 107, 243; Local 327,
38-39; Local 560, 197; Local
807, 12-13; Local 991, 65
Teamsters, Warehousemen and
Production Workers, Local 424,
200
Teamsters, Western Conference
of, 5, 242
Telephone Workers,
International Brotherhood of,
43-44, 170
Textile Workers of America,
United, 5, 16
Tirno, Joseph, 92-93
Tobacco Workers International
Union, 169
Transport Workers Union, 167
Trbovich, Michael, 235; Supreme
Court grants right to intervene
in suit against Mine Workers by
the Secretary, 235-236
Treatise on the Law of Benefit Societies

and Life Insurance (Bacon), 312n
Truck Drivers Local 229, 129
Trusteeships, 278; absence of
emergency, 169; abuse of, 5;
allowable purpose for, 151;
American Federation of
Musicians (AFM), 177;
Brotherhood of Telephone
Workers, 170; Carpenters
Union, 168-169; challenge to by
members, 151-152; conditions
for establishing, 151-152;
constitution and by-laws of
international union, 168;
definition of, 147; disciplinary,
147-148; denial of free speech
and, 160; diversion of funds,
157-160, 173; dual unions and,
163; due process and, 176-177;
duration of, 152; election abuses
and, 160-161; enforcement of,
279; failure to abide by
constitution, 162-163; failure to
fulfill responsibilities, 161; fair
hearing necessary for, 174;
good faith and, 170, 172;
imposition of, 149-150;
inadequate bonding of officers
and, 162; International
Association of Machinists (IAM)
Lodge No. 837, 172;
International Union of
Electrical, Radio and Machinery
Workers (IUE), 173;
International Union of
Operating Engineers (IUOE)
Local 150, 179; International
Woodworkers of America, 175;
investigations of, 153-154;
Laborers Union, 173-174, 178;
McClellan Committee, 151;